# MODERNIZING A
# SLAVE ECONOMY

CIVIL WAR AMERICA  Gary W. Gallagher, editor

# MODERNIZING A SLAVE ECONOMY

*the Economic Vision of
the Confederate Nation*

JOHN MAJEWSKI

University of North Carolina Press CHAPEL HILL

© 2009
The University of
North Carolina Press
All rights reserved

Parts of this work were previously published in "Imagining 'A Great Manufacturing Empire': Virginia and the Possibilities of a Confederate Tariff," *Civil War History* 49 (December 2003): 334–52; and "The Environmental Origins of Shifting Cultivation: Climate, Soils, and Disease in the Nineteenth-Century U.S. South," *Agricultural History* 81 (Fall 2007): 522–49.

Designed by Courtney Leigh Baker
Set in Minion by Keystone Typesetting, Inc.
Manufactured in the United States of America

The paper in this book meets the guidelines for permanence and durability of the Committee on Production Guidelines for Book Longevity of the Council on Library Resources.

The University of North Carolina Press has been a member of the Green Press Initiative since 2003.

Library of Congress Cataloging-in-Publication Data
Majewski, John D., 1965–
Modernizing a slave economy : the economic vision of the Confederate nation / John Majewski.
    p. cm. — (Civil War America)
Includes bibliographical references and index.
ISBN 978-0-8078-3251-6 (cloth : alk. paper)
    1. Confederate States of America—Economic conditions.
    2. Confederate States of America—Economic policy.
    3. Slavery—Economic aspects—Southern States.
    4. Agriculture—Economic aspects—Southern States.
    5. Economic development—Confederate States of America—History. 6. Confederate States of America—Politics and government. I. Title.
HC105.65.M25 2009
330.975′03—dc22
2008038371

CLOTH   13 12 11 10 09   5 4 3 2 1

*To Lisa and Sam*

CONTENTS

|  |  |
|---|---|
|  | Acknowledgments xi |
| *introduction* | Imagining a Confederate Economy 1 |
| *one* | Shifting Cultivation, Slavery, and Economic Development 22 |
| *two* | Agricultural Reform and State Activism 53 |
| *three* | Explaining Lieber's Paradox: Railroads, State Building, and Slavery 81 |
| *four* | Redefining Free Trade to Modernize the South 108 |

| | |
|---|---|
| *five* | Economic Nationalism and the Growth of the Confederate State 140 |
| *statistical appendix* | The Origins and Impact of Shifting Cultivation 163 |
| | Notes 181 |
| | Secondary Literature and Primary Sources 221 |
| | Index 233 |

# ILLUSTRATIONS, TABLES, GRAPHS, AND MAPS

### ILLUSTRATIONS

1. A poor southern farm   49
2. Edmund Ruffin in Palmetto Guards uniform   55
3. John Townsend of South Carolina   115
4. George W. Randolph of Virginia   127
5. Examples of Confederate currency   142

### TABLES

1. Percentage of Improved Land in Farms, 1850–1920   24
2. Cultivated Acreage as a Percentage of Total Area, 1860   30

| | | |
|---|---|---|
| 3 | Intensive Cultivation in Selected Virginia and South Carolina Counties, 1860 | 33 |
| 4 | An Activist Economic Policy: Cumulative Government Investment in Southern Railroads up to 1860 | 83 |
| 5 | Confederate Imports in 1860 and Confederate Tariff Revenue Projections for 1861 | 134 |
| 6 | Confederate National Investment in Railroads | 147 |
| A.1 | Determining the Percentage of Improved Land: County-Level Regression Results for Nine Southern States, 1860 | 166 |
| A.2 | Rural Population Densities, 1790–1890 | 171 |
| A.3 | Shifting Cultivation, Slavery, and Per Capita Value Added for "Demand-Driven" Manufacturing | 172 |
| A.4 | The Continuing Importance of Environmental Factors in the Postbellum Era: County-Level Regression Results for Nine Southern States, 1890 | 176 |

GRAPH

| | | |
|---|---|---|
| A.1 | The Relationship between Slavery and the Percentage of Improved Land in Farms | 169 |

MAPS

| | | |
|---|---|---|
| 1 | Ultisols in the South | 34 |
| 2 | Railroads in Virginia and the Carolinas | 87 |

ACKNOWLEDGMENTS

Writing a book is filled with long hours of solitude, yet the final product often reflects help and advice given from many different quarters. This is especially true of *Modernizing a Slave Economy*. A number of colleagues read portions of this manuscript, often disagreeing with specific arguments in ways that strengthened the book. Gary Gallagher and Stanley Engerman, my readers at UNC Press, made a number of suggestions that significantly improved the manuscript. Other scholars who took the time to read chapters or talk to me about the substance of the book include Sean Adams, William Blair, David Carlton, Peter Coclanis, Dan Bogart, Joyce Appleby, Shearer Davis Bowman, Susanna Delfino, Colleen Dunlavy, Michele Gillespie, Jeff Hummel, James Huston, Naomi Lamoreaux, Claire Strom and William Shade. Dan Klein belongs in a category all his own: he supported this project from the beginning, and he gave me the opportunity to try out my ideas on his students at Santa Clara University. My colleagues at the University of California, Santa Barbara (UCSB), provided a supportive environment; I received useful advice at several faculty brown-bag seminars. I am especially grateful to Ken Mouré and Carl Harris; both read the entire manuscript and gave me many helpful comments. I was fortunate enough to have had the help of Todd Wahlstrom and Nichole Sater, two graduate students at UCSB who read the entire manuscript and made numerous suggestions that saved me from many errors, both great and small. Several UCSB undergraduates provided important research assistance, especially Verena Breker, Angela Prattas, Lindsay Cooper, and Jarad Beckman. Dorothy McClaren helped prepare the maps for publication.

Before writing this book, I coauthored two different articles, one with Viken Thackerian on shifting cultivation and one with Jay Carlander on the Confederate tariff. Viken helped develop the statistical data on the relationship among shifting cultivation, market size, and local industry, while Jay generously shared his immense knowledge on southern political economy. While I take full responsibility for the writing, ideas, and errors in *Modernizing a Slave Economy*, I am grateful to both of them for their help and encouragement.

I presented various chapters of this book at scholarly conferences, where I invariably received useful feedback. The venues where I presented my work include the Business History Conference, the Southern Industrial Project, the Von Gremp Workshop for Economic History at UCLA, the annual meeting of the Southern Historical Association, and the Social Science History Conference. I was fortunate enough to give papers at several conferences sponsored by the All–University of California Group in Economic History. The All-UC Group is an invaluable resource, and I received expert advice from Peter Lindert, Alan Olmstead, Richard Ransom, Gavin Wright, and a number of other topflight scholars associated with the organization. The Berry Lecture at the University of Richmond gave me another forum to present some of my findings. I greatly appreciate Robert Kenzer's gracious hospitality as well as his insightful comments.

The staff of the University of North Carolina Press did a terrific job in seeing this book through the publication process. I especially want to thank David Perry, Zach Read, and Jay Mazzocchi for all of their help.

Several sources provided financial assistance that helped get this project completed. A fellowship from the Howard Foundation provided me with a sabbatical that helped get the research and writing started. The

Academic Senate at UCSB allowed me to visit archives in Virginia, North Carolina, and South Carolina. A Mellon Fellowship at the Virginia Historical Society financed a productive visit, where I had the fortune of meeting fellow Civil War historian Paul Anderson. I especially appreciated the opportunity to talk to Nelson Lankford, who was working on his own study of secession. In addition to the staff at the Virginia Historical Society, archivists at the Virginia State Library, the Southern Historical Collection at UNC–Chapel Hill, the South Carolina State Archives, and the South Caroliniana Library all provided superb assistance. Sherri Barnes at UCSB's Davidson Library showed me the most efficient way to use a range of electronic resources. I also thank Kent State University Press and *Agricultural History* for allowing me to reprint parts of previous articles. The comments of the editors and referees improved my work considerably.

Kenneth Sokoloff, a friend and mentor, died as I was writing this book. It will come as no surprise to those who knew him that Ken generously provided comments and advice, especially in regard to the statistical evidence. His exacting standards, innovative scholarship, and intellectual generosity will continue to influence his many colleagues, students, and friends.

Two other people deserve special mention. Sam Majewski (age ten) constantly kept me grounded in the present as well as the past. Lisa Jacobson, my wife and colleague, patiently listened as I developed my arguments and then read through multiple drafts of the manuscript. Her constructive criticisms greatly strengthened both the substance and style of the book. Perhaps even more important, her unflagging and enthusiastic support helped me finish it. I will always be grateful for her love and encouragement.

MODERNIZING A
SLAVE ECONOMY

*introduction*

IMAGINING A CONFEDERATE ECONOMY

As a son of a prominent Tidewater planter, Virginian John C. Rutherfoord had established himself in the 1850s as an up-and-coming politician. Rutherfoord was part of a cadre of young Virginia Democrats who enthusiastically supported southern secession. For him, southern independence was not an abstract question of political theory or constitutional interpretation but an enterprise of the imagination: what kind of nation would an independent South become? This question inspired Rutherfoord to begin planning a futuristic novel that he titled "A Century Hence." His notes had no characters and no real plots—perhaps accounting for why he never wrote the novel—but his rough outlines nevertheless revealed how Rutherfoord envisioned a southern nation-state. Reflecting an imperialistic mindset, Rutherfoord predicted that two rival nations would dominate North America in 1950: a vast slaveholding Southern Confederacy (consisting of the South, California, New Mexico, Mexico, and Central America) and an equally sizeable Northern Confederacy (including the free states of the old Union as well as Canada). Within the Southern Confederacy, Missouri, Maryland, and Virginia would gradually end slavery. He made clear, however, that all southerners would have a "thorough appreciation of the pecuniary value of slavery as well as its moral, social, and political blessings." Slavery, in fact, would provide the social and political foundation of a modern economy. Rutherfoord imagined that his Southern Confederacy would benefit from "direct trade between Asia & the Southern seaport towns on the Pacific; a Pacific railroad; a United Confederacy held firmly together by the conservative influence of the institution of slavery." New York, in fact, would "find a successful rival in one among the giant cities of the South." Riddled with dissension, the Northern Confederacy would eagerly "return to the Union which her own folly had dissolved."[1]

Rutherfoord was not the only Virginian to imagine what the South would look like in 1850. The anonymous "L.C.B.," hailing from Westmoreland County, published an 1856 essay titled "The Country in 1950" in Richmond's *Southern Literary Messenger*. He did not have the same breathless enthusiasm for secession that Rutherfoord did; he hoped that current sectional tensions would heal, but he nevertheless believed that "separate destinies ultimately await the North and the South." Like Rutherfoord, "L.C.B." predicted that the North's free labor society would eventually fragment, leading the section "to gradually wander from the path of true republicanism."[2] Slavery, though, gave the South an essentially conservative character that discouraged centralization of power and prevented the growth of socialism, feminism, and other dangerous "isms" that supposedly flourished in the North. Despite the conservative tone and substance of his essay, "L.C.B." still embraced a more modern southern economy. Southerners, he argued, must develop commerce and manufacturing. In Hungary and Poland, the failure to diversify agricultural economies had "compelled a retirement into secondary positions," while Great Britain and the Netherlands combined agriculture, commerce, and manufacturing to become world powers. The development of commerce and manufacturing would raise land values (thus giving agriculture "corresponding energy and lucrativeness") and provide wealth to support southern arts and literature.[3] Manufacturing and commerce, in short, would cement the economic and cultural power of the South.

Rutherfoord's notes and the article by "L.C.B." highlight how secession, as a momentous and controversial political decision, compelled southerners to concretely outline the future of their region. Such writings also indicate how economic questions attracted the attention of secessionists. For secessionists, economics was more than abstract theory and dry statistics; it was, above all else, an act of imagination. The focus on economic issues made perfect sense for those attempting to forge a new nation. If nationalism, as many scholars argue, involves the creation of an "imagined community" that provides a sense of connection among a large group of people, Confederates quite logically conceived of an "imagined economy" that provided a viable material basis for nationhood.[4] George Wythe Randolph—grandson of Thomas Jefferson, successful Richmond lawyer, and keen supporter of the Confederacy—put the key question before Virginia's secession convention: "Will the material interests of Virginia be promoted by adhering to the North or by joining the Southern Confederacy?"[5] Throughout the South, secessionists and their opponents asked this fundamental question, sparking a lengthy debate that revealed the aspirations of the men most responsible for creating the Confederacy.

The central argument of *Modernizing a Slave Economy* is that many secessionists envisioned industrial expansion, economic independence, and government activism as essential features of the Confederacy. Secessionists imagined that an independent Confederacy would create a modern economy that integrated slavery, commerce, and manufacturing. Political independence, in essence, would unleash the South's economic potential that the Union had restrained through discriminatory taxes on southern commerce and unfair subsidies to northern industry. As South Carolina planter John Townsend put it in 1850, southerners had all the necessary elements to become "a great, flourishing, and independent nation."[6] Secessionists, though, did not simply want to release their economy from the constraints of the old Union; they embraced state action that would guide economic development. In the antebellum period, many secessionists endorsed state-supported agricultural research and state-funded internal improvements, which indicated a predisposition to accept government intervention in their economy. During the secession crisis, secessionists often focused on controlling trade through a Confederate tariff, which would systematically penalize northern "imports" that had once entered the South duty-free. Far from endorsing laissez-faire, most secessionists believed that some form of collective action would strengthen the long-term prospects for slavery and the southern econ-

*Introduction* 3

omy. The ideological preconditions for a strong Confederate state, I argue, were more firmly rooted in secessionist ideology than many historians have acknowledged.

To understand the economic vision of southern secessionists, this book focuses on South Carolina and Virginia, two of the most important states of the Confederacy. South Carolina was the ideological birthplace of southern secession; the state's rice and cotton planters developed a radical proslavery position that would become the cornerstone of Confederate ideology.[7] Virginia, with a much larger proportion of nonslaveholding whites, was one of the last Confederate states to leave the Union. As part of the upper south, Virginia also had much stronger economic ties with the North. Unionists and conditional Unionists (those who believed that Virginia should secede only in response to an overt military threat) dominated Virginia's politics. Despite these important misgivings about secession, the Old Dominion would become a "crucible of war" and perhaps the single most important state within the Confederacy.[8] Virginia's Shenandoah Valley became the breadbasket of the Confederacy; Virginia's manufacturers, such as the massive Tredegar Iron Works, helped supply Confederate armies; and Virginia provided some of the Confederacy's most important military leaders and units. How secessionists crafted economic arguments and policies to appeal to more moderate Virginians while still remaining true to South Carolina's radical principles can tell historians much about the varied rationales for secession. Analyzing Virginia and South Carolina, however, reveals how important commonalities—the need to protect slavery, the fear of population loss to the West, and an ardent belief in the desirability of economic progress—transcended geographic differences within the Confederate South and created the widespread (if mistaken) belief in a homogeneous white South.

### THE CONFEDERACY IN THE HISTORICAL IMAGINATION

*Modernizing a Slave Economy* presents an interpretation of the Confederacy that is at odds with much of the Civil War literature. Many historians insist that the Confederacy was an agrarian nation fundamentally hostile to industry and commerce.[9] Historian James McPherson, for example, argues that leaders of the Confederacy "fought to preserve its version of the republic of the Founding Fathers—a government of limited powers . . . whose constituency comprised an independent gentry and yeomanry of the white race undisturbed by large cities, heartless factories, restless free workers, and class conflict."[10] A growing body of work on nineteenth-century public policy—focusing on the antimodern tendencies of southern republicanism—supports McPherson's arguments. According to this literature, southerners adopted political doctrines that stressed states' rights, limited government, and the strict construction of the Constitution. According to historian John Lauritz Larson, conservative southern planters—"who frequently envisioned no society more complex than the tidewater plantations on which they were called master"—generally opposed federal initiatives in the antebellum period.[11] It is all too easy to conclude that secession represented the logical outcome of an antigovernment, antimodern southern mindset.

Other scholars have recognized important modernizing elements within the South but still downplay those elements within the secessionist movement. John McCardell's important work on southern nationalism highlights how secessionists such as J. D. B. De Bow, the influential editor of the business journal *De Bow's Review*, focused on economic diversification as a means of removing "the degrading shackles of commercial dependence." In McCardell's rendering, though, modernizers such as De Bow represented a distinct stream of secessionist thought that most Confederates rejected or ignored.[12] Other historians portray secession as a reaction against southern commercial development. Lacy K. Ford's classic study of Upcountry South Carolina, for example, carefully documents the growth of towns, banks, and railroads that accompanied the cotton boom of the 1850s.[13] Ford argues that most South Carolinians supported these developments, but modernization and development produced internal tensions that fed the secessionist movement. Who would control the railroad and banking corporations which increasingly influenced local economies? Such questions helped heighten southern sensitivity to outsiders (such as Yankee abolitionists) who threatened to undermine slavery and a southern way of life. Ford writes that "by 1860, the threat of concentrated and unchecked power, and active governments with their own agendas for progress, loomed larger in the minds of [South Carolina's] Upcountry whites than ever before because of the changes of the 1850s."[14] In Ford's view, secessionists embraced some forms of economic development, but they also reacted vigorously against it.

Historians, of course, have not been the only ones writing about the Civil War. Popular culture has reinforced images of tradition-bound southerners fighting against centralization and modernization. In the aftermath of the Civil War and Reconstruction, southerners nostalgically depicted an Old South of stately plantations, chivalrous cavaliers, and contented slaves. In the lore of "Lost Cause" mythology, southerners fought the Civil War out of philosophical commitments to states' rights and strict construction of the Constitution. The Lost Cause view of the Civil War has often seeped into popular culture, as exemplified in Margaret Mitchell's *Gone with the Wind* (1936). In Mitchell's portrayal of the Old South, "raising good cotton, riding well, shooting straight, dancing lightly, squiring the ladies with elegance and carrying one's liquor like a gentleman were the things that mattered." When Mitchell's southern cavaliers raised their voices to support secession, they cried "States' rights, by God!"[15] Modern-day inheritors of Lost Cause mythology continue to insist that states' rights and antigovernment attitudes motivated secession. "Our ancestors were a little off in their timing, but their rebellion against federal government is finally seeing fruition," a Republican legislator from South Carolina told journalist Tony Horwitz in the 1990s.[16]

However widely held, the belief that the Confederacy represented a rebellion against economic modernity and political centralization runs up against a number of inconsistencies. Historians have had particular difficulty reconciling the Confederacy's supposed rejection of modernity with the decidedly businesslike mentality of southern planters. Southern planters generally managed efficient and profitable plantations, invested in railroads and other internal improvements, and supported the growth of southern towns and cities.[17] If economic development created social tensions, it also produced civic boosterism—an intense loyalty to the economic fortunes of a particular place—that often animated southern politics on the state and local levels.[18] The South's commercial boosters had long cast an envious eye at the wealth and power of northern commercial centers. Secessionists, as we will see, incorporated the booster mentality into their case for secession. Richmond, Norfolk, and Charleston, secessionists argued, could only achieve commercial success outside the Union. Charleston would move at a "snail's pace," wrote one South Carolina secessionist in 1850, as long as it remained in the Union, but political independence would "throw off the *incubus* upon her prosperity, and she will leap forward with an energy far surpassing her present most sanguine expectations."[19]

The large and powerful Confederate state presents another anomaly for the "limited government" interpretation. Although southerners rebelled against growing centralization of the federal government, they had no qualms about establishing a strong national state of their own. Scholars have classified the Confederate central government as a form of "war socialism." The Confederacy owned key industries, regulated prices and wages, and instituted the most far-reaching draft in North American history.[20] The Confederacy employed some 70,000 civilians in a massive (if poorly coordinated) bureaucracy that included thousands of tax assessors, tax collectors, and conscription agents.[21] The police power of the Confederate state was sometimes staggering. To ride a train, for example, every passenger needed a special government pass. Designed to ferret out deserters and draft dodgers, the pass system curtailed civil liberties and inconvenienced travelers, who often had to wait in long lines to get their passes.[22] Political scientist Richard Franklin Bensel writes that "a central state as well organized and powerful as the Confederacy did not emerge until the New Deal and subsequent mobilization for World War II."[23]

To explain how supposedly states' rights secessionists ended up establishing a powerful central state, historians such as Emory M. Thomas conceive that the Civil War was a "revolutionary" experience. As Thomas explains, "The Confederate government, albeit unwittingly, transformed the South from a state rights confederation into a centralized, national state.... The [Jefferson] Davis administration dragged southerners kicking and screaming into the nineteenth century."[24] Although immensely influential, Thomas's argument is not completely persuasive. Affirmations of collective action and a positive evaluation of state action, he implies, suddenly sprang into existence during the war. It is never quite clear how southerners so quickly jettisoned their states' rights baggage. Indeed, an air of inevitability hangs over the argument. Because of the wartime crisis, Thomas implies, the Confederates had no choice but to establish a strong central state. The problem, of course, is that many other governments (including the colonists during the American Revolution) have fought wars without forging large, bureaucratic states. Why, then, did the Confederacy choose that path?

I argue that the strong Confederate state was not a radical disjuncture but a natural outgrowth of southern attitudes established during the antebellum period. Secessionists, it is certainly true, never imagined creating the kind of bureaucratic central government that emerged during the Civil War. On the other hand, southerners had long believed in the necessity of government action to protect slavery. In the antebellum period, southerners routinely supported various forms of police action—including local slave patrols, statewide censorship of mails and newspapers, and national fugitive slave laws—to ensure the safety of slavery and the masters who benefited from it. As South Carolinian Armistead Burt wrote in 1851, "Property in slaves, of all other property, can least endure aggression, and most needs the arm of government."[25] William Lloyd Garrison and other northern abolitionists, in a roundabout way, essentially agreed with Burt. They believed that if the North left the Union, slavery would soon collapse because it would not have the support of a strong central government. Runaways, slave revolts, and other forms of black resistance would soon make slavery unprofitable.[26]

Slavery, though, needed more than police protection to survive in an increasingly ideologically hostile world. A vigorous, diversified economy, secessionists believed, would stimulate population growth, providing southerners with the military might to better defend their peculiar institution. Why not, then, use government power to accelerate economic development? Secessionists believed that state-supported agricultural research, government investment in railroads, and interventionist trade policies would strengthen slavery in the long run. Virginia political economist George Fitzhugh approvingly noted the propensity for southern-state action during the antebellum period. Southerners may have preached free trade, laissez-faire, and "Let Alone" policies, he wrote in the *Charleston Mercury* in 1856, but in actual practice they supported state activism. "We build roads and canals, endow colleges, aid education, encourage commerce and manufactures, prohibit peddling, and, in a thousand ways, endeavor by interfering with, encouraging and controlling private pursuits, by *State Legislation*, to enhance State wealth, intelligence, and well being." Southerners decisively rejected "laissez-faire" when it came to controlling their slaves, Fitzhugh argued, so it was hardly surprising that southerners would reject laissez-faire in other elements of their lives.[27] Fitzhugh was hardly representative, but his observations captured an important element of the southern mindset. Before Confederate mobilization began in earnest, the English journalist William Howard Russell noted in May 1861 that "a strong Government must be the logical consequence of [southern] victory ... for which indeed, many Southerners are very well disposed. To the people of the Confederate States there would be no terror in such an issue, for it appears to me they are pining for a strong Government exceedingly."[28]

The "strong government" that Russell referred to, it should be stressed, was quite different from our twenty-first-century notions of strong government. Thomas and other historians are quite correct to note that before the war, secessionists never imagined creating extensive bureaucracies, high taxes, or centralized planning. When it came to economic policy, Confederates hoped that the central government would nudge and encourage private interests down the path to economic modernization. The secessionist mindset differed from reactionary governments in Japan and Germany, who in the late nineteenth and early twentieth centuries, in the famous phrase of Barrington Moore, used authoritarian means to advance "a revolution from above."[29] Confederate secessionists instead believed that government policies should manipulate (as opposed to supplant) private interests to build a stronger economy. Secessionists supported state investment in railroads, for example, as a way of encouraging individual investors and local communities to contribute to such projects. In a similar vein, secessionists believed that a Confederate tariff would encourage more domestic manufacturing without necessarily resorting to widespread government ownership of industries. Such policies reflected the widely held belief that individualism alone could not create a modern slave economy, but they still left much of the economy in the hands of private interests. I use the terms "state activism" and "government activism" to describe Confederate political economy. One might think of state activism as somewhere between an individualistic, decentralized political framework and the far more powerful central state that the Confederacy created during the war itself. Widespread support for state activism did not inevitably lead to the formation of an authoritarian bureaucratic state, but it helped prepare Confederates to build such a government when military circumstances dictated it.

Perhaps the best historical analogy to Confederate-state activism was Alexander Hamilton's financial programs of the 1790s. As a nationalist, Hamilton sought to use the power of the central government to guide the new nation's economy. Under Hamilton's funding program, the Bank of the United States not only supported a stable currency; it also made loans to manufacturers and merchants. Government bounties and a mildly protective tariff also encouraged industrial expansion. The underlying

*Introduction*

goal was to create a modern, diversified economy that would give the United States the financial and economic muscle to survive in a world of potentially hostile European powers.[30] Secessionists used a slightly different mix of government policies to reach the same end. They imagined that the Confederate state would implement trade policy (especially moderately protective tariffs aimed at northern goods) to establish a more balanced, industrial economy. Instead of importing goods via northern cities, southerners would buy them directly from Europeans, thus jump-starting the growth of southern commerce and southern cities. The goods not imported from Europe would be produced within the Confederacy, enabling southern manufacturing to expand. A more balanced economy would become, in true Hamiltonian fashion, the economic foundation of a powerful nation. Secession, then, was something more than a conservative "counter-revolution" against liberal, egalitarian forces emanating from the North and Europe.[31] Political independence represented an exhilarating opportunity to restructure what secessionists saw as a weak economy (at least relative to the North) into a source of national greatness. Secession, according to Charleston newspaper editor L. W. Spratt, would allow southern cities to begin "a career of greatness" so that they could stand in "metropolitan splendor."[32]

The language of economic rebirth—talk of bustling cities, new factories, and more diversified agriculture—was not the only rhetoric southerners used to justify secession. Like all broad political movements, secessionists used a wide variety of appeals to make their case to other southerners and the world at large. One arrow that secessionists frequently pulled from their rhetorical quiver was republicanism. With roots stretching back to well before the American Revolution, republicanism was a body of thought that stressed the corrupting influences of cities, commerce, and political centralization. In republican thinking, the virtue of independent farmers and planters was the only effective bulwark against corruption and despotism. Decentralization (in the form of states' rights, for example) provided the best political structure to keep power from concentrating in the hands of a few corrupt individuals. Too much commerce and too much urbanization, on the other hand, created class conflict and servile dependency, setting the stage for general moral decline and political despotism. Republicanism also gave secessionists a way of touting their agrarian society while critiquing the more industrial, free-labor society of the North. As historian William J. Cooper argues, republicanism allowed southerners to see the Confederacy as "a continuation of the government of the founding fathers, a government that protected basic southern interests and guaranteed the liberty of southerners."[33]

Although secessionists sometimes used republican rhetoric to justify secession, I argue throughout *Modernizing a Slave Economy* that secessionists did not interpret republicanism (and the corresponding states' rights and nullification doctrines) as a rigid political philosophy. By the antebellum period, southerners used republicanism as an instrumental set of arguments, readily abandoned or embraced depending on particular contexts. Southerners found republicanism and states' rights arguments particularly appealing when facing political opposition in a heterogeneous nation filled with conflicting economic and political interests. A powerful federal government, especially one controlled by northerners, might abolish slavery. On the other hand, states' rights doctrines did not prevent southerners from seeking a strong Fugitive Slave Act to ensure that the federal government tracked down runaways. A surprising number of southern politicians also supported federal aid to a transcontinental railroad, provided that the railroad in question connected a southern city to the Pacific.[34] Southern politicians could live with such intellectual inconsistencies as long as federal activism served their interests.

Some southerners, it is true, used republicanism to oppose centralization within the Confederacy; but such opposition proved surprisingly weak because secession itself inadvertently undermined the appeal of republicanism, especially in debates over the size and scope of the Confederate state. According to secessionists, white southerners shared a common Anglo-Saxon ancestry, a common Protestant religion, and, most importantly, a common interest in preserving slavery. The common interest in slavery, secessionists asserted, provided far more dependable national bonds than abstract patriotic devotion. John C. Calhoun, for example, told a Charleston audience in 1848 that "the North is rich and powerful, but she has many elements of division and weakness. . . . The South, on the contrary, has a homogenous population, and a common bond of union, which would render us powerful and united."[35] Such constructions of Confederate nationalism—based on white racial superiority and broad economic interests rather than traditional conceptions of public virtue—undermined republican critiques of centralized power.[36] If all Confederates held the same interests, then what was to fear from a strong central state? The South's homogeneity of interests, in essence, threatened to make republicanism obsolete.

The secessionist focus on the homogeneity of interests and the protection of slavery speaks to how Confederates could support a modern economy without supporting what scholars often label as "modernization." Modernization theory sees economic growth creating distinct periods or phases of development in which "traditional" beliefs are cast aside in favor of modern notions of rationality, scientific thinking, and political liberalism. In contrast to modernization theory, secessionists saw a modern economy in concrete terms—more factories, more cities, more wealth, more political and military power—in a way that allowed them to reject the dichotomy between modernity and "traditional." Even as they worked toward a more modern economy, secessionists often touted the "conservative elements" in their society, including slavery, evangelical religion, and (when convenient) various forms of agrarian republicanism. Secessionists, in fact, believed that the conservative nature of their slave society established the best possible political foundation for a modern economy. Unlike the free-labor economies of the North or Great Britain, the South could industrialize and urbanize without class conflict or fear of socialist revolution. An independent Confederacy, in essence, would reap the benefits of modern economic development without sacrificing political stability and conservative political principles.

DEFINING THE SECESSIONIST IMPULSE

To understand the economic imagination of secessionists, it is first necessary to define exactly who the secessionists were. Creating a discrete category of individuals called "secessionists" is a surprisingly complicated task. In South Carolina, the state's well-deserved reputation as a hotbed of southern radicalism obscured the ambiguity with which many of the state's leading political figures approached outright disunion. In the 1830s and 1840s, Calhoun earned his reputation as South Carolina's most famous exponent of proslavery ideology and state nullification. Calhoun, though, frequently reiterated his long-held goal of devising a constitutional means of protecting southern interests within the Union. Even in the 1850s, when secessionist doctrines dominated South Carolina politics, a large number of Carolinians remained wary of unilateral withdrawal from the Union. Such "moderates" preferred that the South leave as a united block, a position that fragmented the secessionist movement. In 1851 South Carolinians decisively rejected separate-state secession.[37] Although separate-state secession gained strength over the course of the 1850s—especially with the growth of the Republican Party in the aftermath of the Kansas controversies—important politicians could still take rather puzzling turns. Senator James Henry Hammond, long considered a supporter of disunion, shocked his fellow South Carolinians when he counseled against outright secession in 1858.[38] Hammond and most other "moderates" ultimately supported the Confederacy, making it difficult to classify them as outright secessionists or outright Unionists.

In Virginia, the situation was even murkier. For most of the antebellum period, only a small group of planters from the eastern half of the Old Dominion supported disunion. Virginia's most notable secessionist was Edmund Ruffin, a Tidewater slaveholder who worked tirelessly on behalf of agricultural reform and southern independence. Ruffin and his fellow travelers, though, often seemed lost in Virginia's political wilderness. The tumultuous controversies over the Kansas-Nebraska Act in the mid-1850s breathed new life into Virginia's secession movement, but many politicians remained elusively difficult to categorize. Democrat Henry A. Wise—one of the most influential political figures in the state—rejected disunion for much of his career, but he then emerged as one of the most powerful supporters of secession in the secession winter of 1860–61.[39] Should historians classify Wise as a Unionist (his position over most of the 1850s) or as a secessionist (his position on the eve of the Civil War)?

To respond to such questions, I often use the category of "southern extremist" to characterize a broader range of southerners who aggressively defended slavery. Whether or not they supported secession, southern extremists believed that slavery was a positive good that benefited master and slave alike.[40] Extremists regularly denounced northern abolitionists as dangerous fanatics, voiced support for measures such as a stronger Fugitive Slave Act, and believed that slaveholders had an unambiguous right to take their property into the western territories. Southern extremists often articulated a distinct regional identity, calling on southerners to patronize their own region's merchants, manufacturers, literature, and educational institutions. Even if extremists opposed secession, they almost all believed that southerners had the right to dissolve the

Union whenever they wished. In 1858 Hammond counseled against secession, but he nevertheless believed that southerners "must be prepared . . . to take care of ourselves, whatever may come. . . . [Southerners] can never permit any foreign or hostile power to legislate in reference to their peculiar industrial system, whether to abolish or modify, or impose undue burdens on it."[41]

To understand the economic imagination of southern extremists, I analyze the writings, speeches, and policies of an articulate and educated group of leaders. Most of the men (and it was an overwhelmingly male discourse) who wrote and talked about the future Confederate economy were planters with legal training and substantial political experience. Merchants, manufacturers, and newspaper editors also took part in the conversation. A short list of those Virginians who articulated a vision of an independent southern economy included Wise (former governor), John B. Floyd (another former governor), Edmund Ruffin (noted agricultural reformer), Willoughby Newton (another noted agricultural reformer who also served in Congress), Muscoe H. R. Garnett (congressman and up-and-coming politician), George W. Randolph (grandson of Thomas Jefferson and wealthy Richmond lawyer), Matthew F. Maury (naval officer and distinguished oceanographer), and Daniel London (prominent Richmond merchant). The list for South Carolina would include Calhoun (the South's most prominent extremist), Robert Barnwell Rhett (U.S. congressman and prominent secessionist), Whitemarsh Seabrook (planter, governor, and noted agricultural reformer), John Townsend (prominent planter-politician), and L. W. Spratt (well-known Charleston newspaper editor). These influential political figures and writers certainly did not speak with a unified voice on economic issues, but they often supported various forms of state activism to promote a more modern southern economy. Historians usually associate the drive for economic modernization with the Whigs, but many of the secessionists supporting government activism belonged to the Democratic Party.[42] These Democrats, as we shall see, readily abandoned their party's traditional antipathy to state activism when it came to promoting *southern* development via agricultural reform, railroads, and a Confederate tariff.

Another way of thinking about the importance of these secessionists is by considering the venues for which they wrote. While I sometimes use personal letters, most of my analysis centers on public discourse. The economic case for secession was not confined to a few obscure publications but found its way into the most important public venues of the antebellum South. Prominent newspapers such as the *Richmond Enquirer*, the *Richmond Daily Dispatch*, and the *Charleston Mercury* published speeches, letters, and editorials about the Confederacy's economic future. Many of the most important secessionist pamphlets outlined a vision of a prosperous and dynamic southern economy. Garnett's 1850 pamphlet *The Union, Past and Future*, for example, used trade and census data to argue that the Union smothered the economic potential of the South. Southern independence, he believed, would ignite the growth of the region's cities and industry.[43] A legion of writers approvingly cited Garnett's work, including the South Carolinian Townsend. The Association of 1860, a wealthy and well-organized group of Charleston secessionists, distributed 165,000 copies of Townsend's *The Doom of Slavery* and *The South Alone, Should Govern the South* to slaveholders and politicians across the region. A number of historians have noted the importance of Townsend's pamphlets in popularizing the secessionist cause.[44] The economic case for southern independence was so prevalent that some secessionists sought to dispel the notion that only economic interests motivated their movement. In 1860 South Carolina minister James Henley Thornwell rather defensively argued that "dreams, however dazzling, of ambition and avarice" did not motivate secessionists; deeper issues (including the defense of slavery) accounted for the South's desire for independence.[45]

The public discourse over secession may not have necessarily represented the wishes of rank-and-file voters within South Carolina and Virginia. It is quite possible that even those voters who supported secession may not have attached great weight to economic appeals. Only a small fraction of the southern population had the time, money, and inclination to engage in debates about the future of the southern economy.[46] While true, the importance of this point can be exaggerated. I argue throughout this book that the secessionist economic vision tapped more general impulses emanating from southern society. A strong consensus in Virginia and South Carolina, for example, supported railroads and other internal improvements.[47] Many rather ordinary Virginians and South Carolinians also believed that the South should become less dependent on northern manufactured goods. In the aftermath of John Brown's 1859 raid, for example, local meetings in Virginia often issued resolutions supporting more industrial self-sufficiency to give the Old Dominion the means of defending itself.⁴⁸ As these examples suggest, the secessionist economic imagination flowed from debates over concrete economic policies, policies that could influence the daily lives of yeoman farmers as well as wealthy planters. The economic imagination of secessionists, in other words, had real meaning (and real consequences) for many southerners.

## THE ORIGINS OF STATE ACTIVISM: SHIFTING CULTIVATION AND SLAVERY

*Modernizing a Slave Economy* assumes that economic imagination is not exclusively a phenomenon of the mind. Rather, imagination takes shape within a particular material reality. However much secessionists imagined the economy they wanted, they faced a concrete set of conditions that influenced their outlook. Perceptions of that economic reality could differ greatly from observer to observer, but many Virginians and South Carolinians believed that the South was falling behind the North in terms of population, commerce, manufacturing, and urbanization. To better understand the material reality that southerners faced, I incorporate a detailed economic and environmental analysis of the South's plantation economy. Quantitative methods, including a series of regressions detailed in the statistical appendix, are an essential part of that analysis. This book attempts, in short, to integrate political, economic, and environmental history to better understand both the real world in which secessionists lived and the imaginary world that they hoped to create.

The link between secession and state activism was, quite literally, rooted in the land, or at least in how southern planters and farmers used their land. Chapter 1 focuses on the southern environment and the resulting patterns of land use to help explain why the South fell so far behind the North in population, trade, and industry as the Civil War approached. Virginia and South Carolina had much different economies, but both shared an important similarity: the continuing importance of shifting cultivation. Farmers and planters who used shifting cultivation burned forest growth to quickly release nutrients into the soil. After five or six years, when the nutrients had been exhausted, the old field was abandoned until it was cleared again in twenty years. Given the constraints of the southern environment—the region's poor soils and inhospitable climate—shifting cultivation worked well for individual farmers and planters. The drawback of shifting cultivation, though, was that southerners had to hold large tracts of unimproved land in prolonged fallow for up to twenty years. Whereas northerners held only one-third of their farmland in unimproved acreage, southern farms and plantations left nearly two-thirds of their land unimproved.

The large holdings of unimproved land acted as an economic black hole that drained the vitality of the southern economy. Whereas entrepreneurs in the North could serve a densely populated countryside, the rural population of the South lived on disconnected islands surrounded by an economic "dead space" that reduced population densities and increased transportation costs. Slavery, of course, further restricted the growth of rich, deep markets that had done so much to spur northern development. The combination of shifting cultivation and slavery severely limited the size of markets for southern merchants and manufacturers. Cities such as Richmond, Norfolk, and Charleston, serving sparsely populated hinterlands, lagged behind northern rivals. The southern economy certainly generated substantial profits for the region's many planters and farmers, but the slower growth of cities, industry, and population created a sense of relative decline. Saddled with an economy unable to generate opportunities for many of their children and grandchildren, Virginians and South Carolinians watched with alarm as tens of thousands of residents emigrated to the West every year. Southern extremists expressed their anxiety in a calculus of demographic growth and political power. Northerners would eventually be able to dominate every branch of the federal government, they predicted; abolitionists would then be able to use the post office, military, and judicial system to spread their nefarious doctrines. On the national political stage, these fears encouraged southerners to embrace states' rights, limited government, and strict construction. On a regional level, however, southern extremists often supported activist state policies that would encourage economic development and population growth.

Chapter 2 focuses on a network of prominent agricultural reformers in Virginia and South Carolina that sought to counter shifting cultivation. Virginians such as Ruffin and Newton and South Carolinians such as Seabrook and Hammond circulated important pamphlets, published agricultural journals, and promoted agricultural societies. The central thrust of the movement was to promote the use of marl, lime, and other sources of calcium to neutralize the acidity of southern soils. Southerners could then focus on fodder crops, legumes, livestock, and manures to adopt more intensive cultivation methods. These reformers, not coincidentally, aggressively defended slavery and southern rights, and many became outspoken advocates of secession. For these men, agricultural reform was a means to increase the political and economic power of the South.

Agricultural reformers believed that private interests alone would be insufficient to revitalize southern agriculture, and they enthusiastically sought to enlist the aid of state governments. Agricultural education, they believed, should be carried out in state-subsidized schools or by state-subsidized agricultural societies. The state should also own experimental farms that could carry out far more expensive experiments than individual farmers. Reformers lobbied for agricultural surveys carried out at state expense and for agricultural professorships at state universities. Ruffin, Virginia's most ardent secessionist, supported government efforts to drain swamps to provide additional acreage for southern planters and improve the health of the southern countryside. Ruffin's quest to reduce malaria in the Tidewater region of Virginia, in fact, led him to advocate a "Commission of Sanitary Police" to collect information to better understand the disease. To an extent generally unrecognized in the historical literature, southern agricultural reformers anticipated the development of state-sponsored education and research that would become an important feature in twentieth-century agriculture.

### RAILROADS AND TRADE POLICY

Agricultural reform was linked to another important legislative agenda: government investment in railroads and other transportation projects. Chapter 3 shows how Virginia and South Carolina enthusiastically embraced state investment. Important extremists such as Calhoun, Floyd, and Wise saw railroads as a means of achieving economic equality with the North. Improved transportation, they argued, would expand local markets of planters and farmers, enabling them to diversify production into fruits, vegetables, and dairy products. Railroads would also stimulate the growth of southern cities, allowing merchants and manufacturers to reach the growing markets of the Midwest. With their own interstate connections, southerners could encourage direct trade with Europeans interested in selling in the wider American market. Instead of sending goods to New York City and other northern cities for distribution, Europeans would sell their goods directly to southern ports such as Norfolk and Charleston. To further encourage direct trade, many southerners also advocated government subsidies for steamship lines that would carry trade and information between southern ports and European cities. More was at stake than simply dollars and cents; railroads would allow southerners to keep pace with northern development and thus enable the South to become independent of northern economic influences. Interregional railroads, southerners imagined, would also create bonds of mutual interests between the West and the South that would isolate New England abolitionists.

To succeed, however, southern railroads needed substantial government investment. With vast stretches of the region's land in long-term fallow and a large proportion of its population enslaved, the southern countryside produced fewer passengers and less traffic than the northern economy. The resulting lack of revenue made southern railroads unprofitable investments, necessitating that state governments provide much of the capital. State governments, however, proved to be inefficient planners. State legislators, facing heated competition between local interests, found it difficult to allocate funds in a rational manner. While vital trunk lines remained uncompleted, legislators often subsidized new projects. The large number of incomplete lines did little to spur development. Nor did railroads significantly reduce shifting cultivation. Despite harboring dreams of western connections, direct trade, and bustling cities, many Virginians and South Carolinians still worried that they were falling behind their northern rivals in the 1850s.

Rejecting railroads as a panacea, secessionists focused their attention on federal trade policy, the subject of chapter 4. Secessionists claimed that in the Union, tariffs, bounties, and other subsidies unjustly transferred hundreds of millions of dollars from southern planters to northern merchants and industrialists. In South Carolina, secessionists believed that an independent Confederacy with relatively low tariffs would attract European goods, finally establishing direct trade between southern ports and Europe. Midwestern states, weary of paying high tariffs that benefited northeastern capitalists, would soon ally themselves to the Confederacy. Some of South Carolinian's secessionists also embraced the reopening of the African slave trade. The exponents of the slave trade argued that it would not only enable more white southerners to become slaveholders, but it would also help stimulate the growth of southern commerce. The Confederacy's control of the world's cotton supply, the free traders argued, ensured that the rest of the world would speedily recognize the Confederacy and the beneficial results of the international slave trade. The economic interests of Europe and the North, secessionists confidently predicted, would quickly blunt "fanatical" abolitionist doctrines.

South Carolina's radical free traders faced stiff political opposition in Virginia and other states in the Upper South. Many Virginians worried that firmly embracing free trade would allow European competition to wipe out their small but growing manufacturing sector. Reopening the African slave trade was especially controversial because many states in the Upper South (particularly Virginia) benefited from exporting slaves to Alabama, Mississippi, and Texas. When delegates from the seceding cotton states drafted a permanent constitution, they explicitly banned the African slave trade. Although the Confederate constitution outlawed tariffs "to foster or promote any branch of industry," the failure to set a maximum tariff rate made the clause essentially toothless. Complete free trade, secessionists realized, ran counter to their goal of establishing a strong sense of Confederate nationalism. Could the South really claim political independence if it still relied on northern industry, northern merchants, and northern banks?

To foster greater independence, many secessionists enthusiastically embraced a Confederate revenue tariff of 15 to 20 percent. Such a tariff was low enough to encourage direct trade with Europe but high enough to give southern manufacturers a decisive edge over northern competitors. Support for a Confederate tariff was especially strong in Virginia. Northern industry, secessionists argued, had an insurmountable lead on Virginia's manufacturers as long as the Old Dominion remained in the Union. A Confederate tariff, on the other hand, would make Virginia the "New England of the Confederacy." Cities such as Richmond and Wheeling would become great manufacturing cities; their wealth and population would make the Confederacy into a world economic power whose influence would go far beyond King Cotton. Virginia, in the words of one secessionist, would become a "great manufacturing Empire."[49] A revenue tariff, as will be made clear in chapter 4, harmonized the economic interests of South Carolina and Virginia. It placated most free traders (thus garnering strong support in South Carolina) while offering significant protection to Upper South manufacturers (thus satisfying most Virginians).

## ECONOMIC INTERESTS AND CONFEDERATE DEFEAT

In many respects, the secessionist economic imagination fit well with the general mentality of southern slaveholders. Southern planters imagined that they seamlessly controlled their slaves through a system of carefully crafted rewards and punishments. Their word and authority, slaveholders perceived, directed the actions of a supposedly docile labor force. Slaveholders came to believe that they could manipulate and control the economic destiny of other regions and nations in the same way they controlled their slaves. The shackles of economic interest, secessionists asserted, would bind the world to the Confederacy. They imagined that Europeans would bow down before the power of King Cotton; northerners would hopelessly watch as Confederate merchants took their trade and Confederate manufacturers undermined their industrial dominance; midwestern farmers would eagerly support the South to maintain connections along the Mississippi River system; and even the slaves would loyally support their masters in the unlikely event of war. Chapter 5 argues that such predictions, however inaccurate, flowed naturally from the basic tenets of Confederate economic thinking. In reducing economic and political attachments to "interests," Confederates allowed themselves to believe that other groups had no real agency. Historian Drew Faust has summarized the basic impulse of southern planters as "a design for mastery." Secession reflected the same attitude, but on a global scale.[50] The simplistic understanding of economic interests that underpinned the secessionist movement ultimately contributed to the defeat of the Confederacy.

*o n e*

# SHIFTING CULTIVATION, SLAVERY, AND ECONOMIC DEVELOPMENT

Landownership, like slavery, was one of the pillars of southern society. Land was not merely an economic asset; it was a sign of respectability and a marker of citizenship.¹ Yet, however much southerners valued land, they managed to cultivate only a small fraction of what they owned. Take, for example, South Carolina rice planter William E. Sparkman, who in 1844 purchased the Springwood and Cottage plantations for $16,000. Buying these plantations at an estate sale, Sparkman reckoned that he had made a good deal. But most of the land Sparkman purchased was uncultivated, and it would remain that way for many years. The Springwood plantation alone held some 2,140 unimproved acres, which meant that Sparkman (or, more precisely, his slaves) cultivated slightly more than 12 percent of its total acreage. The large tracts of unimproved land might have been used as a source of firewood or foraging area for the plantation's hogs but seems never to have been cleared and planted in consistent fashion. During the relatively slack winter months, Sparkman ordered his slaves to clear more land. Consider the following journal entries for 1845:

> December 9: "All Hands clear new ground."
> December 10: "All Hands list up new ground."
> December 13: "All Hands work part of day in new ground. Rain."
> December 15: "All Hands work in new Ground."

Such efforts seemed to have only made a negligible difference. "I have got only 25 acres of upland listed and 95 acres of Rice Land dug," Sparkman recorded on February 24, 1845. "I am *more backward* than I ever have been on Black River."[2]

Some 340 miles to the north, Julian Ruffin engaged in a similar pattern of cultivation. In 1843 Ruffin took control of "Ruthven," a plantation in Prince George County, Virginia. Ruffin was hardly a typical planter. As the son of the famous agricultural reformer Edmund Ruffin, Julian seems to have inherited his father's desire to rationalize plantation operations. Julian noted, though, that only a small portion of the farm consisted of improved acreage: "This farm consists of 351 acres. . . . [O]nly about 40 acres are cleared & and a great part of this will require heavy grubbing." For the next six weeks, Ruffin and his workforce of six slaves did indeed grub the land—which entailed laboriously removing stumps and roots—while also plowing fields, building fences, and hauling manure.[3] Ruffin never indicated how much land he and his slaves managed to clear, but given the size of his labor force, it seems doubtful that he made significant inroads into his plantation's large number of unimproved acres. Even this reform-minded planter would continue to burn and clear land for many years.[4]

The small percentage of cultivated land on these plantations was typical of nineteenth-century Virginia and South Carolina. Planters and farmers in these two states cultivated less than one out of every three acres of their farmland in 1860. Northerners, on the other hand, cropped more than half of their acreage. Even the recently settled Midwest had a far higher percentage of improved land than Virginia, South Carolina, and other states along the southern Atlantic coast (see Table 1). These substantial differences reflected two distinct agricultural regimes. Northern farmers generally practiced what might be called continuous cultivation. Fertilizers and rotations kept a high proportion of land in use, either for crops or improved pasture. Southerners, on the other hand, practiced

TABLE 1  Percentage of Improved Land in Farms, 1850–1920

| States | 1850 | 1860 | 1870 | 1880 | 1890 | 1900 | 1910 | 1920 |
|---|---|---|---|---|---|---|---|---|
| Northeast | 61.6 | 63.8 | 65.5 | 68.2 | 67.5 | 59.5 | 58.1 | 56.8 |
| Midwest | 44.8 | 53.3 | 60.9 | 70.4 | 74.3 | 73.1 | 75.4 | 74.3 |
| Border South | 38.1 | 39 | 45.4 | 56.8 | 61.4 | 65.8 | 68.4 | 68.6 |
| Maryland | 60.4 | 62.1 | 64.6 | 65.3 | 68.9 | 68.0 | 66.0 | 65.9 |
| Delaware | 60.8 | 63.4 | 66.3 | 68.5 | 72.2 | 70.2 | 68.7 | 69.1 |
| Kentucky | 35.2 | 39.9 | 43.4 | 49.9 | 55.2 | 62.5 | 64.7 | 64.7 |
| Missouri | 30.2 | 31.3 | 42.1 | 60.1 | 64.3 | 67.4 | 71.1 | 71.4 |
| Upper South | 31.7 | 32.8 | 33.5 | 36.3 | 41.7 | 45.6 | 48.3 | 51.2 |
| Virginia | 39.6 | 36.8 | 45.0 | 42.9 | 47.8 | 50.7 | 50.6 | 51.0 |
| West Virginia | — | — | 30.1 | 37.2 | 44.1 | 51.6 | 55.1 | 57.7 |
| North Carolina | 26.0 | 28.2 | 26.5 | 29.0 | 34.6 | 36.6 | 39.3 | 41.0 |
| Tennessee | 27.3 | 32.9 | 35.0 | 41.1 | 46.4 | 50.4 | 54.3 | 57.3 |
| Arkansas | — | — | 24.5 | 29.8 | 36.8 | 41.8 | 46.4 | 52.8 |
| Cotton South | 29.5 | 30.8 | 29.9 | 32.3 | 38.9 | 41.3 | 47.0 | 51.5 |
| South Carolina | 25.1 | 28.2 | 24.9 | 30.7 | 39.9 | 41.3 | 45.1 | 49.8 |
| Georgia | 28.0 | 30.3 | 28.9 | 31.5 | 38.0 | 40.2 | 45.6 | 51.3 |
| Mississippi | 32.8 | 32.0 | 32.1 | 32.9 | 40.0 | 41.6 | 48.5 | 51.3 |
| Alabama | 36.5 | 33.4 | 33.8 | 33.8 | 38.8 | 41.8 | 46.8 | 50.5 |
| Louisiana | 28.8 | 29.1 | 29.1 | 33.1 | 39.5 | 42.2 | 50.5 | 56.2 |
| Overall North | 53.4 | 57.7 | 62.6 | 70.4 | 72.4 | 71.7 | 71.6 | 70.8 |
| Overall South | 32.1 | 33.3 | 31.1 | 39.9 | 45.6 | 49.1 | 53.0 | 56.0 |

Source: Census statistics at Geostat Center, University of Virginia Library, <http://fisher.lib.virginia.edu/collections/stats/histcensus/>.

shifting cultivation, in which a substantial portion of acreage rested in prolonged fallow. The basic routine of shifting cultivation began with the burning of forest growth to release nutrients into the soil. After five or six years, when the nutrients had been exhausted, the old field was abandoned to weeds, shrubs, and eventually trees. In the meantime, new fields would be burned and cropped. After fifteen to twenty years, the planter would return to the original "old field" and begin the process anew.

Many antebellum observers considered shifting cultivation wasteful and inefficient, but it was a rational response to the soils, climate, and topography of the South. This chapter documents the environmental constraints that led planters and farmers to adopt shifting cultivation. Most southern soils were highly acidic and lacked key nutrients, which made it impossible for planters and farmers to use continuous cultivation. Southern farmers and planters also found it difficult to raise cattle and other livestock, which constituted a crucial link in recycling soil fertility in continuous-cultivation regimes. Debilitating livestock diseases flourished in the warm southern climate, while hay, clover, and other fodder crops wilted in the South's heat and humidity. As was the case of many tropical and semitropical environments, the South's environmental constraints proved exceedingly difficult to overcome.[5] Even the introduction of railroads, the growth of nearby cities, and the introduction of new fertilizers did little to encourage more intensive cultivation practices in the antebellum decades. The fact that shifting cultivation flourished in some parts of the South well into the twentieth century indicates the degree to which the southern environment discouraged continuous cultivation.

Shifting cultivation often benefited individual farmers and planters, who profitably used land-intensive regimes to grow staple crops such as tobacco and cotton. For the South as a whole, however, shifting cultivation deterred development. The vast tracks of unimproved land resting in long-term fallow acted as a black hole that sapped the South's economic vitality. Working in conjunction with slavery, shifting cultivation inhibited the growth of southern markets for manufactured goods and urban services. Cities such as Richmond, Norfolk, and Charleston, with sparsely settled hinterlands, languished in the shadows of Boston, Philadelphia, and New York. Traversing large stretches of land that generated little economic activity, railroads and other transportation corporations often generated fewer profits for investors. To make matters worse, shifting cultivation and slavery both dampened incentives to build institutions that could diffuse useful knowledge. The South's widely dispersed free population made it difficult to establish schools and libraries, organize agricultural societies and mechanics' institutes, and circulate periodicals and newspapers. In many measures of long-term economic development —urban growth, manufacturing output, and mercantile activity—Virginia and South Carolina ranked far behind most northeastern states.

Shifting cultivation and its interaction with slavery helps explain why Virginians and South Carolinians readily turned to state activism to remake their economies. Unable to generate sustained economic development and wedded to a land-hungry agricultural regime, Virginians and South Carolinians watched with alarm as many of their neighbors, family, and friends migrated to western states. From the standpoint of practical politics, slow population growth meant the loss of power and influence. Perhaps more importantly, the westward migration reinforced a pervasive sense of decline that took a heavy psychological toll on politicians, editors, and other public intellectuals who attached great significance to economic progress. The sense of relative decline was especially marked in Virginia. Once the most powerful state in the Union, the Old Dominion (at least politically speaking) fell into second-tier status during the 1830s. The growth of antislavery activism in the North accentuated the sense of crisis. Northern critics, in fact, often made an explicit link between slavery and shifting cultivation; attacks on southern agricultural practices became standard fare for northerners who opposed the spread of slavery into western territories. It is not surprising that many prominent Virginians and South Carolinians came to believe that the survival of slavery—whether inside or outside the Union—depended on finding some way to encourage more intensive cultivation patterns.

IN THE PRESENCE OF OLD FIELD

In the colonial period, shifting cultivation was used in both the North and the South. Borrowing and modifying techniques from Native Americans, colonists from New England to Virginia burned woodlands and forest to quickly clear new fields.[6] Shifting cultivation made especially good sense in an environment where land needed to be cleared quickly. Lewis Cecil Gray and other historians of southern agriculture, in fact, have understood shifting cultivation as a "pioneer" stage of agriculture that was replaced with continuous cultivation as soon as population densities increased and access to markets improved.[7] In New England and the Middle Colonies, for example, farmers did not abandon older fields but converted them to pastures of clover and other fodder crops that helped revitalize the soil. In many areas of the Chesapeake, though, farmers rarely improved their exhausted fields. Seventeenth-century tobacco planter Robert Cole, for example, planned his farming operations around the basic fact that after six years, "the land had to lie fallow for twenty years before its fertility returned." As a result, Cole owned a large reserve of land that would be cleared once cultivated fields had become exhausted.[8] A lengthy scholarly literature has documented that Cole was not alone in employing this approach. The "Chesapeake system" of long-term fallow dominated agriculture in colonial Maryland and Virginia.[9] Agricultural historian A. R. Hall succinctly describes the agricultural techniques in early Virginia: "Virgin lands just cleared of the forest were planted to tobacco for 3, 4 or 5 years until they would no longer yield a profitable crop. They were then abandoned at once or planted to corn for a number of years until that crop would no longer pay for the labor devoted to it."[10]

Significantly, shifting cultivation remained a fixture in the Chesapeake for generations. Some planters, especially those on more fertile land, made the transition to continuous cultivation.[11] Long after other areas had "filled up," however, and the sons and daughters of local farmers and planters had begun searching for fresh lands elsewhere, shifting cultivation remained the norm. Historian Jack Temple Kirby, for example, has documented that "fire culture" became a customary cultivation technique among Virginia's small farmers and planters.[12] One such small planter was Daniel Cobb, a Southampton County slaveholder who recorded in January 1853: "I fired a parsel of logs in oald land with 2 hands where I am going to put Cotton."[13] The "oald land" that Cobb referred to was often called "old field." Northern observers such as Frederick Law Olmsted, traveling through eastern Virginia in the 1850s, noted the telltale presence of "old field":

> Old Fields—a coarse, yellow, sandy soil, bearing scarce anything but pine trees and broom sedge. In some places, for acres, the pines would not be above five feet high—that was land that had been in cultivation, used up and "turned out," not more than six or eight

years before; then there were patches of every age; sometimes the trees were a hundred feet high. At long intervals, there were fields in which the pine was just beginning to spring in beautiful green plumes from the ground, and was yet hardly noticeable among the dead brown grass and sassafras bushes and blackberry-vines, which nature first sends to hide the nakedness of the impoverished earth.[14]

Olmsted found much of the same land in South Carolina. Traveling on a broad and straight "thoroughfare," Olmsted observed that "there was very little land in cultivation within sight of the road." Most of the land "had been worn out and deserted."[15] Another northern observer, Solon Robinson, noted a similar landscape when he traveled on the South Carolina Railroad in 1850: "The traveler is constantly impressed with the idea that he is passing through the wild forests of some new country, instead of along one of the oldest railroads in the United States, and through one of the oldest states."[16]

The journals and records of South Carolina's planters confirm Olmsted's observations. John. D. Ashmore, an Upcountry cotton planter, is a good example. Ashmore was hardly a traditional planter. He owned an extensive library of nearly 1,500 volumes, some 650 of which focused on "Mechanical and Agricultural" subjects. His farm journal shows an inquisitive, curious mind continually experimenting with new fertilizers, planting techniques, and implements. The same journal, though, also indicates that Ashmore used shifting cultivation. On January 29, 1853, for example, he recorded: "Five hands cutting & hauling wood and Lightwood. Two hands cleaning out stable & heaping manure. Balance hands cleaning & burning off cotton land." When Ashmore moved to a new farm in Anderson, South Carolina, he planted his first corn crop on "about 30 acres of old & worn out fields covered with wire briers & sassafras and broomsedge. Land apparently not been broken thoroughly in 20 years."[17] When South Carolina cotton planters migrated even farther west to the fresh lands of Alabama and Mississippi, they frequently brought shifting cultivation to their new locales. In antebellum Mississippi, historian John Hebron Moore notes, "wise cotton growers anticipated the destruction of land by acquiring tracts larger than they planned to cultivate at the time they were setting up plantations, so that they would have a reserve of virgin soil to exploit in the future."[18]

Wealthy slaveholders were not the only southerners who used shifting cultivation. Farmers in southern Appalachia also used fire to clear wooded hillsides and slopes. As was the case in plantation districts, the ash from burned trees and shrubs effectively fertilized the land. In many cases, Appalachian farmers did not even remove the tree stumps, planting their corn in untidy mounds scattered throughout their burned land. Although such practices struck many contemporary observers as unsightly, the upland form of shifting cultivation made environmental sense because the root systems from the deadened trees delayed the onset of soil erosion. Once the fertility of the land had been exhausted either through crops or erosion, the farmer abandoned the tract to long-term fallow and burned another section of the farm. As late as the 1980s, farmers in the Ozark Mountains practiced this form of shifting cultivation.[19] In contrast to slaveholding planters, who produced staple crops for national markets, many farmers in western Virginia and other parts of southern Appalachia used shifting cultivation to grow corn and wheat for household use and local trade. Higher transportation costs, which dampened the incentive to produce surpluses for commercial markets, undoubtedly discouraged these farmers from adopting continuous cultivation even when they owned more fertile soils.[20]

Census statistics provide a rough measurement of land in old field sitting unused in fallow and ready to be burned and cropped at some future date. Beginning in 1850, census marshals recorded the number of improved and unimproved acres for each farm and plantation. Improved land was defined as land "reclaimed from a state of nature, and which continues to be reclaimed and used for the purposes of production," including all land cleared for "grazing, grass, and tillage."[21] Most farms, both northern and southern, contained at least some unimproved land, such as woodlands to provide firewood and lumber. Southerners, though, held a far higher percentage of unimproved land in their farms and plantations than cultivators in other regions. In every census year between 1850 and 1890, the percentage of improved land invariably declined as one moved south (Table 1). Virginia and South Carolina exemplified this trend. In 1860 Virginians cultivated less than 37 percent of their total acreage, while South Carolinians cultivated just over 28 percent of their total land. If we examine improved land as a percentage of total area (as opposed to total farmland), the story remains essentially the same. In 1860 Virginians cultivated 28 percent of their state's total land area, while South Carolinians cultivated 24 percent of their state's total area. In the

TABLE 2  Cultivated Acreage as a Percentage of Total Area, 1860

| State/Region | Cultivated Land as % of Total Area | State/Region | Cultivated Land as % of Total Area |
|---|---|---|---|
| New England | 47 | Border South | 34 |
| Massachusetts | 43 | Kentucky | 30 |
| Connecticut | 59 | Delaware | 51 |
| Rhode Island | 50 | Maryland | 48 |
| Vermont | 48 | Upper South | 25 |
| Middle Atlantic | 42 | North Carolina | 21 |
| New York | 48 | Tennessee | 26 |
| Pennsylvania | 36 | Virginia | 28 |
| New Jersey | 41 | Cotton South | 18 |
| Midwest | 40 | Alabama | 20 |
| Ohio | 48 | Georgia | 22 |
| Indiana | 36 | Louisiana | 10 |
| Illinois | 37 | Mississippi | 17 |
|  |  | South Carolina | 24 |

Source: Census statistics at Geostat Center, University of Virginia Library, <http://fisher.lib.virginia.edu/collections/stats/histcensus/>.

North, the percentage of total area in cultivation ranged from 40 to 46 percent (Table 2). The low levels of cultivated land in the South stubbornly persisted into the twentieth century. One historical geographer has concluded that "clearing, depletion, and abandonment of land remained a general practice in much of the South until the 1930s."[22]

Perhaps southerners held large amounts of unimproved land for reasons entirely unrelated to shifting cultivation. Lumber appears to be the most likely alternative, yet the South lagged behind in lumber production until well after Reconstruction had ended. In 1859 the South accounted for only 17 percent of the value of the nation's lumber, which suggests that southern forests were burned for their ash and not cut for their timber.[23] When the South became a prominent producer later in the nineteenth century, large-scale lumber camps, not individual farms, became the center of production.²⁴ One might also imagine that planters and farmers used their unimproved woodlands to feed livestock, but cattle were generally of secondary importance for most southern cultivators. The value of southern livestock in the antebellum period was quite low relative to the North, and some plantation masters imported beef and pork to feed their slaves.²⁵ The fact that southern planters let their livestock and swine forage on low-quality forest growth rather than graze on far more nutritious grasses growing in improved pastures is itself a telltale indication of shifting cultivation. Cattle grazing on improved pastures produced manure to revitalize fields; livestock subsisting in forests or unimproved fields provided little fertilizer for corn, cotton, and other crops.²⁶

Perhaps the best evidence of shifting cultivation comes from southerners themselves. A flourishing agricultural reform movement—analyzed at length in chapter 2—mournfully observed the popularity of shifting cultivation throughout the South. Correspondent "S.D.M.," writing in Richmond's *Southern Planter* in 1846, complained: "In my county the quantity of waste, or land given up to reclaim itself in pine, is a large proportion of almost every tract I have seen in market." The large acreage in wasteland, S.D.M. argued, depressed real estate values and encouraged western emigration.²⁷ Another Virginia correspondent made a similar point a few years later: "Everything is taken up in the planting, the cultivation, and the getting in of a bad crop spread over an immense space."²⁸ South Carolinians also noted their reliance on shifting cultivation. Robert Mills, who visited every district in the state to gather material for his 1826 gazette, bemoaned the state's backward agricultural practices. Mills characterized agriculture in the Upcountry cotton district of Marlborough as "the same ruinous system of cultivation practised in other places. . . . One piece of land after another is exhausted and abandoned . . . forest after forest is felled, and reduced to ashes, without regard to the consequences of such waste."²⁹ The apparent "waste" of shifting cultivation frustrated other South Carolinians as well. In 1840 an agricultural survey of St. Matthews Parish (also located in the cotton Upcountry) noted that "the lands in this Parish were once uncommonly fine and productive . . . but by improvident culture they have greatly deteriorated. . . . The fields were worked as long as they produced any thing, and then abandoned, and other fields cleared and exhausted."³⁰

## THE ENVIRONMENTAL ORIGINS OF SHIFTING CULTIVATION

If southerners had such disdain for shifting cultivation, why did they continue to use it throughout the nineteenth century? Historians have frequently pointed to some combination of slavery, cheap western lands, and ingrained traditionalism. According to one interpretation, slavery discouraged southerners from becoming attached to their land. To maximize profits, planters "mined the soil" before migrating with their mobile labor force to inexpensive lands in the West.[31] Other historians have similarly argued that the South's "relative abundance of land and high cost of labor" created low land prices, which encouraged extensive cultivation techniques.[32] Still another interpretation posits that southerners, influenced by a Celtic cultural heritage, avoided the hard work of building barns and improving pastures, preferring instead to enjoy a leisurely life as cattle and swine roamed the woods.[33] To some extent, these interpretations reflect the attitude of northern observers, who castigated southern cultivation techniques as lazy and wasteful.

These explanations are hard to square with the different levels of improved land *within* Virginia, South Carolina, and the rest of the South. Not all southerners allowed their cattle and swine to roam in uncultivated wastes. In areas with particularly good soils—northern Virginia, the Shenandoah Valley, and in several Upcountry districts in South Carolina—the percentage of improved land greatly exceeded southern norms (Table 3). Farmers and planters in these regions, in fact, collectively cultivated some 61 percent of their land, a figure that exceeds the overall northern average. In other southern states, the same pattern held true. In Kentucky, for example, farmers and planters in the limestone Bluegrass Region improved nearly 70 percent of their land. The presence of continuous cultivation in these areas raises important questions for the current literature. If slavery was to blame for shifting cultivation, why did the slaveholders in limestone counties improve such a high percentage of their land? As Table 3 indicates, slavery flourished in many of these highly fertile counties. On a per-square-mile basis, in fact, these limestone areas contained some of the densest slave populations in the entire South. If cheap western land led to shifting cultivation, why did farmers and planters in these selected areas apparently ignore the siren call of the frontier? If southern culture created shifting cultivation, why did planters and

*Shifting Cultivation and Slavery*

TABLE 3  Intensive Cultivation in Selected Virginia and
South Carolina Counties, 1860

| County | State | Percentage of Improved Land | Total Population Per Square Mile | Slaves Per Square Mile |
| --- | --- | --- | --- | --- |
| Jefferson | Va. | 78 | 69.2 | 18.9 |
| Clarke | Va. | 77 | 40.4 | 19.1 |
| Loudoun | Va. | 74 | 41.9 | 10.6 |
| Fauquier | Va. | 70 | 33.4 | 16.1 |
| Rappahannock | Va. | 68 | 33.1 | 13.2 |
| Berkeley | Va. | 69 | 39.0 | 5.14 |
| Culpepper | Va. | 64 | 31.7 | 17.5 |
| Laurens | S.C. | 67 | 33.0 | 18.5 |
| Virginia | | 37 | 25.1 | 7.7 |
| South Carolina | | 28 | 23.4 | 13.4 |

Source: Census statistics at Geostat Center, University of Virginia Library, <http://fisher.lib.virginia.edu/collections/stats/histcensus/>.

farmers in these areas practice continuous cultivation while agriculturalists in neighboring localities did not?[34]

What made the intensive-cultivation counties unique was their excellent soils and hospitable climate, which were particularly well suited for continuous cultivation. The rest of the South typically did not enjoy these advantages. Northerners often blamed shifting cultivation on slavery, but even the fiercest critics of the slave South sometimes recognized the generally poor fertility of southern soils. Olmsted, when traveling in South Carolina, ran into a fellow northerner working as a stagecoach driver. Olmsted reported their conversation as follows:

> I asked, "How do you like the country, here?"
> "Very nice country," said the agent.
> "Rather poor soil, I should say."
> "It's the cussedest poor country God ever created," snapped out the driver.[35]

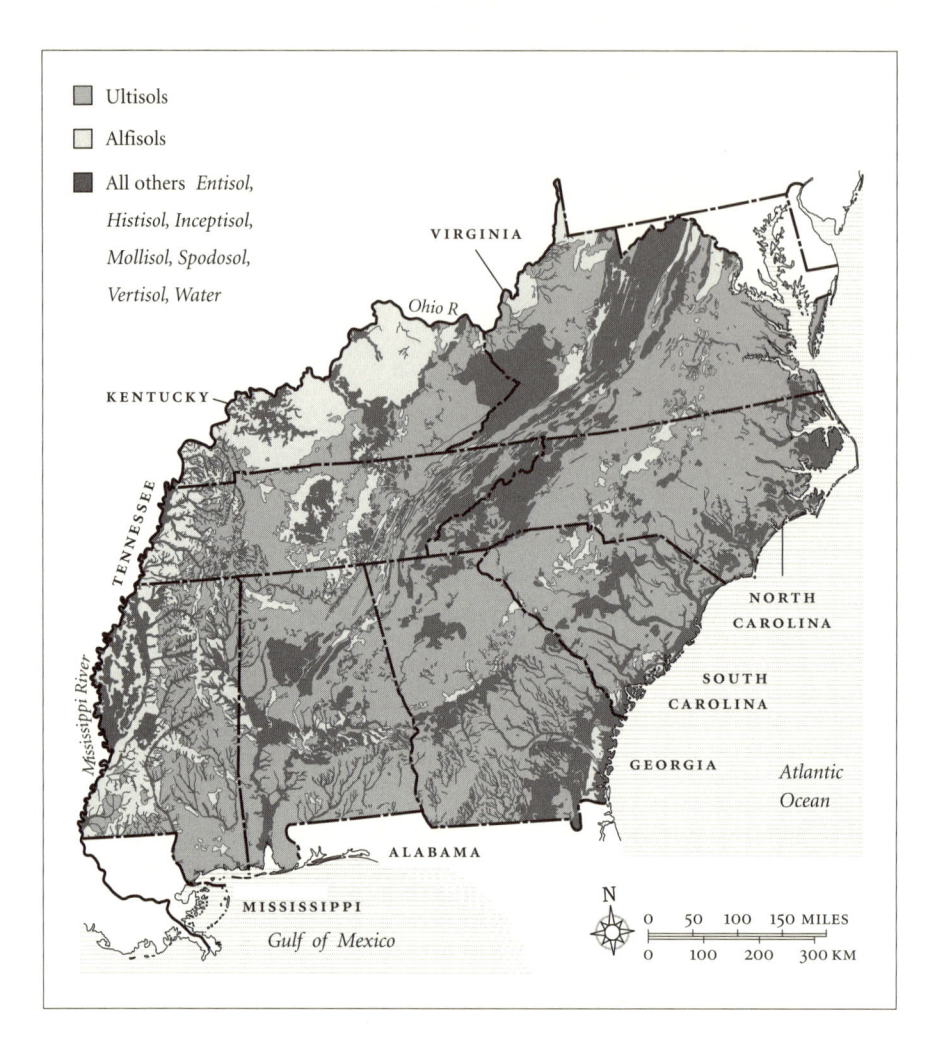

MAP 1   ULTISOLS IN THE SOUTH
*The ultisol soil order predominates in the South. The few nonultisol areas, not surprisingly, had the highest ratios of improved acreage in the region. (Original map by Jarad Beckman; modified for publication by Dorothy McClaren)*

Soil scientists have classified the "cussedest poor country God ever created" as part of the ultisol soil order. Ultisols generally lack key nutrients for plant growth and tend to be highly acidic.[36] The acidity makes it difficult for plants to fully utilize whatever nutrients are present, which means that fertilizing the soil will not raise crop yields unless the acidity is first neutralized. Even a cursory examination of a soil order map (Map 1) shows that the South is heavily burdened with ultisols. Their poor fertility and high acidity explains why southerners burned forest and undergrowth to "fertilize" their land. The ash provided a quick infusion of important nutrients, and its calcium content helped neutralize the acidic ultisol soils.[37] Agricultural writers, in fact, praised ash as a fertilizer precisely because it increased the productivity of soils lacking "calcareous matter."[38] The effectiveness of ash as a cheap, efficient fertilizer (at least before it is leached out of the soil) helps account for why scientists have found a strong correlation between shifting cultivation and ultisols in the tropics today.[39]

The most successful northern cultivators, on the other hand, farmed soils that scientists have classified as alfisols. Alfisols contain an abundance of phosphorus, potassium, calcium, and other essential plant nutrients. Using a highly developed system of mixed husbandry, northern farmers made excellent use of these soils.[40] Field rotations usually included clover and other legumes, which added nitrogen to fields planted in wheat and corn during previous seasons. Cattle grazing in improved pastures, meanwhile, provided tons of high-quality manure that recycled key nutrients to maintain the farm's long-term productivity.[41] Farmers cultivating alfisols could thus produce a diversified output of grains, hay, meat, and diary products while cultivating an exceedingly high proportion of their land. The most populous agricultural hinterlands of major northeastern cities—southeast Pennsylvania (Philadelphia), central and western Maryland (Baltimore), and upstate New York (New York City)—all contained significant stretches of alfisol land ideally suited for continuous cultivation.

Northern farmers enjoyed other advantages as well. Important fodder crops such as hay and clover that supported continuous cultivation failed to thrive in the warm and humid southern climate. Planters and farmers in the cotton states (including South Carolina) fed their cattle the best they could—most often with cow peas and low-quality grasses—but the relatively low nutritional value of such feed meant that southern cattle produced less dung than northern cattle. The warm southern climate also created a hospitable environment for ticks that spread southern cattle fever (more popularly, if less accurately, known as "Texas cattle fever").[42] Southern cattle exposed to such infections at an early age developed immunity to the worst effects of the disease. The price for developing this immunity, though, was high. Southern cattle fever stunted growth and decreased milk output, which made cattle less valuable. The disease also made it exceedingly difficult for southerners to improve their stock; high-quality breeds from Europe or the North without immunity quickly succumbed to cattle fever.[43] Even in areas not suffering from southern cattle fever, the South's hot and humid climate suppressed milk production in cows and made it far more difficult for southerners to produce fresh butter and cheese.[44] Under these adverse conditions, southerners devoted relatively little time and energy to managing livestock and creating improved pastures. Leaving swine and cattle to roam the forest, while ecologically sensible, left southerners without a crucial link necessary to practice continuous cultivation.

Erosion was another important factor that limited continuous cultivation in the South. In the nineteenth century, almost all areas of the United States experienced some erosion, but the problem was particularly severe in the South because of the region's unique rainfall patterns. Simply put, it rained harder in the South. Soil erosion experts have developed a "Rainfall Erosion Factor" (R-factor) to measure the intensity and duration of storms. The higher the R-factor, the more likely that local rainfall will intensify soil erosion. The Southeast has the highest R-Factor in the nation, with intense, pelting storms creating a particularly high rate of soil erosion.[45] The greater risk of soil erosion put southern cultivators in a difficult situation. Continuous cultivation was problematic because row crops such as cotton and corn created channels that carried away precious topsoil. On the other hand, shifting cultivation, which left soil without a protective vegetative cover for several years, could also exacerbate erosion. The resulting erosion of uncultivated fields created a gullied and scarred landscape that shocked northerners and southerners alike.[46] As early as 1799, planter John H. Craven noted that land in Virginia's piedmont was "worn out, washed and gullied, so that scarcely an acre could be found in a place fit for cultivation."[47]

The census data on improved/unimproved acreage in southern farms and plantations bolsters the case that environmental factors resulted in shifting cultivation. Using 1860 and 1890 census data for counties in nine southern states, the tables in the statistical appendix show the results of several multivariate regressions. The dependent variable (the one whose behavior is to be explained) is the percentage of unimproved land in a county. The independent variables (the factors that may or may not influence the dependent variable) include measures of soil quality, topography, and the presence of livestock disease. Economic factors, such as the presence of a nearby city or railroad, are also included. Multivariate regressions, while certainly not perfect, are an exceptionally good way of assessing the impact of a particular variable because the effect of all other specified variables is held constant. The railroad variable, for example, shows the impact of a nearby railroad on the percentage of improved land after soil quality, topography, livestock disease, and other factors have been taken into account.

Readers interested in the details of the regressions may want to study the tables in the statistical appendix more closely. In summary, the regressions indicate that the environmental factors (soil types, typography, and climate) greatly influenced levels of improved land; they show a particularly strong association between alfisol soils and high levels of improved land. Ultisols and rugged topography (such as the mountains of Appalachia or the marshes of the coastal regions), on the other hand, led to low levels of improved land. The regressions predict that a planter in the South Carolina piedmont cultivating cotton on ultisol soils would have improved only 40 percent of his land, while a Virginia planter growing tobacco on alfisol soil would have improved some 62 percent of his acreage. What makes the statistical results for 1860 even more telling is that the same basic relationship holds for 1890 as well. Despite the greater availability of fertilizers, farmers in counties with poor soils cultivated far less land than farmers located in areas with more favorable soils. The 1890 results cast further doubt that slavery and cheap western land caused shifting cultivation. Shifting cultivation, simply put, outlived both.

In contrast to the environmental variables, economic factors such as railroads and urbanization—the product of human choice and action—had relatively little impact on the percentage of improved land within the South. This was a major regional difference. The North's vibrant urban and manufacturing sector, as well as its rapidly improving transportation network, created larger markets for farmers, which gave them a greater incentive to improve more land.[48] A self-reinforcing dynamic developed in which intensive cultivation encouraged urban growth and transportation improvements, which then allowed farmers to improve an even higher percentage of their land. Farms in close proximity to large cities had especially high levels of improved land.[49] Farmers in the six counties near Philadelphia, for example, cultivated nearly 83 percent of their improved acreage. In the South, on the other hand, urbanization made little difference. In 1860 farmers and planters in twenty-seven southern urban counties (defined as having cities with a population greater than 5,000) cultivated 37.3 percent of their land, a figure far below national averages. In the nine counties containing the South's major port cities (including Norfolk and Charleston), planters and farmers cultivated less than 20 percent of their land.

Outside of a few agricultural reformers, hardly anyone recognized the environmental factors that led to shifting cultivation in the antebellum period. Agricultural reformers certainly picked up on problems with specific soils and specific livestock diseases, but few believed that the southern geography and climate encouraged shifting cultivation in a generalized way. Northerners and southerners, in fact, often agreed that the South was naturally more fertile than the frigid climes of the Northeast. Olmsted, for example, quoted at length the noted oceanographer Matthew Maury of Virginia, who was an enthusiastic booster of southern commercial development. The hinterland of Norfolk, according to Maury, had far more advantages than the area surrounding New York City: "The back country [of Norfolk] . . . surpasses that which is tributary to New York in mildness of climate, in fertility of soil, and variety of production." Olmsted concurred: "There is little, if any exaggeration to this [Maury's] estimate."[50] For Olmsted (the northern partisan), the blighting impact of slavery erased the South's natural advantages; for Maury (the southern partisan), national commercial policies such as the tariff accounted for Norfolk's backwardness. Both missed the point that the sandy, infertile soils surrounding the city necessitated shifting cultivation, which created a sparsely populated hinterland. Maury, Olmsted, and other antebellum writers conflated the ability to grow staple crops such as cotton, tobacco, rice, and sugar with fertile soils and other favorable environmental conditions. The reality was far different. In the long run, the South's soils, climate, and topography prevented intensive agriculture and slowed long-term development.

## DEADENING DEVELOPMENT: THE ECONOMIC CONSEQUENCES OF SLAVERY AND SHIFTING CULTIVATION

From the standpoint of an individual planter or farmer, shifting cultivation was not necessarily a problem. Although erosion and other factors might lower long-term fertility, land subjected to shifting cultivation could still produce sizeable profits, especially if crop prices remained high. In the 1850s, for example, many planters and farmers in Virginia and South Carolina experienced sustained prosperity on land that had been cropped for generations because of high prices for cotton, tobacco, and wheat.[51] Other parts of the South—such as the Black Belt of Mississippi and Alabama—produced even greater riches for the planting class. In 1860 nearly two out of every three men who left estates of $100,000 or more resided in the South.[52] Not only was shifting cultivation compatible with the accumulation of great wealth; it was also compatible with innovation. In the colonial era, when most planters used shifting cultivation, agricultural productivity increased substantially over time.[53] In the antebellum period, the widespread use of shifting cultivation did not deter experimentation with new cotton seeds and labor routines to improve productivity.[54] Historians have sometimes associated shifting cultivation with semisubsistence agriculture or traditional folk practices, but southern farmers and planters made this regime part of a highly successful system of commercial agriculture that incorporated a substantial degree of innovation.[55]

The success of southern agriculture, though, came at a high price. Adding unimproved acres required larger farms and larger plantations without increasing the size of the workforce, thus stunting rural population growth. In terms of *rural* population per square mile, southern states such as South Carolina and Virginia lagged far behind most northern states. In 1860, for example, the South Atlantic region (Virginia, North Carolina, South Carolina, and Georgia) contained 20.3 total rural residents per square mile and 11.7 free rural residents per square mile, which was lower than the population density of New England (thirty-three rural residents per square mile), the Middle Atlantic states (forty-nine rural residents per square mile), and the old Northwest (thirty-five rural resident per square mile).[56] The fact that shifting cultivation dispersed population was well known in the colonial period. "By the middle of the eighteenth century," writes historian T. H. Breen, "most [Virginia] planters accepted that dispersed settlement was an inevitable product of a particular type of agriculture."[57]

Adam Smith's 1776 *The Wealth of Nations* provides a way of understanding how the South's low population densities helped stifle overall development. The Scottish economist famously argued that long-term increases in national wealth depended upon the division of labor and the extent of markets. To make his point, Smith gave the rather mundane example of pin manufacturing. Even a skilled artisan, Smith argued, could barely produce twenty pins per day. The lone worker would have to straighten the wire, cut it into tiny parts, make the heads, carefully attach the heads to the wire, and then package them for sale. A workshop, however, could subdivide the task of making pins into distinct operations. Because workers specialized in each operation, productivity in the workshop rose dramatically; a single firm with ten employees might make 48,000 pins a day. Smith's argument, though, contained an important catch: the workshop needed a market so that it could sell its 48,000 pins. With no market, there could be no division of labor and no corresponding increase in productivity.[58]

In the North, a prosperous and deep rural population provided the stimulus needed for early industrialization. The "extent of markets" was a key variable stimulating manufacturing in the Midwest and Northeast. As the population increased and transportation improved, manufacturing firms competing in larger markets had greater incentives to expand output and improve productivity. Dense networks of farms in southern New England, upstate New York, and southeastern Pennsylvania provided particularly rich markets for manufactured goods. These local markets—rather than more distant trade with the West or South—spurred manufacturing in cities such as New York and Philadelphia. The chapter titles of David R. Meyer's recent synthesis of early northern industrialization—"Prosperous Farmers Energize the Economy" and "Agriculture Augments Regional Industrial Systems"—testify to the vital contribution of deep and rich rural markets to the rapid expansion of northern manufacturing.[59] Meyer builds on a long line of scholarly research that shows how deep rural markets generated market towns that supported blacksmiths, carpenters, tanners, and other small manufacturers. The small market towns, in turn, became incorporated into the hinterlands of larger regional centers to form a complex urban network. The northern urban network generated powerful metropolitan industrial centers such as New

York, Philadelphia, and Baltimore, but a wealthy and densely populated countryside provided the economic foundation for the North's large and prosperous cities.[60] Economic historians have labeled northern expansion "Smithian industrialization" to denote the importance of relatively modest workshops that subdivided labor and raised productivity as markets continued to expand.[61]

Shifting cultivation effectively precluded Smithian industrialization. A sparsely settled countryside meant fewer people, smaller markets, and, ultimately, less manufacturing and urban development. A population spread thinly over a wide area discouraged local manufacturing. The lack of local manufacturing and urban development in turn reinforced the incentives of slaveholders to achieve self-sufficiency. With few towns and cities to provide goods and services, slaveholders had a greater incentive to use their slaves to produce textiles, shoes, and other goods for home use when the demands of the plantation slackened.[62] Southerners thus failed to develop the local pools of capital, skilled workers, and entrepreneurial ability that had helped sustain northern industrialization. To provide quantitative evidence on this point, the regressions in the appendix test the relationship between levels of improved land in southern counties and different types of manufacturing output in 1860. The question, at its most basic level, is whether counties that improved more land also manufactured more goods. As we might expect, the regressions show that higher percentages of improved land within a county was associated with greater production of agricultural implements and consumer goods (including textiles, hats, and shoes). More improved land also meant more buildings, which generated higher output for construction and building trades. The regressions imply that if southerners had improved the same percentage of their land as did the nation as a whole in 1860, they would have significantly increased the production of manufactured goods.

Shifting cultivation, though, was not the only factor inhibiting the growth of markets. A great deal of scholarship has noted that the inequality inherent in slavery depressed local markets for manufactured goods. Historian Eugene Genovese, for example, has argued that a large number of slaves and poor whites consumed little in the way of manufactured goods, while a small number of wealthy plantation owners purchased luxury items directly from the North or from abroad. Serving only limited markets, southern manufacturers failed to reap the same economies of scale that northern industry enjoyed. The South was thus caught in a frustrating quandary: it provided a market for outside industry, but that market was too small to sustain local producers that could compete with more productive northern firms.[63] Scholars have highlighted several problems with Genovese's argument, but the quantitative evidence in the appendix nevertheless suggests that his general approach was correct.[64] The same regressions that show that unimproved land deterred manufacturing output also indicate that the presence of slavery discouraged the production of consumer goods. Slavery and shifting cultivation, working in tandem, depressed local manufacturing.

The plantation records of rice planter J. D. Sparkman (referred to at the beginning of the chapter) provide a concrete example of how shifting cultivation interacted with slavery to limit local development. Sparkman's Springwood Plantation included 2,139 acres, 139 of which were rice lands and 2,000 of which were uplands. Sparkman reported that only 120 of the 2,000 upland acres were improved when he purchased Springwood. At the time of the sale, sixty slaves worked Springwood's lands. If we generously assume that ten whites (Sparkman's family and any overseers) lived at Springwood as well, then the overall population density of the plantation (white versus slave) was only twenty-one people per square mile, which was about the same for the South Atlantic region as a whole. In contrast, the same 2,139 acres that Sparkman owned would have supported twenty-six farms in Lancaster County, Pennsylvania, a rich limestone area about fifty miles west of Philadelphia. Farmers in the Lancaster area improved almost 83 percent of their land, which created a rural population far larger than Sparkman's mostly unimproved plantation.

The percentage of improved land and the density of settlement was not the only difference between Lancaster County and Springwood. Lancaster farmers used the profits from their intensively cultivated farms to purchase clothes, furniture, books, clocks, and a long list of consumer goods. Sparkman, on the other hand, provided his slaves with relatively little in the way of consumer goods. According to his plantation accounts, slaves received a new blanket every other year and cloth twice a year. In November 1844, for example, Sparkman recorded that men received an allowance of 6.5 yards, women received 5 yards, children 2 to 4.5 yards, and infants 1.75 yards. Notice, too, that Sparkman only provided the cloth; the slaves themselves had to cut and sew their own clothes. A notation regarding "60 pairs Negro shoes" appears in the journal in 1844 but not 1845 or 1846. Sparkman also gave rations of molasses and whiskey, but he was not overly generous with these small luxuries: "I recommend in the future no Whiskey—but Tobacco for those who Smoke—and extra rations of Rice to those who prefer it."[65] Serving a thinly populated hinterland, southern ports specialized in the collection and exportation of staple crops. Plantations such as Springwood created what historian Peter Coclanis has termed "market disarticulation"—the inability to generate market towns and local manufacturing that could set the stage for more widespread industrialization.[66]

The slow and uneven growth of cities in Virginia and South Carolina highlights the difficulty of sustaining commercial and industrial development in a rural economy with a dispersed population and a large number of slaves. Between 1790 and 1860, port cities in Virginia and South Carolina, lacking large markets to simulate development, declined in relative importance. In 1790, for example, Charleston ranked as the fourth-largest city in the United States. By 1840 it had fallen to ninth, and by 1860 it ranked twenty-third.[67] In Virginia, Norfolk matched Baltimore's population on the eve of the American Revolution. Baltimore, which could tap a rich alfisol hinterland in western Maryland and southern Pennsylvania, grew to become the nation's third-largest city by 1860. Norfolk, with a population of less than 15,000, did not rank in the top fifty in 1860.[68] Richmond exhibited far more growth than either Charleston or Norfolk, and its bustling manufacturing sector earned it the title of "Lowell of the South." Yet with a population of less than 38,000 in 1860, Richmond was slightly smaller than medium-sized northern cities such as Troy, New York, and New Haven, Connecticut.[69] Focusing on tobacco, grain milling, and iron processing, Richmond never produced the diverse array of goods (such as textiles, boots and shoes, ready-made clothing, agricultural implements, and machinery) emanating from large northern cities.[70] The "Lowell of the South" had a long way to go to compete with northern giants such as New York, Philadelphia, and Boston.

Improved transportation might have been one way to overcome limited local markets. If one could imagine an antebellum world with no transportation costs, local market size would have mattered little and southerners could have easily sold goods in the more densely populated Midwest and Northeast. In the real antebellum economy, though, transportation costs remained significant. Transportation projects such as canals and railroads were more difficult to finance and build in the South. Chapter 3 analyzes the impact of slavery and shifting cultivation on the

South's transportation network, but it is worth noting here that a canal or a railroad or even a country lane in the South had to meander through large stretches of unproductive land to connect plantations, farms, and cities. The large swaths of unimproved land generated little traffic, which dramatically reduced potential revenue per square mile. Slavery compounded the "lack of demand" problem. Slaves could not ride as passengers or buy consumer goods that might have helped fill canal boats and railroad cars. Southern railroads, not surprisingly, lacked the revenue and capital to reach many parts of the southern Upcountry, much less the markets of the Midwest.

Low population densities also made it more difficult for southerners to create institutions that could create and disseminate productive knowledge. A region composed of isolated farms and plantations generated fewer subscribers for periodicals and newspapers, had fewer potential members for mechanics' institutes or literary associations, and provided fewer students for schools and colleges. Economic historians have found a strong correlation between low population density and illiteracy in the antebellum period, whether one considers the North or the South. In the North, low population in rural areas was a temporary phenomenon associated with recent settlement.[71] In the South, shifting cultivation created the demographic equivalent of a permanent frontier in which vast amounts of land remained uncultivated for generations. Slavery, of course, made it even more difficult to support institutions that generated human capital. Slaves could not subscribe to newspapers, join voluntary organizations, or attend schools. The South, as many historians have noted, was behind the North in the number of schools and libraries as well as other indicators of educational achievement.[72] Southerners themselves often felt overly dependent on northern newspapers and northern literature, and calls for an authentically "southern" literature became commonplace in the antebellum period.[73] Cultural and political factors undoubtedly contributed to the southern lag in literary institutions, but the combination of slavery and shifting cultivation added to the difficulty of publishing southern newspapers, periodicals, and books.

Southern dependence on northern publishers and other northern firms helps put into context the economic boom of the 1850s. High crop prices created widespread prosperity that many southerners regarded as conclusive proof that a slave economy could flourish. Prosperity, though, did not translate into economic and political security. During the 1850s,

Virginia's population grew 12 percent and South Carolina's population grew 5 percent, well behind the national growth rate of 36 percent. The national political standing in each state declined steadily over the antebellum decades. In 1790 about one out of four Americans (whether slave or free) lived in either Virginia or South Carolina. In 1830 the number had fallen to one out of every seven, and by 1860 it was one out of every fourteen. Political declension had special significance for Virginians: a Virginian had occupied the White House for thirty-two out of the first thirty-six years of the nation's existence, but in the 1830s the Old Dominion seemed relegated to second-rate status. So, too, was South Carolina, where competition from fresh cotton lands proved particularly intense. In the bustling antebellum economy, where northerners touted their economic accomplishments and even planters in the new cotton states could boast of great fortunes, stagnating Virginia and South Carolina seemed decidedly out of place. Nullification and radical states' rights ideology flourished in South Carolina and in some parts of Virginia just as the sense of political decline became noticeable in the 1820s and 1830s. Unable to keep pace with the North's expanding population, southerners turned to political theories that focused on protecting the rights of (white) political minorities.[74]

THE NORTHERN CRITIQUE OF SLAVERY AND
SHIFTING CULTIVATION

In some respects, the agriculturalists of Virginia and South Carolina differed little from their northern counterparts. Many rural communities in the North faced the same specter of relative decline. Northern farmers, on average, cultivated a higher percentage of their land, but more intensive farming practices only delayed the exodus of young men and women seeking cheaper land and greater opportunities in the West. Seeing their sons and daughters move elsewhere, many northern communities had to come to grips with population loss and declining or stagnant land values. Residents of towns bypassed by the transportation revolution were especially vulnerable, as a canal or railroad located even a few miles away might attract trade, growth, and population to a nearby rival.[75] Even in prosperous areas, relatively few farm families established a sense of rooted stability. By the middle of the nineteenth century, less than 50 percent of northern households "persisted" from one decennial census to the next.[76] Many observers in the North, like Vermont congressman Justin Smith

Morrill, worried about "the tendency to desert the rural districts and to shun manual labor."[77] No wonder many northerners wanted to keep the western territories free of slavery and open to free labor. Western migration was just as important to northern farm families as it was to southerners.

Unlike in Virginia and South Carolina, western migration in the North did not create intense political anxieties or a sense of economic and political decline. Immigration into fast-growing cities more than made up for those who departed to the West. The waves of new migrants certainly created important social tensions and economic divisions, but northerners generally celebrated the industrial and technological accomplishments of their free-labor economy. Middle-class northerners believed that northern economic superiority stemmed from the entrepreneurship, innovation, and enterprise that this economy generated. In contrast, southern states such as Virginia and South Carolina appeared stagnant and backward. Slavery, northerners increasingly believed, was incompatible with economic progress. Northern critics of slavery may well have exaggerated the supposed stagnation of the South, but census data and other statistics provided powerful evidence of northern economic superiority.

As part of their belief in the superiority of free labor, northerners harshly criticized shifting cultivation. Southern agriculture, northerners believed, lacked the order and refinement that characterized the North's neat and carefully maintained farms. The unsightly nature of southern farms and plantations—the recently burned fields, the seemingly endless forests of pine, and the shockingly neglected livestock—all accentuated the region's apparent lack of development. The South's uncultivated landscape and dispersed population created a ramshackle air about the region—its public buildings seemed less impressive, its farms and plantations less permanent, and its community institutions (including libraries, schools, and churches) less developed.[78] For northerners who believed in the economic and moral superiority of free labor—what historians have called free-labor ideology—the desultory state of southern agriculture became a powerful indictment of slavery.[79] The laziness that seemed to pervade southern agriculture provided compelling evidence that slavery devalued hard work and suppressed enterprise. As early as the Missouri Crisis of 1819–20, northerners openly worried that slavery would ruin farming practices in the West, much to the detriment of northern settlers.

New York congressman John Taylor, for example, considered the border between Maryland and Pennsylvania as the "dividing line between farms highly cultivated and plantations laying open to the common and overrun with weeds; between stone barns and stone bridges on one side, and stalk cribs and no bridges on the other, between a neat, blooming, animated, rosy cheeked peasantry on one side, and a squalid, slow motioned, black population on the other."[80] In similar fashion, the *New Hampshire Patriot* compared New England's "neat and trim houses and cottages, our well covered barns and well stocked granaries" with the slave South, where "the land appears almost as a waste."[81]

Foreign observers often made the same unfavorable comparisons between southern and northern agriculture. None was more famous than Alexis de Tocqueville's comparison of Ohio and Kentucky. De Tocqueville, it should be noted, spent only two weeks in the South; most of his eight-month stay in the United States was spent in New York and New England. Despite his evident lack of familiarity with the South, De Tocqueville saw the Ohio River as a border between two labor systems that created radically different landscapes. On the Kentucky side, "the population is sparse, from time to time one descries a troop of slaves loitering in the half-deserted fields; the primeval forest reappears at every turn; society seems to be asleep, man to be idle, and nature alone offers a scene of activity and life." On the Ohio side, "the fields are covered with abundant harvests; the elegance of the dwellings announces the taste and activity of the laborers."[82] De Tocqueville, a critic of slavery, attributed the differences to the superior efficiency and work ethic of free labor. De Tocqueville's characterization of Kentucky agriculture was overly simplistic. The Bluegrass Region—perhaps the most intensively cultivated region in the nation—did not contain many "half-deserted fields" or much in the way of "primeval forest." Perhaps the desultory state of southern agriculture had become a regional stereotype that observers such as De Tocqueville expected to find.

No single writer solidified the regional stereotypes regarding slavery and southern agriculture more than Frederick Law Olmsted. Olmsted, like De Tocqueville, detested slavery. As a landscape architect who would later design New York City's Central Park, Olmsted had an eye for telling detail that made his critique far more powerful. Olmsted's observations—sometimes wry and humorous, sometimes freighted with moral indignation—appeared in northern newspapers as well as in his own popular books (Illustration 1). When traveling through the Virginia countryside, for example, Olmsted reported that he became lost along the poorly marked roads and isolated homesteads. Getting directions was almost impossible; Olmsted saw more wild hogs ("long, lank, bony, snake-headed, hairy wild beasts") than people when traveling through the pine forests of Virginia. The only dwelling that Olmsted passed was "a house, across a large new old-field." When he finally reached the county seat, he noted that it consisted of thirty or so buildings, including several stores, a law office, a saddler's shop, and two public houses. For the hub of local commerce, the straggling town was slim pickings, indeed.[83] Olmsted found South Carolina to be no better. When attending a religious service among plain country folk, he noted that the "meeting house [he would not dignify it as a church] stood in a small clearing of the woods, and there was no habitation within two miles of it." Groups of men roasting potatoes in campfires outside the meetinghouse—along with the homespun clothing of the congregation—confirmed what Olmsted saw as a rude lack of refinement.[84] For Olmsted, isolation, shifting cultivation, and poverty went hand in hand.

The reports of Olmsted and other northern travelers made shifting cultivation part of an economic critique of slavery that northern politicians frequently articulated within the halls of Congress. David Wilmot, an antislavery Democrat from Pennsylvania, frequently associated slavery with soil exhaustion. "Sterility follows its [slavery's] path," he declared in 1846.[85] A decade later, Representative Israel Washburn of Maine noted that "their [southerners'] lands are being worn out and exhausted. . . . [T]hey have not the enterprise, skill, or means to renovate them, or, as our Yankee farmers would say, 'bring them to.' Under this system, the country grows poorer, year by year." Washburn compared the blighted fruits of plantation slavery to the "smiling farms and pleasant homes" of the North.[86] Edward Wade of Ohio, echoing Olmsted's critique of the rude, unrefined, and uncultivated South, argued in 1854 that northern settlers would populate the West with tidy farms and new schoolhouses— "the germ of the highest order of civilization known to the human race"—while southern settlement would produce nothing but slaveholders, slaves, and "lean and half-famished 'sand-hillers' and 'poor white folks.'"[87] When describing Virginia, Republican William Seward of New York tied "an exhausted soil" to "old and decaying towns, wretchedly neglected roads, and, in every respect, an absence of enterprise and im-

ILLUSTRATION 1   *Taken from Frederick Law Olmsted's* Journey in the Seaboard Slave States *(1856), this depiction of a poor southern farm aptly demonstrates the social and economic isolation that shifting cultivation created. Notice how the ever-present forest seems to envelop the homestead.*

provement."[88] No wonder that many northerners wanted to stop slavery from spreading to the western territories. Shifting cultivation, they believed, was sure to follow.

No politician synthesized northern critiques of southern agriculture and slavery better than Abraham Lincoln. Like many northerners, Lincoln found great pleasure in the order, neatness, and efficiency of an intensively cultivated landscape. He even chided northern farmers (especially those in the West) for cultivating too much land. "Thorough cultivation," Lincoln told Wisconsin farmers in 1859, made far better sense than planting "broad acres." Economically, thorough cultivation required less land, less labor (there would be fewer acres to plow, sow, and harvest), and less "locomotion" of traveling from field to field. Lincoln, though, put even greater stress on the "effect of thorough cultivation on the farmer's own mind." A farmer could take real pride in a thoroughly cultivated farm. On the other hand, men farming too many acres often used poor methods and thus took little pride in their work. Fences began to fall, cattle trampled the crops, and farmers stored the inadequate har-

*Shifting Cultivation and Slavery*   49

vest in poorly maintained barns and granaries. "Mammoth farms are like tools or weapons, which are too heavy to be handled," Lincoln argued. "Erelong they are thrown aside at a great loss."[89]

Lincoln ostensibly focused on farms in his own region, but references to "mammoth farms," unkempt buildings, and slothful, unmotivated workers undoubtedly reminded his audience of southern agriculture. Lincoln made the connection clearer when he linked the cultivation of farms with the cultivation of the mind. To refute southern "mid-sill" theories that equated free labor with the exploitation of the working class, Lincoln associated free labor with what he termed "its natural companion, education." Free labor, Lincoln declared, "insists on universal education."[90] What made farming (or at least the right kind of farming) so special is that it linked labor with the educated mind. The educated farmer, studying matters rationally and scientifically, worked with "profitable enjoyment" to increase the productivity and efficiency of his small farm. "Every blade of grass is a study, and to produce two where there was but one, is both a profit and a pleasure." A nation that combined "cultivated thought" with the "*thorough* work" of the small farmer was bound to prosper: "Population must increase rapidly . . . and ere long the most valuable of all arts will be the art of deriving the comfortable subsistence from the smallest area of soil."[91]

Lincoln's exaltation of northern agriculture and his condemnation of shifting cultivation created a powerful critique of slavery. On one level, Lincoln and other critics of slavery rightly noted that the combination of slavery and shifting cultivation certainly slowed the development of southern industry and commerce. The northern insistence that slavery *caused* shifting cultivation, though, was simplistic and misleading. Attributing economic progress exclusively to enterprise, education, and hard work, northerners failed to see how superior soils and a more genial climate gave them a significant advantage over the South. Simply importing northern free labor and cultivation techniques could not magically transform southern agriculture. Although shifting cultivation slowly declined after the abolition of slavery, progress was far slower than Republicans had so confidently predicted. Free labor, simply put, was not the panacea for shifting cultivation that northerners had imagined. Northern perceptions that slavery invariably exhausted the land would nevertheless help fuel what economic historian Gavin Wright has called the economic "cold war" between the North and the South.[92]

Virginians and South Carolinians might have opted out of this "cold war" and simply shrugged their shoulders at the economic critique of slavery and shifting cultivation. What if lands in Virginia and South Carolina suffered from soil exhaustion? In the worst-case scenario, Virginians and South Carolinians could migrate to fresh cotton lands in the West, where great fortunes could be made. As long as a western "safety value" existed, the developmental consequences of shifting cultivation mattered little—migration would shift population from one southern state to another. The planters who chose to stay behind in Virginia or South Carolina, moreover, were hardly poor; many could still support their genteel lifestyle. Refined planters, some southerners argued, rightly focused on contentment and happiness rather than the northern obsession with industry and efficiency. "What matter it if the State of Rhode Island does make more than South Carolina?" asked one planter in 1856. "It matters not to me what Rhode Island, or Illinois, or Connecticut, or anywhere else makes. ... If we [southerners] are not so rich, we are content."[93]

Many Virginians and South Carolinians rejected such studied indifference. Like northerners, they connected shifting cultivation with economic stagnation. As the popular agricultural journal *Southern Cultivator* put it in 1843: "We have seen and felt the blighting effects upon the interests and independence of Southern planters, which have been produced by the too common and fatal system of Agriculture almost universally adopted."[94] Newspaper editor Jacob Cardozo, who wrote extensively on the mercantile interests of Charleston merchants, realized that the "future prosperity of our State depends greatly upon a system of *thorough tillage*; our lands are susceptible of improvement and must be *improved*."[95] As chapter 2 demonstrates, the most vociferous defenders of slavery were often the most ardent critics of shifting cultivation. Indeed, northern critics of slavery took great delight in citing southern speeches and southern pamphlets decrying the South's reliance on shifting cultivation.[96] Southerners fumed that northerners took such internal critiques out of context, but such defensiveness revealed southern insecurities over its agricultural regime.

Southern condemnation of shifting cultivation created a surprising national consensus. Northerners and southerners who subscribed to agricultural journals, read political pamphlets, and helped shape political discourse found a landscape of abandoned fields and poorly cultivated farms economically irrational and aesthetically unappealing. Admiration for a well-tended and ordered countryside permeated educated opinion in both the South and the North. When enrolled at Dickinson College in Carlisle, Pennsylvania, in 1856, Virginian William Kinzer was impressed by the landscape of "finely cultivated farms." He recorded in his diary that he wished that the "people of Va. would cultivate their farms more and better, and educate their sons and daughters, like the people of Pa."[97] In associating the cultivation of the land with the cultivation of the mind, this young Virginian (who would fight and die as part of the Stonewall Brigade, one of the most celebrated units in the Confederate army) expressed sentiments similar to those of Abraham Lincoln. Northern critiques hit a raw political nerve precisely because southerners such as Kinzer found shifting cultivation indefensible.

If both sides believed that shifting cultivation was a great evil, then leaders in the two regions differed greatly in their assessment of its cause. Many northerners, of course, blamed slavery for the South's blighted landscape. For northerners, slavery's degradation of labor and hard work made shifting cultivation the product of an "original sin" that could only be erased by replacing servitude with free labor. Singling out Virginia—once the mother of statesmen, "now the sister of decay"—Congressman Washburn of Maine argued in 1856 that only emancipation could reverse the decline of the Old Dominion. "Virginia may try as many expedients and palliatives as she pleases," he declared, "but she cannot change her destiny without changing her system of labor."[98] Republicans took these arguments to their logical conclusion. Since slavery inevitably ruined agriculture and short-circuited progress, the territory in the West would become either a lost Eden corrupted by slavery or a haven for the well-cultivated farms of a free-labor economy. Southerners emphatically rejected such arguments. They attributed shifting cultivation to an unfortunate traditionalism that rational reform would soon correct. Through agricultural societies, experimental farms, advice literature, and endowed professorships, southern reformers sought to enlighten large planters and small farmers about the evils of shifting cultivation—often attempting to enlist southern state governments as allies in this cause.

*t w o*

## AGRICULTURAL REFORM AND
## STATE ACTIVISM

President John Tyler was said to have had two portraits over his mantel: one of Daniel Webster, whom Tyler considered America's greatest statesman; and one of Edmund Ruffin, whom Tyler considered America's greatest agriculturalist.[1] Tyler's pairing of Webster and Ruffin might well have produced wry smiles from knowledgeable political observers. Webster, hailing from New England, often represented the interests of merchants and manufacturers. Ruffin, a Virginian, earned his renown by demonstrating that marl, a mixture of clay and fossilized shells, could revive Virginia's exhausted plantations. Webster was a committed nationalist who spoke eloquently on behalf of the Union; Ruffin supported secession in a steady stream of writings, speeches, and even (in the spirit of John Rutherfoord) a futuristic political novel. Ruffin's willingness to promote southern independence had few limits. In 1860 he sent John Brown's pikes to southern governors, where Ruffin hoped that they might "be placed in some conspicuous position . . . to remain and be preserved as abiding and impressive evidence of the fanatical hatred borne by the dominant Northern party."[2] When the Confederacy bombarded Fort Sumter in April 1861, South Carolinians gave the honor of firing the first shot to Ruffin, who at the age of sixty had volunteered his services to the Palmetto Guards (Illustration 2).

Historians have often noted the strong relationship between agricultural reform and southern extremism.[3] Less well known is how the southern agricultural reform movement strongly promoted state activism. Worried that the South's agricultural practices would ultimately undermine the economic and political foundations of slavery, agricultural reformers believed that their cause could not be left in the uncertain hands of private individuals and voluntary organizations. This chapter highlights how Ruffin and other reformers championed legislative action to promote agricultural experimentation and education. These individuals believed that state governments should subsidize experimental farms, agricultural professorships, geological surveys, agricultural societies, and farm journals to disseminate new knowledge. To complement state educational efforts, some reformers also advocated important changes in property law to encourage the drainage of swamps and to prevent the spread of malaria. In their calls for state action, reformers combined scientific reasoning, economic rationalism, and romantic imagery. The rhetoric of southern agricultural reformers, synthesizing both the modern and the traditional, viewed state support for agricultural research as the hallmark of civilized government.

For all its rhetorical and intellectual energy, the reform movement generally failed to transform southern agriculture in the ways that reformers desired. Many southern farmers and planters prospered in the 1850s, but relatively few of them abandoned shifting cultivation. As noted in the last chapter, farmers and planters in Virginia and South Carolina cultivated on average less than one-third of their land in 1860—a sure sign that the clamor for more intensive farming practices had not changed actual behavior. The fundamental problem, this chapter argues, was that the southern environment made reform measures unprofitable. Fertilizers proved exceedingly expensive to transport long distances; torrential rainfall carried away carefully plowed topsoil; cattle fever and other diseases killed improved breeds of livestock; and the intense southern heat wilted legumes and fodder crops. Reformers imagined a pliable

ILLUSTRATION 2  *Few pictures better symbolize the strong association between agricultural reform and southern extremism than Edmund Ruffin's portrait in his Palmetto Guards uniform. (Courtesy of the National Archives)*

landscape, but nineteenth-century technology and practices led to a decidedly incomplete conquest of the southern environment.

Reformers also failed to conquer their state legislatures. The state governments of South Carolina and Virginia, despite a few gestures on behalf of agricultural research, generally paid little heed to the pleas of the reformers. Given the political stature of the reformers and the relatively small amounts of desired funding, the lack of legislative action is puzzling. One might blame traditionally tight-fisted southern state governments, but the same state governments (as the reformers themselves sourly noted) spent millions of dollars on railroads, canals, and other internal improvements. A more convincing explanation is that persistent factionalism and regionalism within each state accentuated fears that the legislature might fund a white elephant. What interest did the yeoman farmers of western Virginia have in funding an experimental farm that promised to benefit the slaveholding planters of eastern Virginia? What stake did Lowcountry rice planters in South Carolina have in research that benefited Upcountry cotton planters? The agricultural reform movement failed to convincingly answer such questions.

On an ideological level, however, the movement's embrace of an ambitious legislative agenda suggests that southern extremism and state activism often went hand in hand. Saving slavery from abolitionists and other enemies, reformers argued, would require the collective effort of (white) southerners to transform their agricultural routines and increase the population, wealth, and political power of their region. Reform signified patriotic devotion to the long-term interests of the South, while shifting cultivation represented the results of a narrow individualism that threatened the very survival of slavery. The same ethos of extolling collective action and condemning excessive individualism played an important role in building the wartime Confederate state, whether as justification for conscription or as rationalization for confiscatory taxation. The rhetoric of the agricultural reformers suggests that the basic principle behind the growth of the Confederate state—that energetic government action was sometimes needed to save slavery—had deep roots in secessionist thought.

AGRICULTURAL REFORM AND THE DEFENSE OF SLAVERY

Ruffin's quest to save southern society through agricultural reform began with his own family. With a growing family to support (his wife Susan gave birth to eleven children between 1813 and 1832), Ruffin faced the same difficult choice that confronted so many of Virginia's planters in the first three decades of the nineteenth century: he could either improve his exhausted plantation or take his family and slaves to richer soils further west. Eager to avoid the latter fate, Ruffin had tried a variety of techniques to renovate his fields. Nothing worked until Ruffin read English author Humphry Davy's *Elements of Agricultural Chemistry* (1813). Davy's discussion of soil acidity led Ruffin to a profound insight. A few brief experiments convinced Ruffin that the acidity of southern soils prevented crops from taking in nutrients. An acidic soil, no matter how well fertilized, would almost always produce poor yields. To correct the problem, Ruffin applied marl, a mixture of clay and calcium carbonate. The high calcium content of marl, Ruffin hypothesized, neutralized the natural acidity of southern soils. Reformers, in fact, classified marl as a "calcareous manure" to underscore its high calcium content. A series of carefully conceived experiments showed that applications of marl doubled and sometimes even tripled wheat and corn yields. Ruffin publicized his findings in a series of articles and in an 1832 pamphlet entitled *An Essay on Calcareous Manures*.[4] The work was a stunning scientific achievement that promised to revolutionize southern agriculture.

Ruffin's energetic efforts put him at the center of a network of prominent reformers whose support for extremist politics matched their fervor for calcareous manures. Fellow Virginian Willoughby Newton, a prominent planter and local politician, shared Ruffin's passion for secession. They both worked to organize and promote the Virginia State Agricultural Society. Ruffin and South Carolinian James Henry Hammond corresponded for years about agricultural practices. Hammond had strongly supported nullification—South Carolina's 1832 decision to overturn federal tariff laws on its own accord—and had written important proslavery works. While serving as governor in 1842, Hammond had appointed Ruffin to conduct an official geological survey of South Carolina. Whitemarsh Seabrook, president of the South Carolina Agricultural Society, helped secure Ruffin's appointment and coordinated his tour of the Palmetto State. A wealthy Lowcountry planter, Seabrook began writing proslavery tracts in the 1820s. In 1850 he used his position as governor to coordinate South Carolina's growing secession movement with other cotton states. Seabrook, according to historian Charles G. Steffen, "epitomized the fusion of agricultural improvement and sectional radicalism."[5]

This relatively small group of reformers helped build a self-reinforcing network of agricultural journals and agricultural societies. The agricultural journals, which could potentially reach audiences throughout the South, were instrumental in publicizing new techniques and products as well as meetings of like-minded farmers and planters. The most important agricultural journals in Virginia and South Carolina included the *Farmers' Register* (published in Petersburg from 1833 to 1842), the *Southern Planter* (first published in Richmond in 1841 and continuing to this day), and the *Southern Agriculturalist* (published in Charleston from 1832 to 1846). The circulation for these journals was not large, ranging from 1,300 for Ruffin's *Farmers' Register* to 5,000 for the *Southern Planter*.[6] Periodicals with particularly small circulations failed in the 1840s because of declining subscriptions. In the case of the *Farmers' Register*, Ruffin's penchant for editorializing on controversial political issues such as banking undoubtedly hurt subscriptions. The farmers' journals, though, had far more influence than their modest circulation numbers would suggest. Articles published in one journal might be reprinted multiple times. Even urban papers carried articles about agricultural reform. During the swirling sectional crisis of the 1850s, the influential *Charleston Mercury* reprinted articles about new crops such as Chinese sugarcane and Egyptian corn, proposals for draining swampland, and editorials advocating state support for agricultural education.[7]

As practical businessmen, southern agricultural reformers often focused their attention on profits and losses. No subject was too small for reformers to scrutinize and debate from the vantage point of a rigorous cost-benefit analysis. Essayists and correspondents carefully judged the profitability of fertilizers, drainage schemes, cattle feeds, crop rotations, plowing techniques, pest controls, seed varieties, and experimental manures. Ruffin's *Essay on Calcareous Manures*, for example, painstakingly documents every possible expense of applying marl, including the wear and tear on the horses and wagons used to haul the clay to the fields.[8] Such exacting calculations became commonplace in southern agricultural journals and usually reached the same comforting bottom-line conclusion that new cultivation techniques paid their practitioners quite handsomely. It is not hard to understand the appeal of such a strategy: to convince their fellow agriculturalists that reform could work, the reformers had to show that it would pay. Enabling farmers and planters to secure higher profits on the soils of Virginia and South Carolina was the only sure way to stem the flow of westward migration.

Far more was at stake, however, than the profits of individual planters. Ruffin and his fellow reformers, historian William Mathew has written, conceived of their program "in institutionally conservative terms."[9] Agricultural change would stem the flow of western emigrants, thus helping to save slavery. Reformers believed that agricultural reform was a patriotic duty that transcended mere dollars and cents. As early as 1822, Ruffin wrote in 1836 that Virginians "will need all the patriotism, zeal, and talents of her remaining sons, to prevent their country from becoming a waste, and almost abandoned."[10] Years earlier, Ruffin had compared two planters called "N—" (an improver) and "F—" (a user of traditional cultivation methods): "Were all our landholders like N—, the wealth and population of the state would quickly be doubled. Were all like F— . . . wealth, and population would rapidly diminish, until the country became a desert."[11] Ruffin more explicitly spelled out the relationship between reform and regional political power in 1852. Speaking in Charleston, Ruffin warned that the inability to generate population growth had left Virginia and South Carolina open to the predations of northern abolitionists. "The loss of both political and military strength," he concluded, was "the certain consequences of the impoverishment of their [Virginia and South Carolina's] soil."[12]

Reformers in South Carolina—operating in a political environment extraordinarily sensitive to potential attacks on slavery—rarely missed an opportunity to link agricultural change to the defense of slavery. In an 1828 address before the United Agricultural Society, Seabrook warned his audience that northern protectionism and the antislavery movement (represented by the relatively moderate Colonization Society) constituted a "poisonous shaft that is already lifted to strike its prey."[13] Eight years later, Seabrook sounded the alarm regarding the northern abolitionist movement, whose "ultimate object" was the "total destruction of our slave institutions."[14] When mixed with calls for agricultural reform, denunciations of the antislavery movement connected agricultural reform to the very survival of the South. "South Carolina is emphatically, an agricultural state," Seabrook noted. "The prosperity and permanency of her domestic institutions are identified with its success. Her weight on national councils rests on its progressive amelioration."[15] In the 1840s

Seabrook continued to connect the "pecuniary welfare" of the South and the "preservation of her domestic institutions" with "a radical change in habits and practices of the tillers of the soil."[16]

Seabrook and Ruffin were hardly unique in conceiving agricultural reform as a means of protecting slavery. Consider, for example, Nicholas Herbemont, a French émigré living near Charleston and a frequent contributor to southern agricultural journals. As a distinguished winemaker, Herbemont promoted vineyards and other reform measures to increase the population of South Carolina. Early in his career, Herbemont believed that agricultural reform was a means of safely abolishing slavery. With hardy yeoman grape growers adding to the state's white population, South Carolinians could emancipate their slaves without fear of an apocalyptic race war. During the nullification crisis, Herbemont revised his position to match the prevailing political climate. Reform became a way of saving slavery. A larger population created through agricultural reform and more intensive cultivation practices, he wrote in 1829, was vital "to the continuance of our very existence." Herbemont ominously warned that "circumstances may hereafter compel us to direct resistance; will not the proposed state of things be the only one by which our resistance may be effectual?"[17] Herbemont expanded on this theme several years later when writing for Ruffin's *Farmers' Register* in 1836 Better farming methods would give rise to a large "middle class of population," he argued, which would enable the South to "defy the worst efforts of our enemies, and rise triumphant from the conflict."[18] On the other hand, a rootless population spread over a vast region seemed patently inadequate to deal with dire threats such as abolitionism. "If this system of emigration is preserved," Herbemont asked, "what is to become of the state—the glorious, the hospitable, the chivalric state of South Carolina?"[19]

As the southern agricultural reform movement became more institutionalized in the 1840s and 1850s, its organizers engaged in an even more aggressive defense of slavery. Some organizers, it is true, sought to cast agricultural reform as an apolitical movement so as to avoid partisan strife. The idea that agricultural reform was a noble calling that rose above mere politics was apparent in the rules of a local Virginia agricultural society, whose bylaws specified that "no subject shall be introduced into the conversations of the Club unless it be akin to agriculture; and politics shall especially be excluded."[20] More extremist reformers argued that nothing was more important to southern agriculture than the defense of slavery. In both Virginia and South Carolina, mainstream agricultural periodicals and agricultural societies regularly defended the institution. The annual fair and cattle show of the Virginia Agricultural Society, for example, attracted thousands of visitors to Richmond in the 1850s. While many of these visitors may have been apolitical, they would have had a hard time avoiding proslavery polemics. Ruffin, for example, delivered the society's first address in 1852, which he entitled "A Defense of the Effects of Domestic Slavery on the Manners, Habits, and Welfare of the Agricultural Population of the United States." Ruffin declared that slavery was of "divine origin" and promoted "the industry, civilization, refinement and general well-being of mankind." The speech was reprinted in the society's *Journal of Transactions* as well as in the *Southern Cultivator*, Virginia's leading agricultural periodical.[21] Nor was Ruffin's speech unique. In both Virginia and South Carolina, addresses before agricultural societies became popular venues to voice support for slavery and southern rights.[22]

## GOVERNMENT SUPPORT FOR EXPERIMENTATION AND EDUCATION

The defense of slavery connected southern extremism and agricultural reform. Agricultural reformers believed that individual planters would profit handsomely from better cultivation practices but that such practices would also provide important general benefits for the region as a whole. Hence the rhetoric of agricultural reform preached both profit (individual benefits) and patriotism (external benefits for society as a whole). Seabrook succinctly summarized the importance of the two impulses, lecturing to his fellow planters that "your individual prosperity and the safety of domestic institutions demand it [agricultural reform]."[23] Focusing on the "safety of domestic institutions" raised important questions. If southern state governments organized patrols and militias to protect slavery, then should not the same governments also subsidize agricultural research and experimentation that promised to do the same —albeit in a more indirect, long-term manner? And if private incentives proved too weak to generate a sufficient level of experimentation and education, then should southern state governments subsidize these activities?

Reformers had no difficulty in answering such questions. They strongly supported government subsidies to promote the work of reform, especially when it came to education and experimentation. In 1822 Ruffin attributed the principal cause of poor agricultural practices to sheer ignorance, which only Virginia's legislature could correct through agricultural education in schools and colleges. Ruffin argued that the legislature would determine "whether Virginia is to rise—or to sink, without a remaining hope."[24] Fifteen years later, Ruffin outlined an ambitious legislative plan that included a state board of agriculture, state support for county-level agricultural societies, state-sponsored experimental farms and agricultural surveys, subsidized agricultural periodicals and textbooks, and a state-supported system for the "facilitating and encouragement of agricultural apprenticeships . . . under the direction of some of the most intelligent and successful cultivators."[25] Few other reformers developed such a detailed, comprehensive plan, but many supported its various elements. The South Carolina reformer Herbemont noted the "criminal" neglect of agriculture on the part of the South Carolina legislature: "The elements of agriculture should be taught in every school, and a professorship established in every college," he wrote in 1838.[26] Seabrook, true to form, invoked the threat of northern abolitionists as justification for agricultural education in both public schools and universities: "If, from unprofitable harvests, the servant should become a burden to his master, the shouts of the fanatic may yet be heard in his own domicil."[27]

Many other reformers echoed Seabrook's call for agricultural schools and colleges. In 1825, for example, a writer using the pseudonym "A Well Wisher to Agriculture" proposed that the state establish a South Carolina Institute to train farmers. In 1839 the novelist and southern extremist William Gilmore Simms recommended that the state endow each district with farms containing up to 5,000 acres of land. These farms would provide vocational education for the state's orphans and indigent students; tuition would be free in exchange for a term of service as "apprentices" on local plantations. As if to better link agricultural reform with the protection of slavery, Simms added a distinct air of militarism to his plan: all students would be dressed in uniforms, with the older boys "provided with light muskets, and be subjected to the drill and instruction once a month, of the neighborhood Captain of the Militia."[28] In 1854 a southern agricultural convention meeting in Columbia proposed an even more visionary scheme: the "Southern Central Agricultural College." The college would educate planters across the South "in all the sciences and learning pertaining to agriculture and its kindred arts." The convention hoped to fund the college with an endowment of $500,000 and planned to ask Congress and the southern legislatures for the appropriate allocations.[29]

Reformers argued that the South's sparse population made state action imperative. The unique handicap of circulating southern agricultural periodicals and organizing agricultural societies in a thinly populated countryside, they maintained, justified state action. Seabrook, for instance, noted in 1829 that "in the Eastern and Northern sections of our country, agricultural associations have been more successful than in the Southern states." He blamed the South's "sparse population" and "aristocratic pride usually incident from wealth." Seabrook called for the organization of local agricultural societies that would regularly report to a statewide body, but he knew that the success of his plan rested "on the patriotism and munificence of the Legislature. . . . I ask the deputed guardians of an oppressed community for their patronage and support."[30] As editor of the *Farmers' Register*, Ruffin knew firsthand the problems of publishing in Virginia. In his autobiography, Ruffin recalled with envy how the North's leading agricultural journal, the Albany-based *Cultivator*, sold its monthly issues for twenty-five cents because the New York Agricultural Society could guarantee 20,000 subscriptions.[31] Ruffin had no such market, which meant that he had to price the *Farmers' Register* at $2.00 per issue. He told his readers in 1838 that state aid could reduce the price of the *Farmers' Register* and thus raise its circulation. "It is doubtful whether any mode of extending the knowledge, and the improvement of agriculture, would be so effectual and so cheap," he asserted.[32]

A central premise of the reformers was that agricultural experimentation and education needed state support because these activities often offered few pecuniary rewards for individual planters. Here the agricultural reformers treated experimentation (and the dissemination of its results) as a public good that governments must provide. Writing in the *Farmers' Register* in 1834, the correspondent who signed his article "R.N." argued that the "individual, who institutes experiments in agriculture, is almost sure to lose by ninety-nine of them in the hundred." The writer supported a government-run experimental farm that would surely lose money but produce windfall profits for Virginia's farmers in the long run. Simply finding the most effective ways of applying barnyard manure, he asserted, would save Virginians enough money "to support an experimental farm in every county in the state and every other public institution that has been ever thought of for agricultural improvements."[33] Virginian James Barbour took a similar position in 1835, writing that experiments should be undertaken at state expense because "there would be but few or none able to encounter the risks, and not infrequently losses, attending all new experiments."[34] Ruffin himself invoked no less of an authority than Adam Smith—"the most-venerated authority for restraining (on a score of policy) all useless legislative"—in justifying government support for agricultural research. According to Ruffin, the celebrated author of *The Wealth of Nations* sanctioned state provision of education when there was "no sufficient demand on the part of the people to secure the supply."[35]

### SYNTHESIZING THE MODERN AND THE TRADITIONAL

Following Ruffin's interpretation of Smith, reformers argued that almost all "civilized" governments supported agricultural research. In portraying agricultural research as an utterly traditional function of civilized government, reformers created an intellectual variant of an "invented tradition." An invented tradition is a ritual of recent origin (but often portrayed as "traditional") designed to strengthen nationalistic spirit or help support a particular government policy.[36] In formulating their own invented traditions, southern agricultural reformers consistently overestimated the degree to which governments in Europe or even the North had supported agricultural research. They also exaggerated the impact of government-sponsored research on actual practices and productivity. The claim that almost all "civilized" governments had supported agricultural research nevertheless allowed southern reformers to synthesize potentially contradictory appeals into a coherent message. Reform was modern and scientific yet also utterly traditional; reform represented the height of Enlightenment rationalism yet also appealed to romantic agrarian impulses. Their interpretation of history allowed reformers to significantly broaden the ideological and cultural appeal of their policies.

In a few cases, southern agricultural writers dated the origins of reform to the ancients. In 1856 South Carolina planter D. F. Jamison traced agricultural reform back to its Roman roots. The slaveholding planter argued (with no hint of irony) that agriculture was the "only independent pursuit. No other is exempted from patronage, dependence, or servility." In a striking departure from Ruffin and other reformers, Jamison conceived of reform as a traditional practice. The Romans—who, like South Carolinians, owned large numbers of slaves—practiced intensive cultivation complete with improved livestock, fodder crops, and generous applications of manure. Although marl was not found in Italy, Jamison told his listeners that "the application of marl to wasted lands was not unknown to the ancients."[37] Modern experimenters, it seemed, merely confirmed what good farmers had known for centuries. Jamison's focus on the Romans was somewhat unusual, but he touched upon wider intellectual and historical currents that reformers often drew from. Jamison portrayed the Roman farm as an idyllic "sylvan retreat," free from the "turmoil of wealth and the struggle of business." Such pleasures, he asserted, could be enjoyed by all: "Who does not sometimes indulge in visions of green meadows, and sunny fields, and yellow harvests, and lowing herds, as pleasures still in reserve for him?"[38]

If agricultural reform promised to create "sylvan retreats," it would also increase the wealth and power of the South. Reformers frequently attributed the higher productivity of British agriculture to state-sponsored initiatives. In 1825 the anonymous "Well Wisher" argued that "the legislators of almost every enlightened, free, and prosperous country, direct to agriculture their peculiar care and attention." The writer singled out Great Britain for particular praise. Government support of agricultural research had led to the cultivation of "immense heaths and large tracts of apparently unarable land. . . . [I]t is astonishing how a territory so small, can give not only subsistence, but so many comforts and luxuries to a population so dense."[39] In similar fashion, Seabrook praised the British Board of Agriculture for producing eighty volumes filled with reports and statistics. The British reports, he breathlessly declared, "cannot fail of producing national advantages, greater perhaps than have been derived from any other political institutions in modern times."[40] Both "Well Wisher" and Seabrook overstated the importance of state-supported agricultural research, however. British farmers had cultivated new crops and new agricultural implements decades (perhaps even centuries) before the Board of Agriculture published its reports. Britain's support of agricultural research nevertheless allowed southern reformers to present their proposals as a safe, conservative means of increasing the wealth and power of the South. If Britain's landed interest (including aristocrats and the gentry) supported agricultural research to increase the wealth and population of the world's most powerful nation, then southern planters should do the same.

The most frequently cited model of agricultural education, however, was not Britain but the northern states. Southern agricultural periodicals frequently published reports and letters from northern sources that highlighted the results of state activism. Northern state governments, in contrast to Virginia and South Carolina, subsidized agricultural societies, funded geographical surveys, and aided agricultural schools. The amount that northern states spent on agricultural research and education was actually quite small (especially in relation to the size of their populations and economies), but southerners nevertheless believed that even small expenditures had made a big difference. Even Ruffin, who had little good to say about northerners in general and New Englanders in particular, raved about the quality of the agricultural reports subsidized by the Massachusetts state government. "But it is vain to expect any such things here," Ruffin bitterly wrote, for the Virginia state legislature "has continually refused the smallest aid to such improvement."[41] Even more remarkably, southern agricultural periodicals continued to praise northern efforts through the 1850s, when sectional divisions often made their way into the farm journals of both the North and the South. In 1859, for example, the *Southern Cultivator* solicited and received a report from B. P. Johnson that summarized the financial support that the New York State Legislature had given the New York State Agricultural Society. Johnson's report noted that the legislature appropriated $8,000 to the society annually, defrayed the costs of publishing the society's annual reports, and had allocated $40,000 to build an agricultural library and museum. The *Southern Cultivator* approved of such policies, recommending Johnson's report to "our legislature, and all who desire the advancement of our agricultural interests."[42]

Southern reformers admired New York's state government because its agricultural policies embraced modern values such as science and rationalism. Southern reformers, in fact, hoped that state-supported education and research would fundamentally change the way that southerners conceived of agriculture. According to reformers, the unthinking embrace of traditional practices was the underlying problem afflicting southern farming. Instead of extolling past practices, reformers argued that cultivators must integrate new insights from chemistry, biology, and botany. State policy, they insisted, could decisively show agriculturalists the superiority of science and rational choice over blind devotion to the past. The failure of the South Carolina legislature to properly elevate agricultural education, declared Thomas Legare in 1836, had left intact "barbarous prejudice" against scientific agriculture. An aggressive state effort aimed at educating planters would demonstrate that "our whole business is a series of illustrations of the principles of Science; and our very plantations, but scientific laboratories."[43] Virginian Clairborne W. Gooch similarly argued in 1836 that Virginians had no hope of "arresting this flood-tide of depletion" unless the legislature acted to elevate agriculture as one of the "most favored arts and sciences."[44] Seabrook sounded a similar theme in 1848, calling for agricultural education in the public schools so that every farmer would have "a true view of the high character of his calling; in a word, to effect a revolution in his habits and practices."[45] Simms put it even more succinctly: "The Good Farmer," he told the Barnwell Agricultural Society in 1846, "must think as well as plough."[46] An activist state policy could help the farmer do both.

However much reformers promoted a modern vision of scientific agriculture, they frequently justified state action through the romantic imagery of "home, sweet home." Reform would stop the restless movement from exhausted plantations to the fresh lands of the West. Firmly rooted to his farm and community, the contented planter (as the reformers imagined him) enjoyed the steady accumulation of wealth while basking in the goodwill emanating from a stable network of friends and relatives. The domestic glory of "home, sweet home" was something to take seriously.[47] The counterpoint to the contented planter was the profit-hungry migrant, whose wasteful practices created an ugly landscape of burned forests, slovenly plantations, and impermanent communities. In sharp contrast to the unthinking and destructive planter, Simms told the Barnwell Agricultural Society in 1840, the good farmer "preserves his forest from those two merciless assailants, so commonly and improvidently employed among us, the axe and the torch." Renovation and reform would allow the good farmer his family "to enjoy a moral grace which the mind as decidedly derives from the contemplation of innocent and lovely objects, as in the daily study of abstractions which have this purpose to their end."[48]

A rather pointed critique of individualism tied together the romantic imagery of Simms and the more scientific rhetoric of Ruffin. Simms's

"Good Farmer," after all, was not only connected to nature but also to his community. The planter who practiced the seemingly endless cycle of shifting cultivation, on the other hand, could be considered greedy and unpatriotic. "His light radiates over but a small and selfish circle," Legare told a local agricultural society. "It goes for the aggrandizement of the individual and his family; but leaves nothing for the coming generation of myriads unborn."[49] In similar fashion, a writer signing his article "A Virginian" criticized rootless migrants to the west: "All the tender ties of *home* are to be severed; all the feelings of patriotism are to be forgotten in this vain and illusive wondering after wealth."[50] As part of their critique of individualism, reformers condemned "speculating mania" in new crops. Ruffin, for example, excoriated planters who, looking for quick and easy profits, rushed to plant mulberry plants and establish silk cocoon nurseries in the 1830s without sufficient knowledge of proper cultivation techniques. Government activism, he argued, would have prevented isolated and independent entrepreneurs from suffering huge losses. "If a mulberry nursery and cocoonry had been established at public expense," Ruffin argued, "then the problem of the amount of products and of profits would have already been established beyond question."[51] Rational, collective action had far more appeal to Ruffin than the apparent chaos of unrestrained individualism.

## THE STATE AND THE BATTLE AGAINST DISEASE

Ruffin's critique of individualism extended in another direction: he deplored the practices that spread malaria and other diseases throughout eastern Virginia. Reflecting the commonplace scientific belief of his day, Ruffin thought that the "effluvia" of rotting vegetable matter from swamps and stagnant water caused "bilious fevers" that seriously threatened the health of those living in the eastern seaboard states. Much like Ruffin's assessment of shifting cultivation, the disease problem was for him at once personal and political. While at his first plantation of Coggin's Point, Ruffin and his wife lost two infants to disease. Ruffin himself suffered recurring symptoms of malaria. Convinced that Coggin's Point was unsafe, he moved to a safer plantation near Petersburg. Connecting his personal experience to the South as a whole, Ruffin believed that malaria and other fevers had greatly contributed to the "great and deplorable decline of most of the lower counties of Virginia." Reformers in

South Carolina similarly saw malaria as a major threat to their state's survival. "Did not the Romans fail," asked Herbemont, "because the fair fields of productiveness became noxious and dismal morasses, yielding deadly malaria, instead of the rich harvests of corn and luxurious gardens?"[52] Instead of being exemplars of sound cultivation practices, the Romans now became a cautionary tale of woe and pestilence.

Ruffin, Herbemont, and other reformers who focused on the prevention of disease constituted a distinct subset of the broader agricultural reform movement. Their justifications for state regulation nevertheless reinforced the bias in favor of state action. When considering the causes of disease, reformers focused on millponds, which farmers and planters created to power watermills that ground their wheat and corn into flour and meal. Ruffin saw these mills as extraordinarily hazardous to public health and offering few economic benefits in return. He reported to Virginia's Board of Agriculture in 1843 that fevers and diseases "are principally caused by the effluvia rising from wet lands." Millponds created more wetlands, especially when flood waters breached dams to contaminate the surrounding area. On the other meteorological extreme, millponds receding after the hot summer months exposed "alluvial mud" that constituted "a fruitful seed-bed and nursery of disease."[53] Ruffin asserted that eastern Virginia had been far healthier in the colonial period than in the nineteenth century because the initial settlers had not yet built pestilential mills. For reformers, millponds represented the short-sighted and ultimately irrational individualism that plagued southern agriculture more generally. The value of the drained land alone, reformers believed, would be worth far more than the mills themselves, which often tended to be small, inefficient enterprises. Labeling millponds as "bogs of death," one reformer wondered how "our laws suffer such nuisances to exist, or that individuals, for fear of risking the loss of few toll dishes of corn, should spread disease and death through a whole neighborhood."[54] The fact that millponds were often unprofitable compounded their irrationality. Ruffin compared millponds with racehorses, which existed "more for amusement and excitement, and to vary the monotony of their lives, than for profit."[55]

Ruffin and other reformers advocated using eminent domain and other state regulation to eliminate millponds. Although he recognized that the "vested rights" of mill owners required full compensation if the state stopped the operation of their mills, he argued that the mills' limited economic utility would make this issue moot in many cases. For larger mills that had a dependable source of water, Ruffin thought that the state should encourage the use of canals rather than ponds. Local juries, which usually approved millponds with little debate, should carefully scrutinize the impact of the mills on public health. Ruffin, in fact, encouraged individuals to sue mill owners on grounds that the mills harmed the health of the neighborhood. Few Virginians had availed themselves of this form of relief, Ruffin argued, because of sheer ignorance. A "General Board of Health" or "Commission of Sanitary Police"—fully funded by the legislature—would help encourage legal action. The health benefits alone would make the "Sanitary Police" a cost-effective program. "At any possible cost of the investigation," Ruffin concluded, "the public improvement and benefit produced thereby would exceed the expenses an hundred-fold."[56]

Eradicating millponds could remove one source of malaria, but Virginians and South Carolinians also needed to drain natural wetlands. Reformers believed that the utility of draining swamps was obvious to all—such policies would improve the region's health and open up particularly fertile land for settlement. A perverse individualism, however, stood as a major roadblock to reform. If a swamp rested within the property of several owners, as was often the case, draining would provide benefits to all of them. The result was a classic free-rider problem, in which each farmer waited until the others took the time, trouble, and expense to drain the swamp. As Ruffin noted, "the want of either the will or the ability by any one proprietor operates as a complete bar to the procedure of all." Depending upon one proprietor to bear all of the costs, after all, was to expect an "excessive degree of liberality." Even worse, an individual landowner "may be so stupid and perverse" as to block the improvement altogether. To overcome the free-rider problem, Ruffin proposed granting the power of eminent domain to groups of landholders so as to "require of all proprietors (under proper safeguards and restrictions) to contribute to the execution of works manifestly for the benefit of each one and all."[57] Seabrook proposed a similar plan in 1828. He called upon the South Carolina Agricultural Society to exert pressure on recalcitrant planters and farmers who failed to drain swamps and clear abandoned fields of malarial ponds. If such pressure failed, he argued, "it will, perhaps, become necessary, eventually to resort to some more powerful impetus to industry."[58]

If judicial action failed to drain swamps and convert them into valuable farmland, Ruffin and Seabrook believed that the state government should intervene more directly. Seabrook compared draining swamps to building railroads and other transportation improvement: both activities deserved state funding. He thus asked South Carolina's superintendent of public works to study the expense and value of reclaiming abandoned swamplands. Ruffin expressed his "unmixed applause" for North Carolina's plan that granted $200,000 to the State Literary Fund to drain the Great Dismal Swamp. The reclaimed land would be sold to fund the state's public schools. Ruffin feared that the enterprise would be poorly managed—"government jobs are, of all in the world, the worse executed" —so he characteristically advocated that only the best-trained experts should oversee the enterprise. He recommended hiring a "competent engineer, as well as a scientific drainer . . . at *liberal salaries*."[59] Nearly four years later, the *Farmers' Register* reprinted a report on the progress of the work, which promised to fulfill its weighty expectations: "No scheme has been or can be devised, that will so effectively stay the tide of emigration which flows like a mighty torrent from this portion of the state."[60]

The reformers' proposals to eradicate malaria and other diseases— whether focused on the regulation of millponds, grants of eminent domain power, or large-scale public works—invoked a potentially revolutionary conception of property rights. The reformers implicitly endorsed an "instrumental view" of property in which the "public good" could trump individual property rights.[61] An instrumental view of property, if pushed from a different direction, might eventually threaten the legal foundations of slavery. Without an absolutist conception of property, antislavery activists could conceivably seek to curtail the rights of slaveholders on utilitarian grounds in the same manner that Ruffin sought to curtail the rights of mill owners. Reformers displayed little fear that a slippery slope in property law would endanger slavery. On the contrary, they believed that draining swamps and eradicating malaria "would be an incalculable gain of pecuniary agricultural value to the people, and an important gain to the state treasury," all of which would presumably strengthen slavery.[62] The issue of public health, moreover, made it particularly important to assert collective rights. Rights to millponds, wrote an anonymous correspondent to the *Farmers' Register*, was similar to having rights "in a tame bear, that was devouring my child." The correspondent was more than willing to accept government regulation to stop such abuses: "If I know any thing that would induce me to accept the dictatorship of country, it would be that of having the power to constrain the inhabitants in the bilious fever region to remove all stagnant water from it."[63]

## THE ECONOMIC FAILURE OF THE REFORM MOVEMENT

The agricultural reform movement, for all of its experiments, periodicals, speeches, and societies, failed to revolutionize southern agriculture. Ruffin and other reformers spoke of the growing popularity of marl, but census data suggests that most southern agriculturalists still used shifting cultivation on the eve of the Civil War.[64] In Virginia, where Ruffin had the greatest impact, the percentage of improved land in farms and plantations actually fell from 39.6 in 1850 to 36.8 in 1860. South Carolinians practiced slightly more intensive cultivation in 1860 than in 1850, but the small increase in improved land (from 25.1 percent to 28.2 percent) hardly foretold of an agricultural revolution. The failure to significantly change cultivation practices did not necessarily mean that Ruffin was wrong, at least in a technical tense. Marl could indeed neutralize the acidity of the South's ultisols, and its use allowed planters to increase the number of improved acres. Planters and farmers in twelve Tidewater counties (eleven in Virginia, one in North Carolina) frequently used marl.[65] When crop choice, soil type, and topography are held constant through regression analysis (see the statistical appendix), the results show that planters and farmers in the marling counties improved a significantly higher proportion of their land than did the state as a whole. Why did the vast majority of farmers and planters outside of these dozen counties ignore marl and its beneficial impact?

The simple answer is that for most southern agriculturalists, marl and associated reforms did not pay. According to reformers, marling was easy and effective. "The results are *certain* and *speedy*," wrote Newton in 1853. "They are also *cheap*."[66] Newton, though, did not consider the high transportation costs that made the heavy clay uneconomical for many cultivators. According to one Virginia planter writing in 1839, marl "is not everywhere to be had, and is a heavy and expensive affair when both land and water carriage have to be encountered."[67] Marling, moreover, only neutralized the acidity of the soil; improving farmers had to add other fertilizers or else the marl would be counterproductive. One of the most popular fertilizers was Peruvian guano, a manure of bird feces mined from Pacific islands and reefs. Guano was effective but costly; its price of $45 to $50 per ton was more expensive than marl.[68] The cost of renovating 100 acres in eastern Virginia was $2,362, a sum greater than the outlay for clearing land in the cotton lands in the Southwest.[69] Ruffin himself noted that it would take five years of increased crops to fully pay the expenses of marling. What if drought, flood, or some other unanticipated disaster ruined the crops in the interim? What if crop prices suddenly fell, decreasing the additional revenue earmarked to pay for the extra expenses, or a planter applied too much marl and "burned" his crops? All of these frightening possibilities led some planters to doubt the gospel of reform. "Show me one of those plantations that have been 'improved,'" wrote one cynical South Carolinian in 1840, "and I will show you in three cases out of four a moth that has made a monstrous hole in the owner's pocket."[70]

Reformers denounced such sentiments as humbug, but their own correspondence reveals that reform was more uncertain than they publicly admitted. James Henry Hammond was Ruffin's most committed disciple in South Carolina. He marled 2,300 acres in the early 1840s, and he reported great results in various essays and articles. His personal correspondence, however, was decidedly less rosy. In 1849 he wrote to Ruffin to report that "I have made another total failure this year and my crop for the last three years taken together would scarcely amount in the aggregate to my crop of 1839." Hammond still believed in marl—"I think on the whole it [marl] has improved my land 50 percent"—but he nevertheless admitted that "there is no process whatever that will enable us to grow cotton on our sandy pine lands [with the price of cotton] at less than 8 cents."[71] His other reform efforts, such as better livestock breeds and greater use of manure, also met with mixed results. He enthusiastically wrote that penning his hogs had been a great success: "They make manure immensely. I shall haul from my yards, stables, and pens 60 to 80,000 bushels."[72] After a few years, though, Hammond's prized Berkshires—an improved breed far larger than typical southern swine—had died of a mysterious illness. By 1850 Hammond was reconciled to buying most of the meat consumed on his plantation, and plans for accumulating more manure, so breathlessly trumpeted in earlier letters, disappeared from his correspondence.[73]

Other evidence from South Carolina suggests that experiments produced the same uneven results. A writer for the *Southern Quarterly Review* lamented the failure of South Carolinians to use marl after Ruffin's

1842 survey of the state. The writer noted that "experiments have not been conclusive with others or altogether satisfactory to themselves."[74] Ruffin himself glumly observed that several South Carolinian experimenters "have failed to realize any *great* improvement." Ruffin blamed the planters themselves for failing to add enough "vegetable matter" (fertilizer) to the marled fields.[75] That experimenters could make such expensive mistakes, though, showed the risks of marl and associated reforms. The reluctance of most southern cultivators to embrace reform made economic sense. Without a cheap and dependable means of alleviating soil acidity, without a cure for various animal diseases, and without a suitable fodder crop that could withstand the region's heat and humidity, most southern farmers and planters stuck with shifting cultivation. Perhaps that is why reformers put so much emphasis on the relationship between better cultivation practices and southern patriotism. Given the unpromising economics of reform, appeals to self-interest alone failed to persuade planters and farmers to abandon shifting cultivation.

### THE FAILURE TO GAIN LEGISLATIVE AID

The ambitious legislative program of the agricultural reformers also failed to generate widespread support. Virginia and South Carolina subsidized agricultural research in sporadic and episodic fashion. In the 1830s Virginia sponsored a geological survey, and in 1841 the state legislature organized a State Board of Agriculture to collect and disseminate information. Neither initiative constituted a sustained effort to promote agricultural research. The geological survey received small appropriations doled out over a number of years; the legislature was so unenthusiastic that it never bothered to fund publication of the final report.[76] The State Board of Agriculture was similarly too weak and disorganized to have much practical consequence. Ruffin recalled in his autobiography that the board was founded "upon a most parsimonious & totally inefficient plan.... I was soon heartily tired of belonging to this inefficient body—& which could not be much better, upon the niggardly existing organization."[77] South Carolina was somewhat more generous in its funding. The state government funded Ruffin's geological survey in the 1840s, expending some $5,600 on the project. In the late 1850s, the legislature appointed Oscar M. Lieber to fill the position of "Geological, Mineralogical, and Agricultural Surveyor of the State" while providing the South Carolina State Agricultural Society $5,000 per year in 1857 and 1858. Altogether, the state spent $40,367 on geological surveys and agricultural research in the 1840s and the 1850s, which amounted to less than 1 percent of total state expenditures in the period.[78]

Given the prominence of the reformers—and the sense of economic crisis that gripped Virginia and South Carolina for much of the antebellum period—the lack of legislative action is somewhat curious. The reformers were neither lonely voices in the wilderness nor outsiders lacking political influence. To the contrary, agricultural reformers possessed wealth, power, and connections. This was particularly true in South Carolina, where both Hammond and Seabrook served as governor. Ruffin, Newton, and Virginia's agricultural reformers never reached the same level of political success, but their message nevertheless influenced important politicians. In December 1849 Governor John B. Floyd (a southern extremist) reminded state legislators that "no occupation will fail to thrive" if agriculture prospers: "If there is in the Commonwealth a pursuit which deserves the encouragement of the Legislature, undoubtedly it is agriculture." Floyd also recommended the appointment of a state agricultural chemist as "necessary to sustain a properly organized State Agricultural Society."[79] The support of influential governors, a steady stream of petitions, and individual lobbying made little difference; state legislators often refused to listen. James Barbour, a Virginian of some influence, proposed a comprehensive plan of agricultural education to the state legislature, but he found that the election of the doorkeeper elicited "ten times as much interest as to the result, as had been exhibited touching my proposition."[80] Herbemont similarly received a less-than-enthusiastic response in South Carolina: "As I could not mingle *currency* and *banks*, or *no banks* and the *subtreasury scheme*, I could not draw the least attention on the subject that I wished to promote."[81]

Some legislators opposed subsidizing agricultural research because of its potentially high cost. The records of South Carolina's legislative committees show that even the most enthusiastic reformers feared opening the floodgates of state spending and higher taxes. When Herbemont petitioned the state legislature for an appropriation to help encourage grape cultivation, none other than Whitemarsh Seabrook chaired the Committee of Legislature. Seabrook strongly endorsed Herbemont's plan and praised "the unwearied perseverance, untiring industry, and botanical research of the memorialist."[82] Seabrook nevertheless regretfully wrote that the "present financial conditions of the state will deter them from recommending, at this session, any specific appropriation in aid of the highly commendable & benevolent scheme of the Memorialist." A year later, Seabrook used similar language while rejecting a more general plan to support agricultural experimentation. Seabrook's fellow reformer Hammond displayed even stronger opposition to state funding. Then serving as governor of South Carolina, Hammond wrote to Ruffin in 1842: "I have myself been uniformly opposed to a Geological & Agricultural Survey & have been instrumental in defeating them for some years past."[83] Only the prospect of appointing his good friend to the surveyor's post had changed Hammond's mind.

Ideological opposition to government spending, however important in individual cases, did not adequately account for the political failures of the agricultural reform movement as a whole. The same supposedly cost-conscious legislators that refused to fund agricultural research and education had no difficulty investing tens of millions of state dollars into railroads and other transportation projects. Agricultural reformers often enthusiastically supported these projects—internal improvements, after all, promised to reduce the costs of marl and other fertilizers—but they wondered why state governments failed to devote the same resources to agricultural education and experimentation. P. T. Spratley, for example, bemoaned the legislature's spending priorities: "I would not be understood as being opposed to internal improvements, but I would say, the greater the agricultural improves . . . the greater necessity will there be for internal improvements, and the better condition will the country be in, to pay for them."[84] Just as railroad supporters argued that transportation improvements would generate large revenues for the state government, agricultural reformers predicted that better cultivation would increase property values and revenues from property taxes. Ruffin argued that any money the state spent on diffusing agricultural knowledge would "return to the treasury itself all the amount thence derived, with more than tenfold increase."[85] While legislators may have feared (with good reason) that certain reforms would fail, lawmakers in both Virginia and South Carolina funded a number of disastrous canal and railroad schemes that cost manyfold more than an experimental farm or an agricultural periodical.

The same basic pattern—large allocations for internal improvements, small sums for agricultural research—characterized fiscal priorities in northern states as well. Southern reformers, as noted above, had glorified the commitment of northern states to agricultural research. Actual expenditures on agricultural research in the North, though, remained quite modest. The Pennsylvania state government, for example, allocated $2,000 annually to the state agricultural society and made a onetime payment of $40,000 to the state agricultural college. The New York state government paid for the publication of the state agricultural journal and subsidized local agricultural societies. Total expenditures of the Empire State rarely exceeded $28,000 per year. In similar fashion, Massachusetts gave the state agricultural society $6,000 each year and local agricultural societies $600 dollars each year.[86] In all of these cases, northern states spent more than Virginia and South Carolina, but annual state spending amounted to far less than a penny per person. Northern states, like their southern counterparts, spent much less on agricultural research than on internal improvements.

The comparison with northern states reveals an underlining political weakness of the agricultural reform movement. Railroads and manufacturers sought legislation that provided clear, defined, and concentrated benefits, resulting in well-organized and highly motivated constituents with a vested interest in a particular improvement. In contrast, the benefits of agricultural research remained diffused and uncertain; it was never clear how much an individual farmer would benefit. Organizing the vast number of farmers into a coherent lobbying organization for agricultural research thus proved exceedingly difficult. Important differences in regard to wealth, soils, topography, climate, and crops also created divisions among planters and farmers that added to the political difficulties of the reform movement. Ruffin knew all too well the impact of these divisions on the movement. He frequently lamented that the small readership of the *Farmers' Register* was highly fragmented: western farmers wanted to read about grasses, meadows, and cattle; Piedmont planters wanted more articles on tobacco; and cultivators in the Lower South wanted more on cotton.[87] Readership for the *Farmers' Register* flagged when the periodical was unable to meet the diverse needs of its potential audience.

Political support for state aid failed for similar reasons. State legislators feared that the specialization needs of their own localities might be ignored. If the legislature funded an experimental farm, where would it be located and who would reap the most benefits? The issue of local advantage fragmented the reform movement. Ruffin drew a parallel between the Virginia legislature and the "closing scenes of the Greek Empire—

when the people, and their rulers, seemingly forgetful that the Turks were thundering at their gates, were divided into implacable opposing factions, and engaging metaphysical subtleties."[88] In the face of northern abolitionists—as threatening to Virginia's slaveholders as the Turks were to Greece—Ruffin doubted whether Virginians could muster the legislative unity to fund agricultural research.[89]

Several concrete examples highlight the intrastate regionalism that bedeviled the political efforts of reformers. An 1836 agricultural convention, meeting in Richmond, advocated a state-funded experimental farm that would be associated with the University of Virginia. According to planter Clairborne Gooch, the legislature rejected the proposal because of "jealousy" over the farm's location in the piedmont county of Albemarle. Gooch nevertheless stood firmly behind the convention's decision: "Is it [the University] not the resort of the great number of youth and regarded as best calculated to add the finishing touches of education? And is not its position most central, as well as in as fine a section of country as any in the State?"[90] The large number of delegates from the piedmont (including Gooch himself) dominated the convention's proceedings. Under these circumstances, it was not surprising that legislators from other parts of Virginia opposed a plan that promised little to their constituents. A similar convention in South Carolina debated a long list of state policies, including the "creation by the Legislature of an Agricultural Professorship in the South-Carolina College" and the "establishment of an Agricultural School in some central and healthy position of the State." Even in a convention full of reformers, both resolutions failed to pass. One wonders if the wording of the last resolution—"some central and healthy position of the State"—might well have raised the hackles of Lowcountry rice and cotton planters.[91] Instead of supporting an agricultural school, the convention voted in favor of a state-sponsored geological survey, a measure more likely to provide benefits for all of the state's various regions.

During the 1850s, reformers faced another barrier to enacting their legislative agenda: the high prices of tobacco, cotton, and wheat that brought prosperity to Virginia and South Carolina. An ambitious and costly agenda to reform southern agriculture was an especially tough sell when most farmers and planters seemed to be doing quite well. Virginians and South Carolinians could downplay the long-term developmental consequences of shifting cultivation when prosperity seemed so widespread. Agricultural reformers themselves, eager to defend slavery and bolster sectional pride, extolled the prosperity of southern agriculture. Newton typified the mixed message of reformers. In an 1852 speech before the Virginia State Agricultural Society, he praised Virginia's cereal crops ("she surpasses them all"), tobacco ("finds a market in every quarter of the world"), corn ("not surpassed"), horses ("equal to the English and superior to the Arab"), cattle ("the cattle on a thousand hills"), and wool ("exceeds in fineness that of Spain or Silesia").[92] In similar fashion, the editor of the *Southern Planter* assured his readers that Virginia showed a "rate of progress for which she [Virginia] might claim the congratulations of her sister states in the North—IF she had sisters there."[93] Such glowing assessments stoked regional pride, but they may well have undermined the rationale for state aid.

INDIVIDUALISM AND COLLECTIVE ACTION
IN SECESSIONIST THOUGHT

State governments may have had good political reasons to avoid subsidizing agricultural research, but reformers found the lack of government support irrational. For some reformers, the failure of state legislatures to fund the reform agenda reinforced a general contempt for democracy. This was particularly true of Ruffin, who early in his career had a short and unhappy stint as a state legislator. As Ruffin grew older, he frequently found many of his political views (including his enthusiastic support for secession) to be outside of Virginia's political mainstream. Always sensitive to personal slights, Ruffin blamed Virginia's increasingly democratic political culture for the rejection of his political views. He also blamed the same democratic political culture for the failure to subsidize agricultural research and education. Ruffin recalled in his autobiography that the Virginia State Agricultural Society sought state funds for its organizational efforts, but the legislature refused to subsidize the organization: "This was no surprise to me, if so to others. . . . Such had always been the course of that despicable assembly. . . . [I]t had been recently rendered worse by the operation of the last change of the constitution, & the enlargement of the constituency to universal suffrage."[94] Scholars have long recognized an antidemocratic streak in secessionist thought, but here was an unusual twist. In Ruffin's critique, democracy failed because of the unwillingness of feebleminded legislators to energetically expand the role of government. In many respects, Ruffin's attitudes resembled those of national Republicans such as John Quincy Adams, who famously told Congress in 1825 that politicians should not be "palsied by the will of our constituents" when voting for government improvements.[95] Both Adams and Ruffin believed that expert legislators, suitably free from the constraints of taxpaying voters, should determine public policy.

Ruffin's faith in state action attests to the forward-looking elements of the agricultural reform movement. In many respects, the antebellum reformers resembled southern Progressives of the early twentieth century. Progressive reformers established a network of agricultural periodicals and experimental farm stations that espoused what historian Gilbert C. Fite has called the "gospel of diversification, science, and efficiency."[96] Much like their antebellum counterparts, Progressive reformers worried about the depopulation of the southern countryside. To modernize southern agriculture, these reformers advocated a northern-style agricultural regime of continuous cultivation that included fertilizers, livestock, fodder grasses, and legumes. They successfully called for the creation of agricultural colleges and experimental stations that would educate ordinary farmers about the latest scientific advances. Progressive reformers even supported the use of prison convicts to mine lime, which could then be used as fertilizer to reduce the acidity of southern soils.[97] Slavery may have been gone forever, but the agricultural reform movement still found a way to promote unfree labor well into the twentieth century.

In mixing science and state activism, secessionists and Progressive reformers alike looked forward to a more rational and scientific future in which collective action sometimes trumped individual interests. Historians have generally recognized the triumph of collective action over individualism as a major theme of the Progressive era, but they have sometimes overlooked similar attitudes in the antebellum period. In the minds of antebellum reformers, narrow-minded individualists destroyed the fertility of the soil, spread malaria through millponds, and refused to join agricultural societies, subscribe to agricultural periodicals, or support state-sponsored agricultural research. Historian Emory Thomas has written that when southerners jointed the Confederacy, "they by necessity circumscribed their individualism and accepted an identity larger than themselves."[98] The efforts of the agricultural reformers suggest that this process had already begun in the antebellum period. Collective action via state activism, reformers believed, was the only way to protect their slaveholding society.

*three*

# EXPLAINING LIEBER'S PARADOX

RAILROADS, STATE BUILDING, AND SLAVERY

In 1861 Francis Lieber, a former resident of South Carolina and a strong Unionist, noted an important paradox that historians have yet to fully explain: "Almost all, perhaps actually all, the most prominent extremists on the State-Rights side . . . have been at the same time strongly inclined toward centralization and consolidation of power within their respective States."[1] Public investment in southern railroads convincingly demonstrated Lieber's point. Southern governments collectively spent more than $128 million on railroads in the antebellum period. Most of the spending occurred in the 1850s, when railroad mileage in seven key southern states nearly quadrupled from 1,800 miles to 7,001 miles.[2] Such government largesse reflected an important regional divergence: just as southerners embraced state investment, northerners retreated from it.[3] Total public investment (primarily state and local governments, with a small federal contribution) provided 57 percent of the capital for southern railroads, whereas public investment in the North and West amounted to 15 to

21 percent of total railroad investment.[4] The difference in per capita terms was even more striking. Public assistance to northern railroads ranged somewhere between $6.33 and $9.14 per person, while public investment in southern railroads came to $16.58 per person (slave and free) and $26.37 per free person.[5]

This chapter attempts to account for this important regional difference. Virginia and South Carolina provide excellent case studies because both states initiated activist investment policies. Virginians formulated a "mixed enterprise" system in which the state government purchased 40 percent (later increased to 60 percent) of the capital stock of railroad and canal companies. South Carolinians enacted a more ad hoc policy but nevertheless invested heavily in favored enterprises. Both states ranked high in per capita government spending on railroads (Table 4). South Carolina, despite its reputation for archconservatism, invested more government dollars per free person than perhaps any state in the Union.[6] South Carolinians and many other southerners railed against *federal* expenditures on internal improvements, yet they apparently had few qualms about enthusiastically endorsing public investment at the state and local level. If railroads, as historian John Larson argues, helped bring about free enterprise in the North, the experience of South Carolina and Virginia suggests that railroads helped create a more activist state in the South.[7]

A combination of economic necessity, local rivalry, and incipient southern nationalism fueled state railroad investment in South Carolina and Virginia. Slavery and shifting cultivation created the necessity of state investment. Slavery and shifting cultivation meant sparse free populations and limited urban growth, thus preventing railroads from generating revenue and profits. Running through a largely uncultivated countryside, southern railroads had little hope of paying dividends for private investors. With financiers and capitalists leery of investing in unprofitable companies, southern railroads relied on government financing. Economic necessity quickly became a political imperative. Even if they did not pay direct returns to the investors, southern railroads nevertheless promised important benefits for local residents, including higher land values and better access to markets. Urban merchants and slaveholding planters alike incessantly lobbied state and local governments for state investment. Legislators and governors, seeking to curry political favor while advancing their own economic interests, gladly complied. The local advantages that

TABLE 4   An Activist Economic Policy: Cumulative Government Investment in Southern Railroads up to 1860 (in Millions of Dollars)

| State | State Investment | County and Municipal Investment | Total Public Investment | Per Capita Public Investment (Total Population) | Per Capita Public Investment (Free Population) |
| --- | --- | --- | --- | --- | --- |
| Tennessee | 17.25 | 8.53 | 25.78 | 25.71 | 33.77 |
| Virginia | 23.73 | 7.93 | 31.66 | 22.27 | 33.36 |
| S. Carolina | 9.66 | 4.01 | 13.67 | 20.45 | 48.21 |
| Kentucky | .75 | 16.30 | 17.05 | 17.35 | 22.10 |
| Georgia | 6.93 | 5.93 | 12.86 | 14.19 | 24.51 |
| N. Carolina | 10.66 | 1.28 | 11.94 | 13.74 | 20.56 |
| Louisiana | 3.39 | 5.06 | 5.45 | 10.52 | 19.96 |
| Alabama | 2.15 | 3.73 | 5.88 | 7.62 | 13.71 |
| Mississippi | 2.12 | 2.06 | 4.18 | 6.89 | 14.10 |
| Total | 76.64 | 51.81 | 128.45 | 16.58 | 26.37 |

Source: State investment and county and municipal investment figures taken from Milton S. Heath, "Public Railroad Construction and the Development of Private Enterprise in the South before 1860," *Journal of Economic History* 10, supplement, "The Tasks of Economic History" (1950): 41.

such investment produced created a powerful political dynamic that drove state spending inexorably higher in the 1840s and 1850s.

From a narrow economic perspective, the story might well end there. Focusing exclusively on interest-group politics, however, ignores the rich rhetorical and ideological context of state investment. Railroad promoters and urban boosters seeking state funds had to explain how government investment in a particular project would enhance the welfare of the entire state. Justification for railroad investment took many different forms, but speakers, editorialists, and pamphleteers invariably focused on the ability of railroads to help white southerners better protect slavery. Railroads would speed the movement of troops to quell slave revolts, encourage more intensive cultivation practices (thus leading to higher population densities and greater political strength), and unite the South and the West into a formidable political alliance. Railroads would encourage more manufacturing and direct trade with Europe, which would transfer economic and political power from the North to the South. Virginia's Thomas R. Dew, one of the South's leading political economists, wrote in 1832 that internal improvements were literally the "great *panacea*, by which most of the ills of which now weigh down the state may be removed, and health and activity communicated to every department of industry."[8]

Dew was wrong. Railroads benefited many southerners, but they failed to transform the region's economy in the way that boosters had imagined. Most southern planters and farmers still practiced shifting cultivation. Southern cities still remained far smaller than their northern counterparts. Southerners still relied on northern producers for most of their manufactured goods, and southern merchants and factors still shipped imports and exports through New York City and other northern ports. The failure of railroads to revolutionize the southern economy inadvertently played into the hands of secessionists. Secessionists could claim with some justification that southerners—no matter how enterprising or industrious—would always be economically dependent upon the North as long as they remained in the Union. For the South's frustrated modernizers, secession became an increasingly appealing option.

The failure of railroads to revolutionize the southern economy should not obscure the ideological significance of state investment. Railroad supporters, much like the agricultural reformers, believed that public investment would create a modern economy that would allow southerners to better protect slavery. The logic of the southern railroad supporters helps explain the tremendous growth of the Confederate government during the Civil War. If the defense of slavery required activist state governments during the antebellum period, then surely the defense of slavery justified an activist national government during a time of war and crisis. For Virginians and South Carolinians, public support of large-scale enterprise was hardly a revolutionary experience born of wartime exigency. It was, in fact, the norm of the antebellum period.

## SLAVERY, SHIFTING CULTIVATION, AND STATE-FUNDED RAILROADS

The history of a single enterprise highlights the difficulties facing many southern railroads in the antebellum period. In 1835 Charleston's merchants and their planter allies set out to build the Louisville, Cincinnati, and Charleston Railroad, a visionary enterprise that would enable South Carolina's merchants to reach the markets of the Midwest. With great effort on the part of the state of South Carolina and the city of Charleston, the railroad had raised some $4 million by 1836 to begin initial construction. The railroad, however, needed far more capital to reach the Ohio. To attract additional investment, the railroad's promoters devised a scheme centered on the Southwestern Railroad Bank. Investors expected the bank, chartered during a great cotton boom, to pay high dividends. The railroad's promoters, though, required potential bank investors to first buy shares in the railroad. The scheme was puzzling, at least from the standpoint of the railroad's promotional rhetoric. The road's boosters claimed that the railroad would pay handsome dividends, but the implicit premise of the bank scheme was that investors needed the additional lure of bank stock. That premise turned out to be all too true. When plunging cotton prices threatened the solvency of the Southwest Railroad Bank, investors refused to buy the railroad's stock. The resulting shortage of capital forced the company to dramatically scale back its operations. The grand internal improvement of South Carolina managed to reach Columbia.[9] The Louisville, Cincinnati, and Charleston Railroad would eventually be renamed the South Carolina Railroad, a more appropriate name given the company's increasingly local orientation.

The failure of the Louisville, Cincinnati, and Charleston Railroad revealed the difficulties of building profitable railroads in the South. Because of shifting cultivation, a canal, a railroad, or even a country lane had to meander through large stretches of unproductive land in long-term fallow. The large swaths of unimproved land generated little traffic, which dramatically reduced potential revenue per square mile. That a high proportion of the population was enslaved made the situation even worse. The vast majority of slaves would never become passengers (unless they became ensnared in the slave trade), would never send or receive mail (an important part of early railroad revenue), and would rarely buy manufactured goods (which were often sent via rail because of their high value relative to weight). Dependent on the shipment of staple crops such as cotton and tobacco, southern railroads tended to have relatively little traffic heading back to the sparsely populated countryside in which slavery and shifting cultivation depressed demand.[10] As one South Carolinian noted in 1848, railroads in the South were unprofitable because "our population is too sparse, and more than that, our peculiar institutions deprive the Roads of the benefit of one-half of what there is, and will continue to do so forever."[11] Southerners essentially built railroads "ahead of demand" in the hope that their very presence would generate more business in the future (Map 2).[12]

The contrast with the North was pronounced. In the first three decades of the nineteenth century, northern state governments heavily financed canals such as New York's Erie Canal and the Pennsylvania Mainline system. Over time, though, the North's dense networks of farms, towns, and cities provided rich markets that supported profitable railroads. A railroad connecting New York to Buffalo in 1850, for example, could count on the traffic of more than 2 million New York customers alone, not including the booming business emanating from the Great Lakes region. (The *combined* white population of South Carolina and Virginia, by way of comparison, was less than 1.2 million). Increasingly profitable, northern railroads could dispense with state aid. Many northerners viewed state funding as a likely source of corruption that favored a few privileged companies at the expense of taxpayers. These attitudes, coupled with large state budget deficits resulting from canal spending in the 1820s and 1830s, helped propel what historians have labeled the "revulsion against internal improvements."[13] In the 1840s and 1850s, large northern states such as New York, Ohio, and Pennsylvania passed constitutions that either limited state debt or prohibited state ownership of stock. Although state investment did not entirely disappear, the overall trend was clear.[14] The 1857 sale of Pennsylvania's state-owned Mainline system of canals and railroads to the privately owned Pennsylvania Railroad for $10 million (a fraction of its cost) symbolized the transition from state enterprise to private enterprise.[15]

The movement toward private enterprise in the South, though, never took place. Both South Carolina and Virginia exemplified the trend. Of the $20 million that South Carolinians raised for railroad construction in the antebellum period, $13.67 million (68 percent) came from direct municipal and state purchases of stock or state-endorsed bonds. With a larger population and greater geographic area to serve, Virginia's state government and municipalities spent some $31.66 million on railroad construction—some 70 percent of the state's total railroad capital. The substantial railroad subsidies made other southern companies dependent on public investment. Richmond's Tredegar Iron Works, for example,

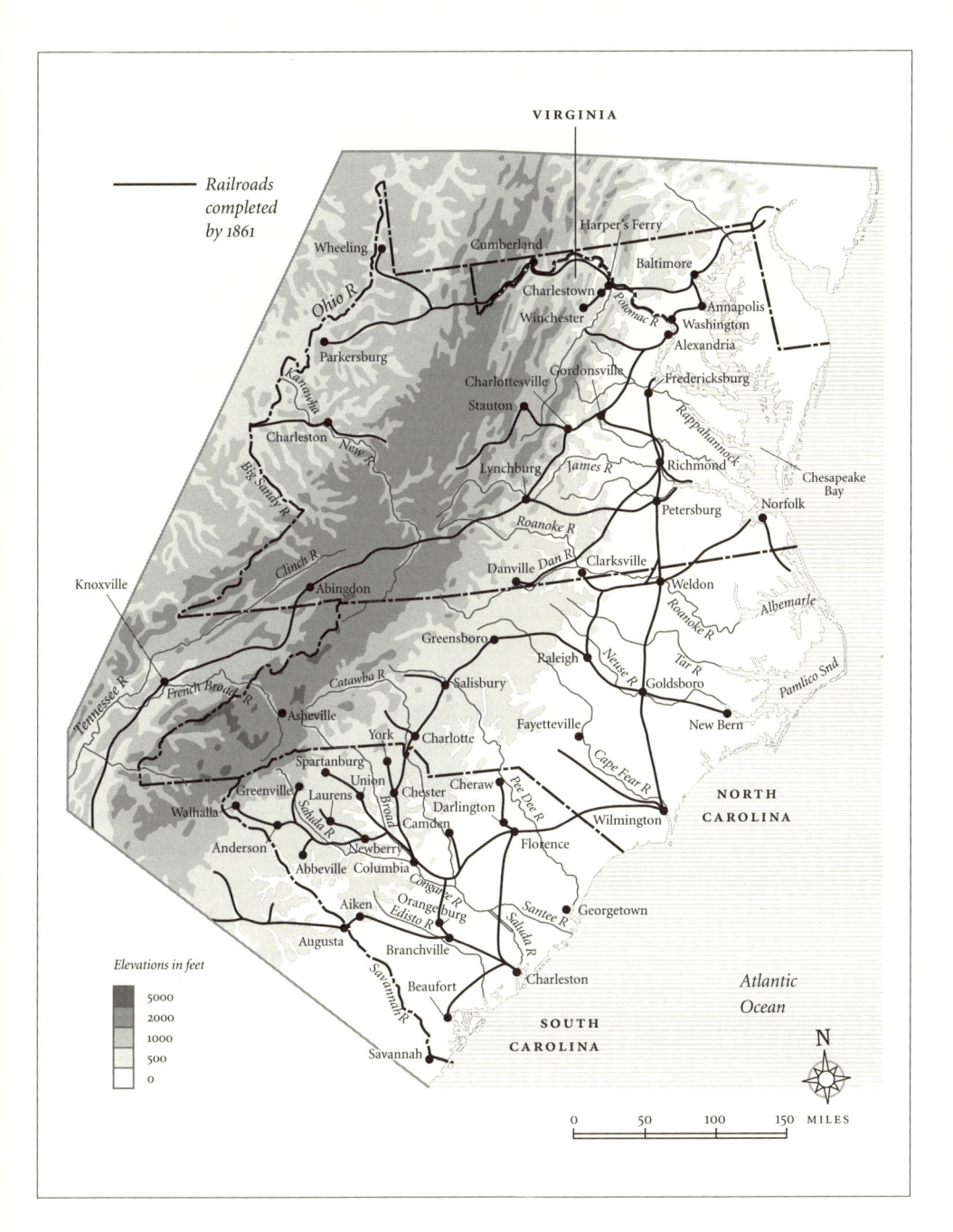

MAP 2   RAILROADS IN VIRGINIA AND THE CAROLINAS
*Despite the dreams of southern boosters, railroads in Virginia and the Carolinas never effectively penetrated the Upcountry to connect port cities such as Norfolk and Charleston to the Midwest. (Map by Dorothy McClaren)*

depended on state-aided southern railroads for orders of rails and locomotives.[16] Without the business of government-supported railroads, the Confederacy's largest ironworks might have gone bankrupt well before the war began. In the antebellum South, big business and state activism went hand in hand.

Public investment remained popular in the South because most southern railroads failed to make money. Government records show that during the 1850s, the Virginia state government received a direct rate of return of less than 1 percent on its railroad investments. A few South Carolina railroads generated higher profits. The South Carolina Railroad, running from Charleston to Hamburg with branches to Columbia and Camden, eventually produced excellent returns. After struggling for much of the 1830s and 1840s, the railroad paid dividends averaging 8 percent from 1849 to 1860. Shareholders, not surprisingly, could find a ready market for the company's stock. The South Carolina Railroad clearly benefited from having a central terminus in Charleston. Whereas Alexandria, Richmond, Petersburg, and Norfolk divided Virginia's small market into even smaller pieces, the South Carolina Railroad funneled almost all of the traffic from the South Carolina piedmont to Charleston without significant competition. William Gregg, a South Carolina textile manufacturer, complained that the absence of competition allowed the railroad to raise freight rates, thus blunting local development: "That the South Carolina Railroad is a monopoly beyond all control, we are willing to admit. That it will remain so until competition relieves us is equally apparent."[17] The legislature refused to charter competing projects, Gregg charged, because it wanted to protect the dividends that the South Carolina Railroad paid to politically well-connected investors. The high cotton prices of the 1850s, which created widespread prosperity in the South Carolina piedmont, undoubtedly added to the company's revenues.

The success of the South Carolina Railroad Company, however, was exceptional; the other nine railroads in the state paid dividends intermittently if they paid them at all. State aid was thus a necessity. In proposing an ambitious scheme of railroad construction in 1847, Governor David Johnson clearly acknowledged the importance of state investment for South Carolina's railroads. "The state is relied upon to contribute, in some form or other towards the completion of these enterprises [railroads]," he declared in 1847, for without state aid "some or all of them must fail."[18] As a general rule, the more ambitious projects required the most state aid, as the fate of the Blue Ridge Railroad attests. The Blue Ridge Railroad was a pet project of Charleston interests in the 1850s; investors once again desired to build an ambitious transmontane project that would link their city to Knoxville, Tennessee. Traversing particularly rugged territory, the central piece of the Blue Ridge Railroad was a one-mile tunnel through solid granite. Private investment was virtually nonexistent. As the company itself explained: "The road lies over a mountainous country but sparsely populated at present and without wealth, and the means required must be almost entirely derived from the State of South Carolina."[19] Despite the expenditure of $5.5 million, almost all of which came from the state government and the city of Charleston, the tunnel was never completed and the project was a complete loss.[20]

Northern companies sometimes faced grim prospects for dividends during their difficult early years as well. In these circumstances, northern railroads turned to a crucial source of private capital: local farmers, retailers, and merchants who sought higher land values, greater local commerce, and other indirect benefits. Individually, local investors living in close proximity to a railroad often invested modest sums ($100–$500 apiece), but the collective effort of hundreds of such stockholders could provide a significant infusion of capital at a critical moment.[21] The Pennsylvania Railroad, for example, depended upon such local investment when poor prospects for direct profits made it difficult to tap the fortunes of large-scale capitalists and financiers. In the late 1840s, the company's organizers took its subscription books door-to-door throughout Philadelphia in a desperate bid to raise capital. The promoters forcefully argued that all residents of the city had an interest in a company that would raise land values for all property owners, large and small. A good many investors apparently believed such promises. The railroad's 1847 annual report boasted that "out of some twenty-six hundred subscriptions near eighteen hundred are for five shares and under."[22]

Southerners, too, enthusiastically trumpeted the local benefits of railroads so that they could raise local capital. In a widely published 1848 letter, John C. Calhoun strongly support a proposed railroad from Columbia to Anderson, South Carolina, which would undoubtedly improve the prospects for a railroad connection within his own county of Pickens. Evaluating the project from the standpoint of direct profits, Calhoun argued, "would be taking a very narrow view." He listed the indirect benefits the project would bring to his community, including high property values, more manufacturing, and even more tourists "attracted by the romantic and fine mountain region."[23] The problem for Calhoun and other railroad promoters was that the combination of shifting cultivation and slavery resulted in far fewer plantations, farms, and towns along a given line, giving southern projects a smaller pool of local investors to draw upon. The consequent lack of urban growth was also an important factor. Charleston (population 40,522) and Richmond (population 38,000) could not hope to match the potential number of investors in a city such as Philadelphia (population 565,000). No matter how enthusiastically they supported railroads, southerner city dwellers could never raise enough money to finance them. Here, perhaps, is one way of understanding the often-repeated assertion that southerners "lacked capital" to finance internal improvements. It was not so much that southern planters and merchants lacked capital; there were simply not enough of them to shoulder the burden of supporting developmental enterprises that paid little in immediate returns.[24]

### SLAVERY, AGRICULTURE, AND THE RHETORIC OF PUBLIC INVESTMENT

Because railroads provided great benefits to local communities, state-level politicians found it politically popular to approve public financing. The political popularity of each individual project, however, did not necessarily justify public railroad investment as a whole, especially when such investments resulted in escalating budget deficits and potentially higher taxes. Even the most cynical railroad promoter knew that asserting naked self-interest on behalf of his enterprise or locality would result in a political disaster. Southern legislators needed to hear a larger justification to unlock the public treasury. Railroad promoters, not surprisingly, focused on protecting slavery. In debates over railroad policy, historian Colleen Dunlavy has observed, "at stake was not only regional prosperity, but ultimately national power."[25] Railroads, according to their southern promoters, would enable the South to maintain or increase its power within national politics.

Promoters sometimes focused on military advantages—the use of railroads to quell slave rebellions or move troops—to justify public investment. Slow travel over wet, muddy roads might well hinder the ability of white southerners to put down their region's peculiar form of domestic unrest, especially given the South's low population densities. Railroads could quickly transport troops to areas that needed help. South Carolinian Robert Hayne, a southern extremist and president of the Louisville, Cincinnati, and Charleston Railroad, declared in 1836 that his enterprise "would put an end at once, and forever, to all apprehension of domestic insurrection, or foreign invasion, while the obvious facility with this intercourse could be interrupted, would afford ample security against its ever being used for hostile purposes."[26] The term "hostile purposes" was ambiguous, perhaps intentionally so. Did it refer to foreign invaders (as perhaps northerners would assume), or did it also include abolitionist fanatics (as southern listeners might infer)? A decade later, South Carolina governor David Johnson warned that the "time may come when we shall be obliged to buckle our armour to repel invasions or quit domestic strife." Railroads would allow the state to quickly mobilize its "united strength."[27] In similar fashion, the Memphis and Charleston Railroad characterized rail lines as "our tower of strength" that could collect men and supplies "with lightning velocity to . . . strike down the servile arm, overthrow the disturber of the State, and expel the invader." The company concluded that state governments should help build "this right arm of national defense." Given that the company made its appeal in the context of the "relative condition of North and South," the word "national" here took on a distinctly southern meaning.[28]

Events proved the Memphis and Charleston right, of course. In several critical situations, railroads transported southern troops and supplies during the Civil War, if not quite with "lightning velocity." Yet taken as a whole, the promotional rhetoric clearly conceived of railroads primarily as economic enterprises and not military projects. Focusing too much on the military value of roads introduced an uncomfortable instability that southern railroad supporters instinctively avoided. Was the threat of slave revolts so grave that southerners needed to build expensive railroads to combat domestic insurrection? To avoid such troubling questions, railroad supporters instead concentrated on the economic value of their companies, and they then tied that economic utility to broader issues of sectional politics and the protection of slavery. Southern railroad supporters conceived general economic development as the best way to secure the future of the peculiar institution.

Railroad promoters stressed that improved transportation would encourage more intensive cultivation of the countryside, which in turn would provide southerners with a larger population and more political power. Supporters believed that railroads would spell the end of shifting cultivation, as declining transportation costs gave farmers and planters an incentive to increase production. Acreage once deemed as waste might be brought into cultivation, especially since railroads would also allow planters and farmers to cheaply transport guano, marl, and other manures. As one correspondent to Richmond's *Southern Planter* asserted, "Let the roads be made better, and one cause, one great cause of the poor condition of Agriculturalists in Virginia, Tennessee, the Carolinas, &c., would be done away with."[29] Improved transportation would also accelerate urban and industrial growth, which would encourage farmers and planters to produce more butter, milk, cheese, fruits, vegetables, and livestock. With more manufacturing and a greater urban population, the *Southern Planter* declared in 1845, the "thousands who are engaged in overproducing the staples of wheat, corn, and tobacco would be employed in making vegetables, butter, cheese, &c. for this new population."[30]

Dew made a similar argument is his well-known *Review of the Debate in the Virginia Legislature of 1831 and 1832*. Published after the Virginia legislature had rejected a plan for gradual emancipation, Dew's book is often cited as an important turning point in the southern defense of slavery. Explicitly refuting Jefferson's view that slavery was a grave national sin, Dew argued that the institution was a positive good for master and slave alike. As a response to those who doubted the economic efficiency of slavery, Dew prophesized that internal improvements would transform Virginia's cultivation practices. By making it easier for planters and farmers to get their produce to market, internal improvements would increase the profits of agriculture and thus discourage emigration to the West: "A general prosperity is diffused over the whole country—new products are raised upon the soil—new occupations spring up—old ones are enlarged and rendered more productive—a wider field is opened for the display of the energies of both mind and body, and the rising generation are bound down to the scenes of their infancy, and the homes of their fathers: not by the tie of affection and association alone, but by the still stronger ligament of *interest*."[31] In Dew's vision, internal improvements would increase the size of Virginia's eastern cities, farm sizes would decline, and free laborers from the North would migrate into the state. Slavery would eventually decline in importance, albeit on the Old Dominion's own terms: "In due time the abolitionists will find this most lucrative system working to their hearts content . . . without those impoverishing effects which all other schemes [of emancipation] must *necessarily* have."[32]

Dew's argument that higher population density would eventually result in gradual emancipation exerted little influence on the debates of railroad funding. Virginia's railroad supporters, in fact, almost always argued the opposite: high population densities would give the Old Dominion political influence to better protect slavery within the Union. In portraying Virginia's slow demographic growth as a major political crisis, railroad supporters used a language familiar to Edmund Ruffin and the agricultural reformers. Joseph Segar, a lawyer and Whig politician from the Norfolk area, declared in 1838 that "there is a drain operating upon us, which is fast weakening the political power of the state and consuming her strength." That New York and Pennsylvania had surpassed the Old Dominion was bad enough, but the fact that Ohio, "a state comparatively of yesterday," threatened to overtake Virginia was particularly galling. Without internal improvements, Segar predicted, "decline and degeneracy must be her doom, and poverty fixed upon her citizens."[33] Fifteen years later—in the aftermath of the Compromise of 1850 and the Fugitive Slave Act controversies—Segar declared that population growth was the "best defence [sic] of our peculiar institutions." Virginians, he declared, "look to happy agency of internal improvements, in keeping our people in the land of the fathers, and attracting the stranger to it."[34]

The rhetoric of demographic disaster, agricultural change, and economic survival was also popular in South Carolina. When seeking state funds, the directors of the Memphis and Charleston Railroad predicted that their company would "revolutionize" agriculture and "in some measure stop the tide of emigration seeking the cheap virgin soil of the Southwest."[35] For Upcountry railroad promoter John B. O'Neall, the railroad's impact on agriculture was literally "*a matter of life and death*. Without it you might as well abandon your homes and seek new residences. . . . The effect of a Railroad will be to place part of this immense wasteland in cultivation, and cover it and the other parts of the Districts with a dense population."[36] Calhoun presented a similarly sharp dichotomy between a region with a railroad "that retains its population and receives emigrants" and a region without one that "sends forth emigrants without receiving them."[37] South Carolinian J. P. Reed, one of Calhoun's correspondents, considered the proposed railroad between Columbia and Anderson as a way for South Carolina to maintain the "equality of her political position in the Union" and "as a very great means of defence [sic] to our country."[38]

A GREAT COMMERCIAL REVOLUTION

According to their southern supporters, railroads would not only generate dramatic agricultural change; they also promised to instigate a commercial revolution. Railroad supporters dwelled on the South's lack of direct trade with Europe, reminding southerners that the vast majority of the region's exports and imports first went to New York City, where northern middlemen took a large cut of southern profits. Southern railroad promoters portrayed the national distribution system as a degrading form of commercial vassalage. While New York grew to become one of the world's most important commercial centers, southern ports such as Norfolk and Charleston stagnated. Building railroads that connected the South's ports to western markets would stimulate direct trade with Europe, as merchants would send goods to Norfolk or Charleston before sending them to the West. An efficient railroad network, railroad promoters argued, would make the South the emporium of the world's commerce. The Charleston and Savannah Railroad, for example, saw itself as part of a chain of railroads linking Asia to New Orleans and then to Charleston. The company imagined that the "powerful and wealthy Oriental kingdoms of China and Japan will be forced to seek the accommodation of these transit lines." The company also believed that it would attract the trade of the "vast and fertile empire of Brazil" to the South, which was an especially important consideration given that Brazilians, like southerners, manfully resisted the "extravagant rhetoric of abolition theorists."[39]

Such arguments, however exaggerated, became an integral part of railroad promotion. Whig politicians, well known for their mercantile orientation and strong support for state activism, eagerly promoted dreams of commercial greatness. Once Virginia completed the Ohio and Covington Railroad, declared Segar, "New York, empire New York herself, beholden to Virginia, will be seen shipping her supplies of merchandise, via Richmond and Covington, to her customers in the west."[40] William M. Burwell, a Whig leader in various commercial conventions held in Virginia, similarly argued in 1851 that Virginians had to improve the "means of intercourse with the markets of the world" to attract immigrants that would increase the state's political power.[41] Such rhetoric served political as well as promotional purposes. Frequently being labeled as "soft on slavery," southern Whigs needed a way of showing off their proslavery credentials. Linking public aid to railroads to the long-term survival of slavery fused the traditional Whig program of state intervention with southern nationalism.

Many Democrats—including strong secessionists—joined Whigs to promote railroads as the commercial salvation of Virginia. Perhaps most notable was Henry Wise, who served as Virginia's governor from 1857 to 1859. The ambitious Wise was something of a political enigma, but he was a warm friend of internal improvements throughout his political career and vigorously embraced a comprehensive plan of public investment. Wise thought of his liberal spending plan as a way of building up a great commercial center within Virginia that could challenge New York, Philadelphia, and other northern cities for control of the western trade. "That control cannot be had without a center of trade," he told the legislature in 1857, "and that center of trade cannot be built up without public works to bring a back country to some point of commerce."[42] Wise supported a modernization program so strongly that he successfully advocated the politically dangerous policy of raising taxes so that the state could better fund its mushrooming investments in public works.[43]

Wise was hardly a lone Democratic voice. John B. Floyd, a southern extremist, also enthusiastically endorsed railroads when he served as governor from 1849 to 1851. In his inaugural speech, Floyd argued that public expenditures should be focused only on major trunk lines that would connect Virginia with the West. Floyd imagined that these western connections would eventually reach the Pacific and capture the trade of China and India. Once Virginia had completed her western improvements, nothing could "hinder a car, laden with rich silks and aromatic spices of India on the shores of the Pacific, from pursuing its continuous and uninterrupted course, until the journey is completed, and rests on the banks of the Chesapeake."[44] Floyd's successor, Governor Joseph Johnson, was somewhat more restrained in his rhetoric, but he firmly believed that Virginia's geographic position would give her control of the "immense trade that will be brought to our shores from the West and Southwest upon the completion of several grand lines of improvement now in progress."[45]

The desire to jump start direct trade led many Virginians and South Carolinians to investigate other forms of state activism. If the state government could invest in railroads, they argued, why could it not subsidize the steamships that would connect European merchants and southern ports? In commercial conventions, legislative petitions, and newspaper articles, Virginians and South Carolinians devised numerous state-supported schemes to encourage direct trade. Southern state governments could invest in steamship lines, grant tax exemptions to foreign goods directly imported into their ports, or even tax northern goods entering their states, thus encouraging European merchants to send goods directly to northern ports. Although state legislatures frequently discussed these measures, local rivalries (such as deciding which steamship company would receive state investment) and entrenched interests (southern merchants with strong commercial ties to the North) doomed their political prospects. That these proposals received so much debate, though, highlights how eagerly southerners sought to revolutionize their economy.[46]

The enthusiasm for far-flung connections also speaks to the geographic determinism that suffused southern railroad rhetoric. Equipped with maps and mileage tables, southerners fantasized that their supposedly unique geographic position entitled their region to become a vast commercial empire that would literally unite global commerce. Perhaps the best example of this type of thinking came from Virginian Matthew F. Maury, a distinguished naval officer and oceanographer. In addition to his notable scientific expertise, Maury wrote extensively on commercial affairs from a decidedly pro-southern perspective. In a lengthy letter to Calhoun, Maury outlined how a railroad from Charleston to Memphis to Monterrey, Mexico, would become the crossroads of international commerce. The railroad, operating in conjunction with a line of steamers linking China to Monterrey, would enable southerners to "drink tea made in Charleston within the same month in which the leaf was gathered in China."[47] Never mind that Monterrey, Memphis, and Charleston could hardly compete against cities such as New York and Philadelphia, whose population, capital, and commercial services made long-distance trade efficient and profitable. What really mattered to Maury was geography— the fact that Memphis and Charleston were closer to the "geographic centre" of the nation. The railroad to Memphis and Monterrey, he observed, would "place us before the commercial marts of *six hundred millions* of people, and enable us, *geographically*, to command them."[48]

For Maury, geography was destiny because geography was power—power that the South could wield with a few crucial railroad connections.

BONDS OF INTEREST

The goods and people traveling along the South's western connections— whether from Asia, Brazil, or the West—would make the South not only the commercial center of the nation, but also the political center. Railroads and the expansion of commerce would create "bonds of interest" between southerners and their various trading partners. Such arguments reflected the widespread belief that commercial interest formed the most permanent political bonds. Regions connected with internal improvements would receive the same news, buy the same goods, and depend on the same trade. Common interests, in essence, would eventually mold them into one people. Many antebellum Americans believed in the political power of interests, but the southern embrace of this economic determinism was striking. In 1831 Virginia's Committee of Roads and Internal Navigation noted, as a matter of fact, that the "history of man of all ages" clearly revealed "that the strongest connection by which men in an associated character, are held together, is a community of interest. . . . Patriotism alone has never been known to bind men together in a political connection, for a great length of time, where their interests were directly opposed."[49]

For Virginians, binding east and west started at home. The Board of Public Works noted that northern states had already embarked on successful programs that had "secured the union of their own people."[50] The implication was subtle but nevertheless clear. Virginia, sometimes bitterly divided between the slaveholding eastern seaboard and the mountainous west, could secure political unity through internal improvements. If western Virginia's iron, coal, and grains came to Richmond rather than to Baltimore or Cincinnati, a common commercial destiny would unite the commonwealth. Failure to build railroads and canals, on the other hand, invited political disaster. If Virginia failed to build internal improvements, Segar prophetically declared in 1838, eastern Virginia should give up any hope of keeping western Virginia as part of the state: "I would cast my vote to give away our western country to any state that would do it justice, by opening for it an outlet for market."[51]

Railroads would both unify Virginia and cement alliances with the

West. As antislavery activists gained strength in the Northeast, railroad promoters argued that southerners must cultivate good relations with the West. Richmond lawyer R. G. Morriss equated intersectional railroads with "bands of gold" that would "produce a unity of interests of the Western States with Virginia."[52] As bloodthirsty abolitionists prepared to free the nation's slaves, Morriss asked whether it was "not the part of the wisdom of Virginia to prepare for the coming storm—to make it the interest of the Western States to stand by her in any difficulties that may occur, and to increase her population and resources as much as possible?"[53] If Virginia did not build western connections, northerners certainly would. Without a competing southern link, the *Richmond Enquirer* warned in 1856, "abolition, along with foreign goods and Yankee notions," would soon dominate the West.[54] Such warnings combined the geographic and economic determinism that suffused southern railroad rhetoric. Westerners did not choose or reject abolitionism of their own accord but adopted the same beliefs and attitudes of their major trading partners. Ideas and beliefs could thus be reduced to the thin black lines of a railroad map. The origin of those lines—the North or the South—would determine what westerners believed and how they would vote.

South Carolinians found such determinism particularly appealing. As a small state with no hope of dominating the Union through sheer size, South Carolinians rarely conceived of political strength in terms of numbers alone. Especially in the 1830s and the 1850s, South Carolinians hoped that railroads would cement southern unity, which was painfully lacking as South Carolina stood precariously alone on its radical perch. South Carolinians, warned Charleston newspaper editor Jacob Cardozo in 1835, "must improve and extend those relations of trade that will enable the entire South and South West to present an undivided front to those who would assail their common interests and institutions." Predicting future sectional tensions, Cardozo believed that the "interchanges of commerce" would make the cotton states "one firm and united commonwealth."[55] Like Virginians, South Carolinians also believed that state-sponsored internal improvements would result in an alliance between East and West. When the Charleston and Cincinnati Railroad raised enough capital to officially begin operations in 1836, Robert Hayne toasted the impending bonds between the two regions: "The South and the West—We have published the banns—if any one know aught why these two should not be joined together, let him speak now, or forever hold his peace."[56] New western states "would not only become reconciled to our institutions (by becoming better acquainted with them)," Hayne asserted, "but would also be interested in defending and maintaining them."[57]

Calhoun wholeheartedly agreed with such sentiments. In his nationalistic phase, Calhoun had vigorously supported the Bonus Bill of 1817, which established a federal fund for internal improvements. "Let us bind the republic together with a perfect system of roads and canals," he famously declared. "Let us conquer space."[58] As Calhoun turned toward states' rights, he retained his enthusiasm for internal improvements, albeit with important qualifications. According to Calhoun, the Constitution prohibited the federal government from directly funding or managing internal improvements, but the federal government could make land grants to specific enterprises in its capacity as proprietor of public lands. Given that railroads and canals would increase the value of the public domain, the land grants constituted a perfectly constitutional means of wise stewardship. To give the national government even more authority, Calhoun argued that Congress should also consider the Great Lakes and the Mississippi River a "great inland sea." Just as the federal government funded lighthouses and harbor improvements along the Atlantic and Gulf coasts, it should shoulder the burden of dredging and otherwise improving the Mississippi River and its various tributaries.[59] Calhoun believed that a federal system of internal improvements would indeed help "bind the republic together," but along distinctly regional lines that would promote an alliance between the South and the West.

Calhoun believed that railroads from South Atlantic ports (especially Charleston) were another way of cementing such an alliance between South and West. In the 1840s Calhoun and his political allies eagerly supported a railroad connecting Memphis and Charleston. F. H. Elmore, who had been selected as a South Carolina delegate to a railroad convention in Memphis in 1845, urged Calhoun to attend the meeting. With Calhoun's prestige, Elmore argued, the South could build railroads that would work to "advance Southern interests—to form & consolidate a right sentiment—to unite our section upon right policy and principles." Elmore made clear that the "right sentiment" involved the protection of slavery. A railroad between Charleston and Memphis, he wrote, would consolidate an alliance between Upcountry southerners (whom he characterized as the "most martial portion of our people & who have, as at present[ly] situated, the least interest of all the South in slavery") with slaveholders in both the South Atlantic and Mississippi Valley regions. With commercial bonds firmly established, "their interests & ours would be indissolubly united. They would be to us a source of strength, power & safety & render the South invulnerable."[60] In his speech before the Memphis convention, Calhoun enthusiastically supported building railroads between the South Atlantic and the Mississippi Valley, declaring that such enterprises would form the basis of a "great internal market."[61] Perhaps mindful of his national political standing and his hopes of cementing an alliance between the South and the West, Calhoun avoided overly sectional rhetoric. Listeners could readily assume, however, that participation in Calhoun's "great internal market" would give westerners strong economic and political incentives to support slavery.

## SOUTHERN CRITICS OF STATE INVESTMENT

Although a strong southern consensus favored state investment, a number of critics raised important questions. Perhaps the most fundamental question was whether more southern commerce and manufacturing might ultimately destroy slavery. In 1854 a lengthy article by the anonymous writer "Planter" maintained that the prosperity of most slaveholders had little to do with railroads and local development; it instead depended on the international price for cotton, rice, and other staples. Cotton prices, he asserted, would be the same whether Charleston's population was 20,000 or 200,000. Politically, the growth of cities would positively harm planters because urban merchants and working men had little interest in slavery and would undoubtedly embrace the free-labor ideology of the North. "Every city is destined to be the seat of free-soilism," he claimed. "It is unconsciously making its appearance in Charleston, and it is destined to increase with every fresh arrival of European immigrants."[62] The writer's arguments drew on a long line of conservative republican thought, which had long maintained that cities, with their large concentration of wage workers, constituted "sores on the body politic." That cities could become hostile to slavery had at least a grain of truth. Virginia slaveholders, in particular, knew that cities generated interests contrary to their own. John Minor Botts, a successful lawyer, became well known for uniting many of Richmond's white artisans and workers into an urban political machine. Although hardly an abolitionist, Botts's politics alarmed proslavery politicians. During the emotional election of 1856, for example, the outspoken Botts denounced southern extremism and supported restricting slavery in the West.[63] If Richmond grew into a large commercial center, it might produce antislavery politicians far more powerful than Botts.

The anxieties over large cities dovetailed fears that railroad spending and exploding state budget deficits would generate political corruption and higher taxes. These fears were especially important in Virginia, where the outstanding debt of the state's internal-improvement fund grew to $34.4 million in 1860, up from $8 million in 1850.[64] Virginia's governors and legislators hoped that railroads and other investments would pay dividends to the state so that the state could pay down the debt without raising taxes.[65] Critics such as Edmund Ruffin argued that such optimism bordered on the delusional. In the 1830s and 1840s, Ruffin supported railroads as a way of lowering the price of marl and other fertilizers, and he made substantial investments in several enterprises in Virginia and North Carolina. Virginia's growing debt, though, worried him. The champion of state-sponsored agricultural research linked state spending on railroads to waste, logrolling, and corruption. "The legislature has appropriated $2,500,000 to different rail-roads & some of them useless & some even injurious to state interests," Ruffin recorded with disgust in his diary in March 1858. "Probably in consequence of this increase to the very large state debt, & fear of 'repudiation,' the state bonds sold yesterday at 90. . . . The finances of the commonwealth have been woefully managed."[66]

South Carolinians avoided Virginia's fiscal problems because of their state's fortuitous investment in the South Carolina Railroad. The company paid relatively high dividends in the 1840s and 1850s, which increased the value of the state government's sizable stake. To finance other railroads, the state gave them large blocks of the South Carolina Railroad stock, which could readily be sold on the open market to raise funds for construction. Another favored policy of South Carolina was to endorse millions of dollars worth of railroad bonds. Endorsing bonds was politically appealing because it did not immediately drain the state's finances. But if companies could not pay the bonds back—a likely possibility, given the poor profitably of many of these enterprises—then the state would eventually have to pay the debt. Critics charged that endorsing bonds would likely bankrupt the state at some future date. As early as 1848, James Henry Hammond (writing under the name "Anti-Debt") proclaimed that the state government has managed "*to coerce the tax-payers without their consent into these rash and ruinous speculations.*"[67] For Hammond, continued investment was a ticking fiscal time bomb that would inevitably explode in the face of South Carolina's taxpayers.

Hammond's rhetoric fit well within the language of traditional republicanism, which feared the union of governmental power and high finance would invariably produce political corruption. Yet in many respects, his arguments reflected a modern libertarian sensibility that extolled the virtues of private enterprise while associating government management with cost overruns and inefficient planning. State investment, he argued, led to "much undue and improper intermeddling" in the affairs of individual companies. These companies would be better off in the long run without state funding, which would inevitably "prove fatal to the economy in their construction and to their successful management when built."[68] William Gregg, the state's largest textile manufacturer, similarly argued that the absence of private capital has "shipwrecked many a promising undertaking." Private capital, he noted, had funded most of the successful northern railroads, while most state works were colossal failures. "Did you ever know a State government to carry on a business right?" he asked.[69] Similar critiques of state enterprise, historians have noted, flourished in the North as part of the revulsion against state-funded internal improvements. Private corporations became an emblem of efficiency, planning, and progress; state-run improvements became symbols of waste, corruption, and political opportunism.[70]

All of these criticisms—whether originating from traditional republican ideology or from the more recent rhetoric of private enterprise—utterly failed to derail state investment in the South. Republican ideology aside, most southern politicians believed that large commercial centers were an indelible part of modern economic life. Having the wealth and power of large commercial centers located in the South would strengthen, not weaken, slavery. Several extremist politicians in Virginia and South Carolina explicitly endorsed the goal of creating a large commercial metropolis. Governor John L. Manning told the South Carolina legislature in 1853 that further expansion of the state's railroad network will "at no remote period, convert the present confines of the city [Charleston] into the more extended limits of a great metropolis."[71] Virginia governor Henry Wise, as noted earlier, made creating "centers of trade" a key element of his legislative agenda. Wise provided a series of statistical tables to show that Virginians should "*build up centres of trade within their own limits.*" Without a commercial center, Virginia and other agricultural states essentially exported their crops to the Northeast, whose merchants and bankers expropriated most of the profits. With "all their surpluses or balances tied up in the vaults of New York, Philadelphia, and Baltimore—cities which will of course take care of their own people or themselves first," Virginians would find it difficult to concentrate capital and credit necessary for long-term development.[72] Wise's argument was essentially Hamiltonian: states and nations with great commercial centers controlled their own destinies; states and nations without them did not.

Just as fears of great cities failed to blunt state investment, criticisms of deficit spending fell on deaf ears. Even ardent critics of deficit spending recognized the necessity of state activism. Politicians and observers who raised the threatening specter of state bankruptcy and higher taxes almost always found a favored enterprise that deserved state funding when other projects did not. Hammond, who so pointedly criticized the "railroad mania" sweeping South Carolina, nevertheless supported a line from Charleston with Chattanooga. "If the State *must* appropriate the public funds to Railroad purposes," he declared, "this is a Road that is needed; that will pay dividends; that will soon make her a chief outlet for the productions of the Great Valley; and *that will bind the destinies of the powerful States of Missouri, Kentucky, and Tennessee, to the destinies of the South.*"[73] In similar fashion, Gregg's criticism of state enterprises did not stop him from advocating that the state legislature should still provide at least two-fifths of their capital for railroad companies. Such a facilitative policy, he declared, would allow Charleston to become the "emporium of the Western trade."[74] In Virginia, extremist John C. Rutherfoord worried that spending on internal improvements threatened to undermine the state's finances, but he nevertheless made clear that Virginia should continue funding the Ohio and Covington Railroad. The Ohio and Covington, Rutherfoord declared, has "an object dear to the heart of every patriotic Virginian—the commercial independence of his State—for it goes to bring us that great Western trade which will free us from our bondage to New York."[75] Sharing the same commercial dreams as the most enthusiastic supporters of government investment, critics of state spending hopelessly compromised their own message.

## THE FAILURE OF STATE INVESTMENT
## AND THE SECESSIONIST IMPULSE

In their unabashed promotion of their own pet projects, critics of deficit spending unintentionally revealed the localism that suffused state investment policies. Political fragmentation—determining which lines would receive the money—necessarily limited the effectiveness of state activism. In Virginia, the substantial support for trunk lines fragmented when boosters from Alexandria, Richmond, Lynchburg, and Norfolk vigorously supported their own projects at the expense of rival enterprises. State legislatures often subsidized new and sometimes redundant projects before previously funded improvements had been completed. A number of trunk-line projects—the James River and Kanawha Company, the Virginia Central Railroad, and the Virginia and Tennessee Railroad—remained unfinished as the Civil War approached. Observers noted that state legislative policy seemed more intent on satisfying politically powerful constituencies than building the most efficient network. Virginia's governors and other observers continually urged completion of key central lines, but state legislators beholden to local interests ignored their pleas.[76] Although Charleston's position as the primary port of South Carolina mitigated the impact of such rivalries, the state government there found it far easier to build branch lines within the state than to focus on a central line to the West. Charleston, much like Richmond and Norfolk, did not have an effective connection to burgeoning western markets as the Civil War began.

Even if Virginia and South Carolina had followed the advice of their more enlightened leaders and built a rational, coherent railroad network, the developmental impact probably would have been limited. Railroads did painfully little to address the two fundamental problems of the southern economy: slavery and shifting cultivation. Even with relatively easy access to rail transportation, many southern farmers and planters still tilled poor ultisol soils, still found fodder crops difficult to grow, still saw cattle fever ravage their livestock, and still faced the problems of leaching and soil erosion. Nor did railroads turn slaves into paying customers who could encourage the growth of local manufacturing and regional urban centers. Failing to correct the region's fundamental economic problems, state activism produced a boom in railroad construction without revolutionizing the southern economy. Direct trade with Europe remained small, and the growth of port cities such as Charleston, Richmond, and Norfolk hardly met the heady expectations of railroad supporters. Industry grew somewhat, especially in Virginia, but southern manufacturers rarely challenged northern dominance even within their own home markets.[77] Instead of cementing a grand alliance between the West and the South, southerners watched in frustration as northern improvements increasingly redirected trade from the Mississippi River Valley to northern ports. Railroads thus failed to increase the South's influence within national politics. The growth of the Republican Party, in fact, had made slavery's survival seem more precarious than ever.

The failure of southern railroads to fulfill the grandiose promises of their supporters ultimately played into the hands of secessionists, who increasingly focused on the Union itself as the South's primary economic problem. For decades, southern extremists had charged that tariffs and the unfavorable distribution of federal funds (including those for internal improvements) had transferred hundreds of millions of dollars from southerners to northerners. The accumulation of capital in the North encouraged industry and trade to locate there, much to the detriment of the southern economy. "When we regard this course of taxation and disbursement," wrote Virginian Muscoe R. H. Garnett, "we cease to wonder at the growth of the cities of the North, or the palaces that cover her comparatively barren soil. . . . In this Government forcing system, the genial climate and luxuriant growth of the South are transported, beneath wintry skies, to the rocks of New England."[78] Such rhetoric was not only a critique of the Union but also an implicit rejoinder to railroad promoters who had promised that railroads would inevitably bring commercial greatness to the South.

The changing nature of southern commercial conventions demonstrates how secession itself became an economic policy that eventually subsumed public railroad investment. In the late 1830s, influential southern merchants, bankers, and planters met to devise ways in which the South could escape its degrading commercial vassalage to the North. Southern commercial conventions passed resolution after resolution calling for the improvement of harbors and rivers, the construction of railroad lines to the West, and the establishment of steamship lines with European cities. The speeches delivered at the commercial conventions articulated the same dreams that motivated state-funded railroads. Delegates were told that building railroads would revitalize agriculture, bind the West to the South, and attract the commerce of Europe and Asia to southern cities. Such grand ambitions went nowhere. If state railroad policy could not transcend the commercial rivalries *within* individual states, the commercial conventions stood little change of curtailing even more intense competition among Richmond, Norfolk, Charleston, Savannah, Mobile, New Orleans, and other southern cities for trade and wealth. It is hardly surprising, then, that by the late 1850s, extreme secessionists such as Ruffin and Robert Barnwell Rhett increasingly dominated the proceedings. Extremist policies—including reopening of the international slave trade—supplanted discussion of railroads to the West and steamships to Europe.[79] The rhetorical shift spoke to how political independence had become an increasingly viable policy (at least in the eyes of many secessionists) for igniting southern economic development.

Secessionists, of course, still imagined that railroads would play an important part in the commercial rejuvenation of an independent South. Garnett, for example, predicted that southern railroads, free from the ice and snow that supposedly slowed locomotives in the North, "will concentrate a vast trade at Norfolk, Charleston, and Savannah" once the South had achieved political independence.[80] Similarly, Rhett's *Charleston Mercury* predicted that in the midst of the great commercial prosperity that would follow secession, "[southern] Railroads will increase their transportation and advance the value of their stocks."[81] Such statements, while clearly supportive of railroads, nevertheless marked an important departure from earlier rhetoric. Railroads themselves would not bring prosperity and commercial independence; they would simply benefit from the economic boom that secession would bring. Secessionists, in essence, demoted railroads from agents of change to recipients of change. Who could blame them? By the late 1850s, the booster rhetoric surrounding railroads seemed old and stale. Virginia governor John Letcher (a conditional Unionist) told the legislature in 1860: "Our internal improvements should be pushed forward to completion as rapidly as the means of the state will warrant, as aids to direct trade and state independence."[82] A year later he asserted that the Old Dominion's "present and prospective system of rail roads" would generate prosperity for the state "whether in or out of the Union as it stands at present."[83] Coming on the heels of two decades filled with similar promises, secessionists remained skeptical. Only political independence, they maintained, would allow southerners to achieve the economic independence they so ardently desired.

Chapter 4 shows how trade policy, not railroads, dominated secessionist rhetoric as the sectional crises accelerated in the late 1850s. On an ideological level, though, the South's railroad boosters had helped solidify the link between economic development and the long-term protection of slavery. Southern promoters argued that railroads would speed the concentration of military forces needed to put down servile insurrections, increase economic and population growth, and cement alliances with western states. The willingness of southerners to embrace state activism to better defend slavery helps explain Francis Lieber's paradox of why southern state governments invested far more in railroads than did northern state governments. The same dynamic also helps explain the emergence of a strong Confederate state when slavery was threatened in a far more direct manner during the Civil War. Southerners, after all, had already embraced the idea that governments could guide and assist private economic interests well before April 1861.

*four*

# REDEFINING FREE TRADE TO MODERNIZE THE SOUTH

Southerners made free trade a central element of their political economy. From an economic viewpoint, southern support for free trade stemmed from the region's status as an exporter of staple crops and an importer of manufactured goods. Southerners argued that high tariffs on European goods decreased the profits of European textile manufacturers, who would therefore buy fewer southern staples. "Those who live without buying must live without selling," warned South Carolina political economist Thomas Cooper. "If we must not purchase the manufactures of Great Britain, the latter will not purchase our cotton, rice, or tobacco."[1] A similar strain of antitariff argument focused on the direct costs that southerners incurred for more expensive manufactured goods. In 1834 South Carolina politician George McDuffie argued that a 40 percent tariff cost southern planters 40 out of every 100 bales of cotton.[2] McDuffie's famous "forty bale" theory undoubtedly exaggerated the impact of the tariff, but his argument contained a kernel of truth. Economic historians have estimated that a tariff of 40 percent in 1859 would have reduced the real incomes of southern slaveholders by at least 20 percent.[3]

The economic critique of protective tariffs was indispensable to free traders, but the debates over trade policy represented something more than dollars and cents. For many southerners, protective tariffs were a clear case of how a more-populous region (the North) exerted control over a less-populous region (the South). If the majority could raise tariffs, many southerners wondered, what could stop them from abolishing slavery? Antitariff sentiment thus became tied to critiques of what southerners termed "consolidated government." South Carolinians, ever alert to threats to slavery, led the charge against tariffs and consolidation. In 1827 a South Carolina legislative petition defined "CONSOLIDATION" as the ability of a "combination of the people of such states as might constitute a majority of all the inhabitants of the United States" to impose their will on unwilling minorities. Such a government "would be the worse species of tyranny which a minority of some states could possibly endure by the oppression of others."[4] To avoid such a calamity, many South Carolinians embraced their state's right to nullify national legislation deemed unconstitutional, including protective tariffs. The tariff issue thus became the first line of defense for slavery and other southern rights. The South Carolina legislature efficiently summarized the relationship between tariffs and slavery in the title of an 1844 resolution: "Regarding Abolition, the Tariff, and Other Issues Threatening the South."[5]

For secessionists wanting to strengthen southern nationalism, their region's free-trade tradition presented a potential challenge. In the nineteenth century, protective tariffs constituted a primary expression of economic nationalism. In Henry's Clay's "American System," high tariffs would encourage domestic manufacturing, thus providing national economic independence and strengthening national defense. In contrast, free traders tended to reject the notion of a transcendent national interest. Virginia political economist Thomas Dew, for example, equated the "interest of the nation" with the "interests of the individuals who compose it."[6] Such arguments hardly seemed sufficient for secessionists seeking to strengthen Confederate nationalism. If Confederates define themselves merely as a collection of individuals, how could they expect citizens to make sacrifices for the public good? Virtue, honor, patriotism, and other values threatened to become meaningless if individualism was taken too far. In a more narrow economic sense, free trade might endanger Confederate nationalism if it allowed northerners to continue their economic domination of the South. Could southerners truly achieve independence if Yankee manufacturers still monopolized southern markets and Yankee merchants still controlled southern trade?

In response to such questions, secessionists in South Carolina and Virginia imaginatively redefined free trade to better fit the needs of Confederate nationalism. In sharp contrast to McDuffie's "forty bales" theory, secessionists rarely mentioned the impact of protection on southern agriculture. Instead, they focused on how protectionism had undermined the growth of southern industry, commerce, and cities. According to secessionists, protective tariffs had transferred hundreds of millions of dollars from the South to the North, where it was lavished upon northern internal improvements, lighthouses, harbors, and fisheries. These policies concentrated capital in northern cities, which gave Yankee merchants a decided advantage in attracting trade. Secessionists argued that an independent Confederacy would end the forced redistribution of capital from South to North, thus removing the fetters restraining southern commerce. Capital that had once funded northern improvements would now be spent in the South, helping to spur the growth of cities, the expansion of internal improvements, and the rebirth of direct trade with Europe. In the words of Virginian Muscoe R. H. Garnett, removing the "unnatural" burdens of the national tariff would allow southern trade and southern cities to "revive and grow, like a field of young corn, when the long expected showers descend after a withering drought."[7] Free trade, in essence, would modernize the South.

Secessionists also redefined free trade by making it considerably less free. Once the Confederacy achieved independence, northern goods formerly considered part of the domestic trade suddenly became defined as foreign goods. A Confederate tariff, no matter how low, might result in a radical change in trade patterns; hundreds of millions of dollars of northern goods would be stopped at the Confederate border, stored in special warehouses, inspected by Confederate customs offices, and taxed a specified percentage of their value. Even a relatively low Confederate tariff would penalize northern manufacturers. What better way, secessionists asked, for southerners to end the colonial relationship with the North? Safely protected from more efficient northern competitors, a Confederate tariff would allow Virginia, in the words of one secessionist, to "become a great manufacturing empire."[8] A tariff on northern goods gave the secessionists the best of both worlds. With little sense of contradiction, they could remain true to traditional principles of free trade while incorporating nationalistic and protectionist rhetoric into their appeals for southern independence.

The Confederate trade agenda thus became a blueprint for the development of cities, commerce, and manufacturing. Confidently predicting future economic glory, secessionists focusing on trade sounded much like the southern railroad boosters of the 1840s and 1850s. Like the railroad boosters, secessionists presented trade policy as a panacea that could single-handedly transform the southern economy and realign bonds of interest so that Europe and the West would defend the South. The Confederate trade agenda, moreover, sidestepped the localism, logrolling, and budget deficits that bedeviled state investment in railroads. Secessionists linked the manipulation of trade to the creation of Confederate nationalism, thereby transcending the provincial interests of particular cities and states in ways that railroads could not.

FREE TRADE AND CONFEDERATE MODERNIZATION

After becoming a central political issue in the 1830s, the protective tariff declined in political significance during the 1840s and 1850s. Controversies over slavery dominated national politics, which made tariffs less significant as a rallying point for southern extremists.[9] Southerners also won important tariff reductions in 1846 and 1857, thereby diminishing regional tensions over trade issues.[10] Yet while tariffs had declined in political importance, southern extremists still believed that the issue could help their cause. As the economic divide between North and South widened in the 1840s and 1850s—and as northerners increasingly criticized the economic impact of slavery—southern extremists needed a ready explanation for their region's relatively slow development. Protective tariffs were one candidate. Precisely how the tariff stifled southern development, John C. Calhoun wrote to James Henry Hammond in 1845, "deserves an elaborate investigation.... It has been often touched on, but has never yet been discussed & presented in the full light." Calhoun made clear what he expected such an investigation to find: "Abolish custom Houses & let the money collected in the South be spent in the South and we would be the most flourishing people in the world.... All we want to be rich is to let us have what we make."[11]

Garnett's 1850 pamphlet *The Union, Past and Future* provided precisely the "elaborate investigation" that Calhoun had recommended. Garnett was well suited to revise the southern free-trade tradition. As the scion of the Tidewater elite, he naturally gravitated toward the southern extremism of his uncle, Senator R. M. T. Hunter. Too young to have participated in the older nullification debates, Garnett approached trade issues from a fresh perspective. Combining red-hot political rhetoric with a dense array of statistics, *The Union, Past and Future* attempted to show that southerners paid most of the national taxes (via tariffs and duties) while northerners received most of the expenditures (via fiscal appropriations).[12] The first part of the argument relied on the common assumption of southern free traders that "duties are paid by the producers, and the several sections, in the ratio of products exported."[13] According to Garnett, the South provided most of the exports of the nation, which in turn provided the foreign exchange that essentially "paid" for the imports of the nation. Using this logic, Garnett calculated that between 1791 and 1845, slaveholding states paid more than $711 million in total duties, while free states had paid only $211 million. To make matters worse, southern taxes subsidized various northern projects, such as canals, lighthouses, and fisheries. "The wages of Southern labor and the profits of Southern capital," Garnett concluded, "are swept northward by this current of Federal taxation and disbursement as steadily and more swiftly than the Gulf stream bears the waters of our shores."[14]

Garnett's claim—that national fiscal policy forcibly redistributed capital from the South to the North—became a standard part of secessionist rhetoric. "Rutledge," an anonymous South Carolinian who supported separate-state secession in 1851, estimated that the Palmetto State alone had paid some $5 million per year in duties, which had been taken "most unjustly" from the state and sent to the North. Over the course of two decades, the writer calculated, the drafts on South Carolina (one of the smallest states in the Union) amounted to $100 million.[15] Charleston newspaper editor L. W. Spratt argued in 1855 that northerners received some $40 million per year in federal expenditures, while the South only received $10 million per year. The bulk of the revenue, he maintained, came out of the pockets of southerners who paid the lion's share of the nation's taxes.[16] Congressman Preston S. Brooks of South Carolina sounded a similar theme, asserting that southerners paid two-thirds of the nation's taxes and received only one-ninth of the nation's expenditures. Brooks considered the South to be the "goose of the golden egg to the North, which Free-Soilers, in their mad cupidity and fanatical tamperings, are threatening to destroy."[17]

The coercive redistribution of capital, secessionists argued, blunted the development of southern commerce, southern cities, and southern manufacturing. Because national fiscal policies had concentrated capital in northern cities, northern merchants and manufacturers enjoyed a tremendous advantage over their southern rivals. Secessionists frequently pointed out that before the nation's first protective tariff in 1818, the two regions were roughly economic equals. Decades of oppressive taxation, though, had created a remarkable economic inequality that had reduced the South to colonial status. In 1851 Robert Barnwell Rhett, echoing Garnett's calculations, told the Senate: "We are colonies" forced "to minister to the aggrandizement and wealth of the North."[18] The image of an exploited colonial South became the quasi-official position of the South Carolina secession convention, which bitterly complained that the tariff and other national commercial policies had "made the cities of the South provincial." The tariff had "paralyzed" southern cities so that they had become "mere suburbs of Northern cities."[19] Northern trade policies, the *Charleston Mercury* similarly editorialized in 1861, "have kept Southern cities stationary, and built up the great emporiums of the Northern merchant princes."[20] By accepting some of the northern critique of the southern economy—but assigning a far different cause than slavery—secessionists strengthened the case for southern independence.

Focusing on trade policy allowed secessionists to put forward a positive vision of the Confederacy's economic future. Political independence would free the capital that the Union had forcibly transferred to the North. The newly released capital, in turn, would transform southern cities. "Restore to her the use of the 130 or 140 millions a year of her produce for the foreign trade," wrote Garnett, and "all her ports will throng with business. Norfolk and Charleston and Savannah . . . will be crowned with shipping, and their warehouses crammed with merchandise."[21] "Rutledge" similarly argued that the independence would create a large pool of capital: "What is to hinder us from rivaling ENGLAND in her prodigious accumulation of capital?" When South Carolinians put that additional capital to work, "Rutledge" predicted, commerce would boom and Charleston would become a "considerable Manufacturing town."²² Other secessionists stressed that the imposition of "double duties" would send European trade to southern cities. Secessionists reasoned that Europeans exporting goods to the South would not want to first pay northern tariffs and then pay Confederate tariffs as well. Europeans would instead ship their goods directly to the South, much to the benefit of southern merchants and the Confederate economy. When the North raised tariffs after the secession of the cotton states, secessionists reacted with joy. The higher the northern tariff, the more likely southern and European merchants would bypass the North altogether. In February 1861, the *Mercury* celebrated the "Prospectus of the Charleston and Liverpool Steamship Company." With its own direct trade, Charleston would become the "natural emporium" of the South: "The agents of the great manufacturers will be here, with their goods in our bonded warehouses. Great jobbing houses will accumulate. The City will be thronged with strangers. . . . Real estate must rise in value."²³

The rhetoric of commercial greatness, it should be stressed, was not the work of a few obscure writers. The most influential secessionist pamphleteers dwelled on the commercial promise of the Confederacy. Perhaps the best example is South Carolinian John Townsend (Illustration 3). A cotton planter hailing from Edisto Island, Townsend owned half a million dollars' worth of real estate and more than 200 slaves, making him one of the wealthiest planters in the state. In 1850 he wrote *The Southern States, Their Present Peril and Their Certain Remedy*, which went through several editions. Like other conservative Lowcountry planters, Townsend rejected immediate state secession as too revolutionary and instead called for a southern convention to discuss joint secession. A relative moderate by South Carolina standards, Townsend nevertheless sketched how commercial greatness would contribute to the "Glorious Destiny" of an independent southern nation. Townsend focused on the unfairness of Union tariff policies: "We are the tax*payers*; whilst they are the tax receivers and the tax *spenders*."²⁴ Townsend, in fact, considered southern states nothing more than "*tributary colonies*" of the North. Ending the tributary association through secession "would bankrupt almost every manufacturing establishment in the North, and would throw out of employment hundreds of thousands of their citizens." Northern capitalists and their workers would soon emigrate to the prosperous South, Townsend asserted, where they

ILLUSTRATION 3

*John Townsend, a wealthy South Carolinian, was one of the most popular prosecessionist pamphleteers in the South. (Courtesy of the South Caroliniana Library, University of South Carolina, Columbia, S.C.)*

"will be eagerly embraced."²⁵ Townsend did not worry that the Yankee migrants would challenge slavery or seek to undermine the southern social order. Northern migrants would presumably become good southerners once they had lived among the slaves and slaveholders themselves.

A decade later, Townsend sketched out an even more glowing commercial vision of an independent South in *The South Alone, Should Govern the South*. The impending election of Abraham Lincoln convinced Townsend that South Carolina must secede immediately from the Union. To help ensure the secession of other southern states, the 1860 Association (based in Charleston) distributed 165,000 copies of *The Doom of Slavery* and *The South Alone, Should Govern the South*. In the latter pamphlet, Townsend devoted most his attention to explaining why the Lincoln administration posed an immediate threat to slavery, but he also offered what was by 1860 the standard secessionist position on trade policy. Within the Union, southern merchants "are too feeble in capital, to contend with the enormous wealth accumulated in Northern cities." Secession, by simply preventing southerners' "wealth from being carried away from" them, would give southern merchants the resources to compete with their northern rivals.²⁶ The imposition of a moderate Confederate tariff would also give Europeans the incentive to export directly to the

Redefining Free Trade    115

South. The imposition of "*double* duties," Townsend predicted, meant that "*Southern* merchants will then do the business of the South, and our Southern cities reap the richest reward."[27]

The economic optimism of Townsend and other southern extremists complemented proslavery ideology. With slaves comfortably cared for or otherwise controlled, the South's social stability would allow commerce to thrive. The instability of free labor, with its ceaseless class conflict, would virtually doom the North to political chaos.[28] "The great sore of modern society," Garnett argued, "is the war between capital and labor. . . . [T]he lower the wages, the higher the profits." Slavery, on the other hand, produced social stability, for masters had an inherent interest in caring for their slave property. Garnett asserted that the "slaves themselves live in a state of comfort—we had almost said of luxury—superior to any northern farmer."[29] Taking away the benefits of the Union's tariff policies, L. W. Spratt argued in 1855, would expose the instability of the North. The northern capitalist must either "yield to the superior advantages of works established on our own soil, or he must bring his capital and labor here, and recommencing his enterprises, must contribute his wealth and energy to sustain the institution and swell the prosperity and greatness of our Southern country."[30] Edmund Ruffin developed this theme at length in his 1860 futuristic novel *Anticipations of the Future, to Serve as Lessons for the Present Times*. In Ruffin's imaginary world, workers loot and burn every square foot of New York City; military authorities establish order only after hanging thousands of rioters. In sharp contrast, southern cities prospered. Norfolk, for example, replaces New York City as the "chief seaport and commercial mart on the Atlantic Coast."[31] The stability of the South's slave society, presumably, enables Norfolk and other southern cities to claim the mantle of commercial greatness without falling victim to the seething tensions that had engulfed New York and other northern cities.

## THE INTERESTS OF KING COTTON

Economic fantasies of northern decline and southern ascendancy dovetailed nicely with the secessionist faith in King Cotton. The tremendous growth of cotton exports in the 1850s convinced secessionists that cotton was an indispensable pillar of the world economy. They thought that Europe and the North would soon grind to a halt without cotton. Manufacturers would go bankrupt, banks would sink into insolvency, and millions of workers would lose their jobs. No nation would dare attack the Confederacy and lose its access to cotton. "Were there no other consideration," wrote South Carolina politician D. H. Hamilton in 1851, "the obligation to keep employed and to feed her [Great Britain's] starving manufacturing population would compel a peace with us."[32] Secessionist Edward B. Bryan calculated that 11,604,443 people throughout the world depended on cotton manufacturing for their livelihood. "What is an army of warriors, when compared to the potent *cotton* in our fields?" he asked.[33] South Carolina senator James Henry Hammond famously declared in 1858: "No, you dare not make war on cotton. No power on earth dares to make war upon it. Cotton is king."[34] The South's exports of cotton and other raw materials created a symbiotic relationship that would result in lasting peace. Referring to Europeans, Townsend wrote that the "Northern States, in all their pursuits, are their rivals; whilst the Southern United States, by their employments, and the rich staples of our agricultural, would be their natural allies."[35]

The elaborate explanations of cotton's economic power and diplomatic influence, however comforting to secessionists, presented a potentially troubling contradiction. As King Cotton grew more powerful in the antebellum decades, worldwide hostility to slavery should have subsided. Instead, antislavery sentiment grew far stronger on both sides of the Atlantic. To explain this apparent contradiction, secessionists drew upon a long line of proslavery discourse that characterized abolitionism as a form of irrational fanaticism.[36] In 1838 William Harper, one of South Carolina's most noted proslavery theorists, painted abolitionists as "fanatical agitators" who steadfastly refused to see the error of their ways. As Harper put it, "fanaticism is in no danger of being convinced."[37] Hammond similarly noted in 1845 that the "rise and progress of this fanaticism is one of the phenomena of the age in which we live." Hammond considered most rank-and-file abolitionists as "silly enthusiasts, led away by designing characters." Such "designing characters," he asserted, "cloak their designs under vile and impious hypocrisies, and, unable to shine in higher spheres, devote themselves to fanaticism, as a trade."[38] Such men cared little for the public good or even the welfare of their own region; they only pursued their own selfish gratification. At once coldly calculating and wildly irrational, fanaticism explained why northerners and the British so willingly risked their economic future over the slavery issue.

Secessionists believed that Confederate independence would be something akin to a hard slap that would awaken rational economic interests and dispel abolitionist delusions. Interests, in other words, would trump ideology. Trescot argued that the "most selfish interests of the foreign world would be prompted to speedily recognize our national independence."[39] The anonymous writer "Rutledge" took a similar position, noting that the "failure" of emancipation in the West Indies had taught the British a valuable lesson about the perils of promoting misguided ideology over sensible interests. "The English nation, often bad at theorizing, but quick to learn from experience," he wrote, "has too much practical wisdom to again attempt such a ruinous course."[40] Even in the North, fanaticism would quickly decline once southerners wielded complete control over their own economic resources. Drawing on stereotypes of the penny-pinching Yankee, Spratt argued that northerners "have a pious regard for their individual interests." Economic interests, in the end, would probably prevent "fanaticism" from indulging in any "expensive eccentricities."[41]

Secessionists speculated that economic interests would eventually lead some northern states to seek an alliance with the South. Southern extremists had long believed that a "natural" alliance between the West and the South would assert itself through the Mississippi River and its many tributaries. The network of waterways provided a ready southern market for western hogs and corn. The agrarian West, like the South, had much to lose from protective tariffs that primarily benefited New England's manufacturers. Secessionists hoped to continue what proslavery Ohioan David Christy called a "*tripartite alliance*" of western farmers, southern planters, and British manufacturers, all "united in a common bond of interest: the whole giving their support to the doctrine of Free Trade."[42] Even during the war itself, secessionists confidently predicted that the pull of interests would invariably dissolve the artificial ties between the North and the West. In June 1861 the *Charleston Mercury*'s western correspondent reported that Lincoln's embargo on trade between North and South had depressed the price of western provisions such as bacon and corn. When banks begin to fail, the correspondent predicted, "you may look out for an uprising in the West." In making such a bold prediction, the *Mercury* asserted that the "true interests of the Western people are all with the South."[43]

The constant invocation of "interests" shows the degree to which secessionists had departed from traditional free-trade arguments. In contrast to mercantilists—who assumed that trade was a zero-sum game in which a nation could only benefit if another nation lost—free traders had traditionally argued that all nations would benefit from open commerce. Free trade would thus encourage peace and cooperation because no nation wanted to lose the benefits of exchange. The most idealistic free traders believed that commerce would gradually dissolve the nationalistic sentiments that allowed mercantilism to flourish. Commerce, wrote free-trade political economist Thomas Cooper in 1830, "must ultimately be indebted for making one family of all the nations of the earth."[44] In the secessionist vision, though, commerce became a way in which one nation imposed its will on another. In its basest form, King Cotton diplomacy was a form of economic blackmail that was at odds with the cosmopolitan openness of free-trade doctrines.[45] Even as the *Charleston Mercury* championed low tariffs and reciprocal trade agreements with Europe, it supported "starving" Europe of a crucial commodity: "The cards are in our hands, and we intend to play them out to the bankruptcy of every cotton factory in Great Britain and France or the acknowledgement of our independence."[46] South Carolinians, as the British correspondent William Howard Russell sarcastically reported, supposed that the "Lord Chancellor sits on a bale of cotton."[47]

## SHOULD THE SOUTH TRADE WITH THE NORTH?

Europeans, of course, viewed such threats with hostility and suspicion. So, too, did many moderates and Unionists in the Upper South, who viewed King Cotton diplomacy as part of a larger secessionist trade regime inimical to their interests. Moderates often presented free trade and King Cotton diplomacy as part of a Lower South conspiracy to bully the Upper South. During Virginia's secession convention, Samuel Moore of Rockbridge County argued that the cotton states "are opposed to the collection on any duties on goods brought into the country, and they want free trade and direct taxation."[48] Free trade would allow European competitors to drive Virginia's white mechanics and artisans out of business, thus increasing the political power of cotton-state slaveholders. "What will become of the promised manufacturing industry and enterprise of Virginia and the other border states of which we hear so much?" asked one Alexandria Unionist.[49] Upper South moderates considered the promises of a Confederate commercial revolution as delusional. John Kennedy of Maryland denounced Confederate free trade, mocking "its phantoms of untold wealth, its free ports, its untaxed commerce, its illimitable cotton fields, its flattering alliances, its swarms of reinforcements from the shores of Africa."[50]

Kennedy's last phrase—"swarms of reinforcements from the shores of Africa"—referred to the proposed reopening of the international slave trade. Charleston newspaper editor L. W. Spratt was part of a group of secessionists (many of them radical free traders) who believed that reopening the international slave trade would lower the price of slaves. Lower prices would then enable more yeoman farmers to become slaveholders, thus widening the support of slavery within southern society. Reopening the slave trade would also provide the South with the necessary cheap labor that would help spur economic development. Spratt compared the southern importation of slaves to the influx of "pauper immigrants" that had settled in the North. Just as access to cheap labor had given northerners the ability to build canals, railroads, and factories, inexpensive slaves would enable southerners to diversify their economy. Instead of simply admiring northern prosperity, which stemmed from "5,000,000 slave foreigners," Spratt argued that reopening the slave trade would allow southerners to stand "still more resplendent in the prosperity to be poured upon us by the teeming thousands from the plains of Africa."[51]

Proposals to open the international slave trade horrified many in the Upper South. Upper South moderates thought that revisiting the brutalities of the international slave trade would damage the paternalistic image that slaveholders wanted to project.[52] From the standpoint of economic interests, reopening the international slave trade would also endanger the booming domestic slave trade, which allowed planters in the Upper South to sell their surplus slaves.[53] Opposition from the Upper South proved so implacable that the Confederacy banned the international slave trade in its constitution. The controversy over the slave trade, though, dramatically highlighted the divergent interests of the Cotton South and the Upper South. Virginia governor John Letcher spoke for many when he predicted in January 1861 that the dissolution of the Union might create as many as four different nations. Virginia would align itself with a confederacy of the Upper South, the midwestern states, Pennsylvania, New Jersey, and Missouri. United by the Mississippi River system, the confederation of middle states had distinctly different "interests" from New England and the Cotton South. In reiterating the independence of Virginia, Letcher made clear his position: "I will resist the *coercion* of Virginia into the adoption of a line of policy, whenever the attempt is made by northern or southern states."[54] The underlying logic of Letcher's stance—that slavery was not enough of a common interest to unite white southerners—threatened to overturn one of the basic assumptions of secession.

To craft an economic vision that recognized their state's more diversified economy, Virginia's extremists proposed policies to restrict or limit the sale of northern goods. Limiting trade with the North through boycotts, taxes, and regulations, they believed, might satisfy moderates as an intermediate step that avoided an outright political break. Restricting northern trade could potentially funnel the economic nationalism of many former Whigs into a prosouthern direction. If Whigs wanted protective tariffs to protect northern industry from British competition, it seemed logical to suppose that they would support protecting southern manufacturers from northern competition.[55] South Carolina's more confident secessionists often denounced schemes to penalize northern goods as a tepid, ineffectual response to northern outrages.[56] Virginia's extremists, operating in a far more hostile political environment, supported such measures as an important first step toward political independence. Policies aimed at discouraging the importation of northern goods, after all, affirmed the diverging political and economic interests of the North and the South. Achieving economic independence from the North was a goal that most southerners could support.

The venerable Virginia statesman William C. Rives inadvertently demonstrated the wide political appeal of trade restrictions to moderate Virginians when he published the 1847 pamphlet *Discourse on the Uses and Importance of History*, which compared the American and French Revolutions. Rives's pamphlet was hardly original—it praised the conservativeness of the American Revolution while condemning French radicalism. Rives sent a copy to William Ballard Preston, a prominent moderate in Virginia politics. Rives's analysis of colonial trade restrictions captured Preston's imagination. Rives noted that the First Continental Congress had "contented themselves with a simple agreement and association against the importation and use of British commodities and trade with England, until the acts of Parliament which violated the liberties of America should be repealed." On the margins of the pamphlet, Preston approvingly wrote: "The remedy proposed was peaceful—the result from interest and trade.... And *now* are not these same remedies the proper ones to secure tranquility & repose at home?" When Rives described how British merchants from "Bristol, Glasgow, and other trading and manufacturing towns" soon rallied on the side of the colonists, Preston scribbled: "Why not northern cities—New York, Boston, Philadelphia?"[57] Punishing northern trade, presumably, would awaken conservative interests in the North before a more permanent rupture occurred. Virginia extremists, on the other hand, emphasized that penalizing northern goods was the first step toward southern independence. During the 1850s, many of Virginia's most prominent southern extremists—men such as Ruffin, Governor John B. Floyd, and George Fitzhugh—supported either boycotting or taxing northern goods.

The Central Southern Rights Association, founded by the young Richmond merchant Daniel H. London, exemplified the different goals of radicals and moderates. The association called for legislative action and voluntary boycotts to prevent northern goods from being sold in Virginia. Many of the more moderate merchants and manufacturers in the organization supported the limited goal of compelling northern states to enforce the Fugitive Slave Act of 1850, thus preserving the Union. London and his allies, meanwhile, viewed taxes and boycotts as a way to establish the economic basis of an independent South. Merchant R. G. Scott captured the ambiguity within the organization when he proposed that northern goods be taxed at a rate of 10 to 15 percent. Such a policy, he argued, would create a more diversified economy, one that "will give us power, strength, equality, and everything that makes a great people." Faced with the prospect of a commercially independent South, "the North will see that we must become two people, and then they may be ready to retrace their wrongful steps. If not, we shall stand innocent of blame, and the responsibility will be with the North."[58] Scott left unstated exactly what the North would be responsible for—increased sectional hostility, greater economic tensions, or outright secession by the South?

Appealing to both conservative and extremist sensibilities, calls for regulating northern trade and establishing Virginia's economic independence received popular support, especially during the political crisis of the late 1850s. In the political tumult following John Brown's 1859 raid on

Harpers Ferry, for example, a committee in Chesterfield declared: "We are in favor of encouraging southern industry and, thereby, as far as we can, make ourselves independent of our enemies."[59] A similar committee in Fredericksburg, Virginia, linked southern military preparedness with policies "to stimulate and foster the industrial and manufacturing arts . . . and retain at home all that patronage, which sends Southern money to a section so regardless of Southern rights."[60] A meeting in Albemarle County recommended that Virginians "purchase no product or manufacture of any non-slave-holding State, or any article imported from a foreign country."[61] The popularity of such sentiments generated a number of specific legislative proposals. The Whig iron manufacturer Joseph Anderson—a rather late convert to the secessionist cause—instigated a "Buy Virginia" campaign to force state-subsidized railroads and canals to buy their supplies from within the Old Dominion. Such legislation, he wrote anonymously in the *Richmond Whig* in 1859, "would more effectually establish manufactories . . . than can be done by any tariff law that Congress ever did or can enact."[62]

Much like the calls for state-supported agricultural research, the desire to tax or regulate northern goods generated a good many speeches but little legislation. Southern states failed to pass discriminatory taxes aimed at northern goods, in part because they threatened powerful vested interests. Many of Virginia's merchants had strong ties with northern merchants and manufacturers. Self-interest aside, these merchants argued that disrupting northern trade might have disastrous unintended consequences. Forcing the state's railroads to buy iron rails produced in Virginia, for example, might stymie the Old Dominion's effort to build interregional transportation lines and hinder efforts to establish direct trade with Europe. Indeed, any trade restrictions on northern goods might force Virginia's trade to competing ports such as Baltimore and Wilmington, where northern goods could then enter Virginia as a "southern" commodity. Instead of becoming the great emporium of the South, Alexandria, Norfolk, and Richmond would see their trade dwindle. Several South Carolinians had highlighted similar concerns when their state debated separate-state secession in 1850 and 1851. Opponents of separate-state secession argued that if South Carolina left the Union alone, it would lose its trade to other southern states. W. A. Owens, for example, predicted that South Carolina's railroads would suffer significant losses because trade "would be diverted to Savannah, and Savannah would become a great exporting and importing city at the expense of the city of Charleston."[63]

If state-level restrictions failed to generate sufficient political support, voluntary boycotts fared even worse. When formed in 1850, the Central Southern Rights Association encouraged Richmond merchants and manufacturers to either buy goods from southern manufacturers or directly from Europe. Even though the organization's goal was to lobby the legislature for a tax on northern goods, Daniel London characterized the association's efforts as the "voluntary and spontaneous resistance of a noble people against the aggressions without a parallel in the history of civilization."[64] The merchants and manufacturers who joined the association pledged not to buy any items from nonslaveholding states. To help these businesses keep their promise, the association provided members with a list of mercantile firms that sold goods either imported directly from Europe or made in the South. Despite assurances that the "patriotism" of Richmond's business community would make the boycott a stunning success, the association's efforts gradually fizzled. From 1854 to 1859, the Central Southern Rights Association did not meet. John Brown's raid stimulated the association to resume its meetings, but its efforts failed to dent the lucrative trade between Virginia and northern cities.[65]

If a relatively small group of merchants and manufacturers in a single city could not enforce a boycott, then organizing action among millions of southern consumers would be next to impossible. Exhortations of newspapers and politicians led southern consumers to make sacrifices for short periods of time, but most people quickly reverted to old habits. Boycotting northern goods inevitably forced southern consumers to pay more for locally produced goods or give up certain high-quality goods altogether. In a society that attached great importance to social status, reverting to homespun or locally produced goods introduced a troubling "leveling" tendency that flattened social distinctions. Would a wealthy planter and his family really dress, eat, drink, and entertain like a humble yeoman farmer over a long period? Southern newspapers noted with disgust that many of the same politicians who called for boycotts on northern goods often wore northern suits and northern fashions.[66] Even during the war itself, wealthy southern families imported hoop skirts and other luxuries to keep alive the social hierarchy. As the *Southern Illustrated News* despaired in 1862, "Not five out of five hundred ladies would be caught in the street in a homespun dress."⁶⁷ It was one thing to tout the virtues of economic independence; it was quite another to actually live those values. If southerners truly wanted to restrict northern goods, they would have to take collective action that transcended the selfish, status-conscience interests of the individual. From the standpoint of Confederate nationalism, individualism would once again fail the South.

The ineffectiveness of voluntary boycotts and state-level regulations highlighted the fact that only a centralized southern government, with the power to levy taxes and tariffs, could realistically wean southerners from northern goods. Using the argument, Virginia secessionists linked political independence to economic independence. Newton, the secessionist agricultural reformer, declared in 1858 that a Confederate tariff aimed at northern goods "would give such protection to manufacturers that all our water falls would bristle with machinery, and the hum of manufacturing industry would be heard in all the inland towns of the state."⁶⁸ Ruffin penned similar sentiments in *Anticipations of the Future*.⁶⁹ Ruffin went out of his way to endorse the "prohibition of the introduction of northern products." As he argued: "If this were the policy adopted, the South would, indeed, pay all the cost of the system—but would receive all the benefits of creating home supplies, and building up home markets for agriculture."⁷⁰ Ruffin's reference to "home supplies" and "home markets" for farmers recalls the rhetoric that Henry Clay and other protectionists had used to defend high tariffs within the old national Union. Such rhetoric, now invoked on behalf of a Confederate tariff, would become standard fare at the Virginia secession convention.

CONFEDERATE TARIFFS AND VIRGINIA'S
SECESSION CONVENTION

After Lincoln's election and the secession of the cotton states, Virginia held its secession convention, which convened from February 13 to May 1, 1861. To persuade a Unionist majority—many of whom still distrusted the cotton states—secessionist speakers articulated their economic vision of the Confederacy, which invariably involved a Confederate tariff. Virginia secessionists had many eager allies in their effort to promote a Confederate tariff, including cotton-state emissaries entrusted with the task of persuading other slave states to join the Confederacy with the promise of future industrial grandeur. One of three emissaries (Henry Benning of

Georgia) offered Virginians a 20 percent revenue tariff so that the Old Dominion could monopolize the lucrative southern market. "Why will not she [Virginia] take the place now held by New England and New York, and furnish to the South these goods?" he asked. Benning painted an alluring picture of prosperity and progress. Virginia's manufacturing industry would flourish and northern mechanics and capitalists would move to Virginia, stimulating the growth of villages, towns, and cities. Property values would rise as farmers and planters would have a profitable home market for their produce. Richmond itself would "take the place of New York" and become nothing less than the "centre of the Earth."[71]

Virginia secessionists echoed Benning's optimistic assessment of a Confederate tariff. These secessionists invoked the hum of machinery and the buzz of progress—not pastoral descriptions of a southern agrarian landscape—when portraying the future Confederate economy. John Goode Jr. of Bedford County, for example, predicted that "our noble water-falls would whistle with machinery, and the spindles of the North would be transferred to the Potomac, the Rappahannock, and the James; and Norfolk, with her magnificent harbor, would become the grandest commercial emporium of the world."[72] Even when sounding a more cautionary note, Virginia secessionists could hardly contain their enthusiasm for a new industrial order. "It would not be in the interest of Virginia to become a great manufacturing State at once," James Bruce of Halifax County warned. Yet later in his speech, he boldly pronounced: "When we are divided [from the North], and become a great commercial and manufacturing people, then we shall fulfill the destinies of Virginia."[73] These predictions of impending economic greatness gave secessionist rhetoric an overtly promotional tone that resembled southern railroad boosters. Secession and the booster spirit went hand in hand.

No secessionist speaker better highlighted the glorious commercial and manufacturing future of Virginia within a new Confederate nation than George Wythe Randolph (Illustration 4), the grandson of Thomas Jefferson. Randolph studied law at the University of Virginia and practiced in Albemarle County for ten years. In 1850 he moved to Richmond, where he married a wealthy widow and built a lucrative law practice. John Brown's raid pushed Randolph firmly into the camp of southern extremists. To defend Virginia against similar abolitionist incursions, Randolph organized an artillery unit named the Richmond Howitzers. When South Carolina left the Union, Randolph enthusiastically advocated secession.[74]

ILLUSTRATION 4

*George W. Randolph, the grandson of Thomas Jefferson, was an ardent secessionist who enthusiastically supported a Confederate tariff that would spur southern industry. (Courtesy of the Library of Congress)*

In the election of delegates to Virginia's 1861 state convention, Richmond voters chose Randolph as one of the city's three delegates. Randolph was the only one of the three to publicly support secession. Many of Richmond's powerful merchants and manufacturers feared that disunion would sever lucrative trade with the North, and a substantial number of artisans suspected that secession would benefit slaveholding planters rather than working families.

To persuade the Unionist majority that initially dominated the convention, Randolph argued that disrupting commercial ties with the North would actually benefit Richmond's commercial development. Virginia, Randolph argued, could never succeed within the Union. Northern manufacturers, he explained, immediately cut prices and took losses to wipe out upstart Virginia firms, only to raise prices once competition had been eliminated. "By means of their vast accumulation of capital, Northern manufacturers can bear heavy losses. . . . [W]e are weak as yet, and require success at the start, in order to accumulate the capital necessary for successful competition."[75] Other secessionist speakers cited variants of this argument. Citing northern advantages in manufacturing, Virginians like James Barbour declared: "As their manufactures increase ours will diminish, because of the impossibility of our competing with them."[76] Bruce similarly asserted that the "North has got a start on us, and we cannot

*Redefining Free Trade*

possibly overtake her under this system of free trade [between North and South]."[77] Given the greater advantages of the North, why should Virginia remain within the Union? As Randolph put it, "If we wish to become a manufacturing State, it will be an extraordinary policy for us to unite ourselves with a people who produce vastly more than they consume, and to decline a union with States who will take everything we produce."[78]

A Confederate revenue tariff, of course, would have provided far less protection for southern manufacturers than antebellum tariffs had given northern industrialists. At its height, the antebellum tariff had exceeded 40 percent on some goods. Virginia secessionists nevertheless asserted that moderate duties of 15 to 20 percent would be sufficient for the Old Dominion to monopolize southern markets. Such a tariff would provide the Confederacy with ample revenue yet at the same time encourage the "manufacturers which Virginia now has, and which hang by a feeble thread."[79] Randolph observed that the market for ready-made clothing, hats, and shoes was almost entirely in northern hands, but "with a very slight protection" it could easily swing to Virginia manufacturers.[80] Such goods could be produced without fear of serious European competition because of high transportation costs and quickly changing fashions. No European manufacturer, Randolph believed, would take the chance of sending outdated and unfashionable ready-made clothing, hats, and shoes to the southern market. Randolph could thus assert that "we impose duties on Northern production and gain, in this way, vastly more protection than we lose by the reduction of the duty on foreign manufactures."[81] It is hard to judge the validity of such arguments, but in some ways Randolph and the other Virginian secessionists had an easy argument to make: whatever tariff level the new Confederate government set, it would offer more protection against northern manufacturers than the Unionists could offer.

The scenario that Randolph and other secessionists predicted—lower duties on European goods, higher duties on northern goods—promised to synthesize both free trade and protectionist arguments. To bring about this synthesis, Virginia secessionists reframed free-trade critiques of protectionism. Virginia secessionists never argued that a tariff rewarded inefficient industries or decreased consumer welfare, as a modern economist might.[82] Instead, they criticized the U.S. tariff exclusively on distributional grounds: it benefited one region at the expense of another. Embedded in this critique was the assumption that the tariff had worked extraordinarily well in promoting northern industry, northern commerce, and even northern agriculture. Why, then, would a Confederate tariff not work for the South as well? As Benning put it: "The same cause that built up manufacture in the north [the protective tariff] will operate similarly in Virginia."[83]

Such arguments allowed secessionists to keep one foot in the free-trade camp while incorporating the modern, nationalist rhetoric of the protectionists. In many cases, Virginia secessionists sounded much like Friedrich List, the German nationalist who believed that manufacturing, suitably encouraged via protectionism, promoted long-term development. A purely agricultural nation, List argued, remained extraordinarily vulnerable: "Its intellectual and political development and its power of defense are hampered. It can have no shipping of importance, no extensive trade. All of its prosperity ... can be interrupted, injured, or ruined by foreign regulations or by war." Barbour of Culpepper County had a similar argument in mind when he declared that encouraging manufacturing with a Confederate tariff was akin to developing the state's "imperial resources." Planters and other property holders who would bear the cost of a Confederate tariff, he argued, should do so happily: "While resolutely protecting slave labor, let us also give the fullest encouragement to the labor of the mechanic and the merchant and the artisan. ... When we build up commerce, manufactures, and trades, the accumulated wealth and population will be a source of strength and safety which will be cheaply purchased."[84]

If the Confederate tariff transformed Richmond and other Virginia cities into the South's industrial center, would conflict between slaves and white workers become endemic? The question was hardly an abstract one, as delegates to the secession convention surely knew that in 1847 Richmond's Tredegar Iron Works had replaced striking white workers with slaves.[85] Randolph argued that white mechanics and artisans had little to fear from slaves, who would occupy lower-order jobs such as miners and manual laborers. Virginia's white workers, he maintained, had far more to fear from the competition of cheap northern labor. "The true competitors of our laboring whites," he declared, "are the gigantic manufacturing corporations of the North which flood our market with everything that white labor can produce."[86] Only a Confederate tariff, Randolph argued, could protect Virginia's white mechanics from these "gigantic manufacturing corporations." Randolph also highlighted how a

*Redefining Free Trade*     129

Confederate tariff would benefit nonslaveholders in western Virginia, who held long-standing grievances against eastern slaveholders over political representation and the distribution of the state's internal improvement funds. With a Confederate tariff to provide protection from the "overwhelming competition of the North," western Virginians "will be what they ought to be—the manufacturers and miners of a great nation."[87] James Bruce similarly prophesized that "Wheeling is to become the Manchester of Virginia.... [I]f there be a disruption of this Union, I have no hesitation in saying that she would command the whole trade, or nearly the whole trade, of the lower Mississippi."[88]

The speeches at the Virginia secession convention—which themselves often received coverage in Virginia newspapers—became part of a larger discussion of Confederate trade polices. Newspapers across the country speculated and debated what a Confederate tariff might mean for regional trading patterns. Newspapers supporting secession took great delight in quoting northern observers who feared that a combination of high tariffs in the North and low tariffs in the Confederacy would divert European trade to the South. Other newspaper reports seemingly confirmed that a Confederate tariff would encourage southern industry. In March 1861 the *Richmond Daily Dispatch* carried a story from the *Boston Shoe and Leather Reporter* that warned northern shoemakers to quickly ship their existing orders before the Confederate tariff took effect: "The tariff on shoes, we believe under their [Confederate] laws, is about twenty-four percent, and of course, the saving [in shipping early] in the aggregate will be very large."[89]

### FORMULATING CONFEDERATE TARIFF POLICY

The protectionist elements of the Confederate tariff, so popular in Virginia, produced tension among secessionists tied to the South's traditional free-trade principles. Some of South Carolina's most radical free traders sought the elimination of all tariffs. The bigger the tariff differential between the North and the Confederacy, the radicals believed, the better chance Charleston and other southern ports had of attracting European trade and diplomatic recognition. Some South Carolinians even wondered whether an industrial Upper South could really be trusted on the issue of slavery. William Gilmore Simms, for example, believed that the Upper South would become another New England, complete with free-labor factories, pro-tariff politics, and abolitionist sentiments.[90] Free-trade radicals, fearing the rebirth of protectionist sentiment in the South, worked to ensure that the Confederacy's new constitution prohibited "any duties or taxes on importations from foreign nations to be laid to promote or foster any branch of industry."[91] Even this injunction against protective tariffs was not enough for some South Carolinians, who unsuccessfully sought to amend the Confederate constitution to ensure that "all expenditures in excess of revenues from imports (which shall not exceed fifteen per cent. ad valorem) and other sources, shall be met by direct taxation."[92]

In the end, most radical free traders surrendered rather tamely to the moderate revenue tariff. Some viewed complete free trade as a form of economic perfectionism better left to heaven than earth. In an 1857 speech, W. W. Boyce of South Carolina declared: "I do not know anything which can contribute more to the grandeur and prosperity of the country than free trade, absolute and unlimited." A few moments later, however, Boyce pragmatically accepted a tariff "if it were reduced in good faith strictly to the revenue standard."[93] In similar fashion, a correspondent for the *Mercury* supported the elimination of the tariff but also made clear that he "would not object to a moderate revenue tariff if not above ten or fifteen percent."[94] Garnett of Virginia considered himself a free trader, but he still supported a tariff of 15 percent while serving in Congress in 1857, reasoning that "this rate is so low as to do no great injustice to any one."[95] Even Garnett's low tariff, however, would provide Confederate manufacturers with some protection from their Yankee counterparts. Indeed, the acceptance of a moderate revenue tariff enabled radical free traders to cheer the incidental protection that such duties provided. Speaking of a South Carolina paint factory, the rabidly free-trade *Charleston Mercury* reported that a "tax of fifteen percent on this class of Northern imports will give our Charleston manufacturing a decided and very apparent advantage."[96]

On February 9, 1861 (four days before the Virginia secession convention opened), the provisional Confederate Congress passed a tariff—almost identical to the U.S. tariff of 1857—that imposed a duty of 24 percent on most manufactured goods. Nine days later, the Confederate Congress amended this act to expand the free list of goods to include most food products as well as arms, ammunition, and gunpowder. On March 15—when the Virginia secession convention was still meeting—the Confederacy lowered the duty on pig iron and other iron products to 15 percent.[97] In May 1861, after Virginia had joined the Confederacy, the Confederate Congress implemented a new tariff schedule with duties ranging from 5 to 25 percent. For the manufactured goods that the Confederacy was most likely to import—iron products, textiles, boots and shoes, furniture, and wagons—the duty was pegged at 15 percent. Reflecting the consensus favoring a revenue tariff, the Confederacy thus enacted duties within the range that secessionists in Virginia had predicted.[98]

Confederate preparations to collect duties showed how the new tariff would significantly hinder trade between North and South. Circulars issued by the treasury department established revenue officers not only in Atlantic ports but also along the Mississippi River and the various railroads that connected the Confederacy with the North. The circulars created formidable bureaucratic regulations, especially for those importing goods via railways. For example, the railroad conductor had to submit triplicate copies of a manifest at the nearest government revenue station and then wait for the revenue guard to inspect the train to ensure that the "goods described therein are placed in separate cars from which mails or passengers are conveyed." The revenue agent then placed Confederate revenue locks on the freight cars, which could only be opened at specified Confederate revenue depots. Once at the revenue depot, the merchandise in question was then moved to a "warehouse of deposit." After executing a bond guaranteeing the payment of duties, the importer was finally granted a "permit for inland transportation" so that the goods could finally reach their destination. The treasury department even authorized Confederate revenue officers to inspect passenger baggage for dutiable goods.[99]

The Confederacy, of course, never really had a chance to collect its tariff. If the seceding states had been allowed to leave without war, however, the Confederate tariff would have had a significant fiscal impact. According to economist Thomas F. Huertas, the South imported $200 million worth of northern goods in 1860 (see Table 5).[100] With an independent Confederacy, northern goods would have been transformed into dutiable foreign trade. Under Confederate tariff schedules passed in May 1861, imported manufactured goods from the North and Europe would have yielded the Confederate treasury almost $34 million. The percentage of collected duties to the value of total imports would have been 14.3 percent, which was only slightly lower than the ratio of 16 percent for the entire United States in 1860.[101] In per capita terms, every free person in the Confederacy would have paid $6.07 in duties. By way of comparison, the entire United States (both North and South) collected duties worth $53 million, or $1.94 per free resident in 1860.[102] If the North had allowed the South to peaceably leave the Union, the Confederacy would still have increased the tax burden on its own citizens—an ironic result for a nation supposedly committed to free trade and limited government.

The high rate of per capita taxation suggests the complex relationship between trade and Confederate nationalism. In some respects, the traditional southern commitment to free trade remained strong. In 1861, for example, South Carolinian G. N. Reynolds wrote in a letter to William Porcher Miles (a South Carolina delegate to the Confederate constitutional convention) that Switzerland was a model of free trade: "The result is that capital and industry flow solely in the most productive channels. So let it be with us."[103] Other secessionists thought in nationalistic terms and conceptualized trade not as a free-flowing river but as a weapon for punishing enemies. Referring to the North, Texas senator and former South Carolinian Louis Wigfall boasted, "Not one pound of cotton shall ever go from the South to their accursed cities; not one ounce of their steel or their manufactures shall ever cross our border."[104] A moderate revenue tariff that lowered duties on European goods while raising duties on northern goods synthesized these two potentially contradictory messages of free trade and Confederate nationalism. In the minds of many secessionists, free trade offered the Confederacy a means of escaping northern economic domination and solidifying international alliances. At the same time, secessionists could tout the ability of their government to penalize northern goods and protect southern manufacturers.

In fusing free trade and protectionist impulses, secessionists spoke and wrote in a Hamiltonian idiom of economic modernization and economic nationalism. Just as Hamilton had imagined the United States becoming a world economic power, secessionists envisioned the Confederacy as a vehicle for promoting economic modernization. Confederate duties closely resembled (and sometimes exceeded) the 10 to 15 percent tariff rate proposed by Hamilton in his famous *Report on Manufacturers* (1791).[105] The similarity in rates reflected shared goals of simultaneously promoting nation building and economic development. Hamilton wanted to make his new nation economically independent while simultaneously encouraging enough international trade to pay for his ambitious fiscal plans. His

TABLE 5  Confederate Imports in 1860 and Confederate Tariff Revenue Projections for 1861

| Item | Imports from North (in Millions of Dollars) | Imports from World (in Millions of Dollars) | Total (in Millions of Dollars) | Confederate Tariff Percentage Rate, 1861 | Projected Revenue from Tariff, 1861 (in Millions of Dollars) |
|---|---|---|---|---|---|
| Canned, smoked fish | 3 | 0 | 3 | 15 | .45 |
| Coffee | 0 | 10 | 10 | 0 | 0 |
| Sugar, brown | 0 | 3 | 3 | 20 | .6 |
| Molasses | 0 | 1 | 1 | 20 | .2 |
| Salt | 0 | 1 | 1 | 0 | 0 |
| Tea | 4 | 0 | 4 | 10 | .4 |
| Soap and candles | 6 | 0 | 6 | 15 | .9 |
| Paper | 7 | 0 | 7 | 15 | 1.05 |
| Cotton woven goods | 27 | 15 | 42 | 15 | 6.3 |
| Woolen goods | 34 | 1 | 35 | 15 | 5.25 |
| Ready-made clothing | 24 | 0 | 24 | 15 | 3.6 |
| Hosiery | 4 | 0 | 4 | 15 | .6 |
| Hats | 7 | 0 | 7 | 15 | 1.05 |

Sources: Confederate imports from Thomas F. Huertas, "Damnifying Growth in the Antebellum South," *Journal of Economic History* 39 (March 1979): 91; Confederate tariff rates from *Tariff of the Confederate States of America on and after August 31, 1861* (Augusta, Ga., 1861).

| Item | Imports from North (in Millions of Dollars) | Imports from World (in Millions of Dollars) | Total (in Millions of Dollars) | Confederate Tariff Percentage Rate, 1861 | Projected Revenue from Tariff, 1861 (in Millions of Dollars) |
|---|---|---|---|---|---|
| Shoes | 30 | 0 | 30 | 15 | 4.5 |
| Linen goods | 4 | 1 | 5 | 15 | .75 |
| Furniture | 1 | 0 | 1 | 15 | .15 |
| Carpeting | 4 | 0 | 4 | 15 | .45 |
| Musical instruments | 2 | 0 | 2 | 15 | .3 |
| Cast-iron stoves | 11 | 0 | 11 | 15 | 1.65 |
| Farm implements | 4 | 0 | 4 | 15 | .6 |
| Nails and spikes | 2 | 0 | 2 | 15 | .3 |
| Bar, sheet, and railroad iron | 8 | 3 | 11 | 15 | 1.65 |
| Pig iron | 6 | 0 | 6 | 15 | .9 |
| Cigars | 0 | 2 | 2 | 25 | .5 |
| Silk goods | 12 | 0 | 12 | 15 | 1.8 |
| Total | 200 | 37 | 237 | | 33.95 |

moderate tariff encouraged domestic manufacturing while generating enough revenue to finance the Revolutionary War debt. Confederates wanted tariffs high enough to penalize northern goods—thus encouraging economic independence—but still low enough to allow for a vibrant trade with Europe.

CONFEDERATE TRADE POLICY:
RHETORIC VERSUS REALITY

Hamilton, of course, did not forge his trade policies during the most destructive war in North American history. Even if the Confederacy had managed to peacefully secede, Confederate trade policy might have had disastrous consequences for the southern economy. Confederate independence would have hemmed southern manufacturers into a small, slow-growing market. Whereas northern manufacturers in 1860 produced for a market of some 27 million free consumers, manufacturers in the Confederacy could rely on a market of only 5.6 million free residents. Shifting cultivation and slavery would still have stunted markets in an independent Confederacy. Without sufficiently large markets, southerners could not develop the large pools of capital, skilled workers, and specialized firms that spurred northern development. In all likelihood, patenting rates and others of measures of innovation would have remained low. The Confederate manufacturing sector would have been composed of small, relatively inefficient firms needing high levels of protection to survive against northern competition.

Secessionist plans to increase direct trade with Europe would have probably failed as well. Europeans, secessionists reasoned, would sell their goods to the nation with the lowest tariffs, thus encouraging merchants to send their wares to southern ports instead of northern cities. Northerners, though, could have easily circumvented the "double duty" plan by offering tariff rebates on European goods eventually shipped to the South. Europeans wanting to sell their goods in the southern market could thus send them to northern cities without the additional tariffs. Sending goods to northern cities (especially New York) made economic sense because of the huge economies of scale that these metropolises provided. With their small hinterlands and inferior transportation links, southern ports could offer no such economies, making direct trade uneconomical. "Suppose a ship laden with silks and the more expensive textile fabrics, were to go to Charleston for a market," wrote northerner Daniel Lord in 1861. "Her cargo would be sufficient to supply the State for years. . . . How long would such a direct trade continue?"[106] Lord's point underscores how secessionists incorrectly identified the source of their frustrations. Southerners treated the lack of direct trade as a major political issue without acknowledging how slavery and shifting cultivation hindered the development of large markets.

Because the Confederacy never had a chance to implement its commercial policies, the South's fate as an independent nation remains a matter of conjecture. Historians need no conjectures, however, to evaluate the success of King Cotton diplomacy. Southerners embargoed cotton at the beginning of the Civil War to force Britain and other European powers to recognize Confederate independence.[107] Withholding cotton, though, failed to bring the world economy to its knees. The cotton famine created considerable hardship within certain segments of the textile industry, but it hardly led to economic panic, widespread starvation, or political violence in the North or Britain. Contrary to the predictions of James Henry Hammond, the North did indeed dare to make war on King Cotton—and proved willing to endure hundreds of thousands of casualties in the process. As for Europe, King Cotton not only failed to bring diplomatic recognition; the Confederate's cotton embargo also created a diplomatic backlash that damaged the Confederacy's credibility abroad. British statesmen such as Lord John Russell considered it "ignominious beyond measure" that King Cotton would coerce Britain to recognize the Confederacy.[108]

Why were the Confederates so wrong about cotton? Secessionists imagined a static world economy in which other economic agents did not make adjustments to changing circumstances. They thus overlooked how higher cotton prices encouraged the British to turn to other sources of cotton in Egypt and India. Secessionists similarly failed to recognize that the cotton shortage would encourage capital and labor to migrate to woolens and other industries, thus partially mitigating the impact of the cotton famine. In characterizing British workers as passive victims with no agency of their own, secessionists missed how textile operatives and factory owners built an impressive array of charitable institutions to lesson the impact of the cotton famine.[109] Cotton-mill workers certainly suffered, but not to the extent that secessionists had predicted. John Bright, a leading British liberal and a textile manufacturer himself, elicited "Loud laughter" and

"Roars of laughter" in 1863 when he quoted secessionist predictions of the impending starvation of England's cotton workers.[110] That Bright delivered his speech as Rochdale—a center of textile production—highlighted the economic reductionism in secessionist thinking. In simplifying complex matters of culture and political ideology into crude notions of economic interests, secessionists overestimated their ability to influence other nations and other regions. The Confederate belief in King Cotton assumed that Britain would act first and foremost to protect its economic interests. "These tall, thin, fine-faced Carolinians are great materialists," wrote the sarcastic William Howard Russell. "Slavery perhaps has aggravated the tendency to look at all the world through the parapets of cotton bales and rice bags."[111]

As the possibility of foreign assistance became more remote and the Union blockade tightened, political sentiment in the Confederacy increasingly favored protectionism and national economic independence. When a correspondent to Richmond's *Southern Literary Messenger* called for a peacetime economy of free trade, a rejoinder from the anonymous "C.R.C." appeared a few issues later. A protective tariff, the writer argued, would allow the Confederacy to extinguish its large debt and, more importantly, establish the industrial power necessary for national independence: "The South should be densely populated, and with manufactories in every region, and with double lines of rail roads in all directions; a future blockade would bring but little of the suffering and heartless speculations in provisions and clothing." Adopt a policy of free trade, he predicted, and a "future blockade would find the South little better prepared for self-defense than at present."[112] Secessionists had always believed that the South needed political independence to achieve economic independence. As "C.R.C." realized, the war and the Union blockade showed that the reverse was also true. To sustain their political independence, Confederates would have to become more economically autonomous.

In many respects, "C.R.C." reiterated a position that had already become quasi-official policy in the Confederacy. In the face of the northern blockade, Confederate leaders touted the ability of their nation to achieve self-sufficiency. Jefferson Davis noted in November 1861 that the Confederacy was "becoming more and more independent of the rest of the world" and confidently predicted that it could fight a protracted war. Davis even believed that the Union blockade, by forcing the South to develop its own industry, would prove to be a blessing in disguise.[113] The

Confederacy's inability to repair damaged railroads and supply its armies underscored Davis's lack of realism. He was not alone in failing to grasp the magnitude of the economic crisis that would grip the Confederacy. Fantasies of great metropolises, bustling factories, and bulging warehouses gave way to a reality of burned plantations, ruined cities, and hungry soldiers and civilians. Politically, the activist state that secessionists hoped to create became something akin to a Confederate Leviathan. The Confederate government did not simply guide economic development (as secessionists hoped); it also controlled entire industries and profoundly influenced the allocation of capital and labor. Chapter 5 explores how secessionist dreams quickly became a wartime nightmare.

*f i v e*

# ECONOMIC NATIONALISM
## AND THE GROWTH OF
## THE CONFEDERATE STATE

Like the colonists during the Revolution, Confederates printed vast sums of money to help pay for their war of independence. Unleashing the printing presses created ruinous inflationary pressures, but the currency itself provided a venue for expressing national identity. Embodying the new nation's sense of self, Confederate currency often depicted idealized visions of past heroes, contented slaves, and stately plantations. Confederate notes also featured representations of a modern slaveholding economy. The popular $100 note issued in Richmond in 1862 shows a larger-than-life locomotive that dwarfs the human figures standing beside it (Illustration 5, top). Modern, powerful, and dynamic, the locomotive aptly symbolized how Confederates imagined their economic future. The telegraph lines running alongside the track strengthen the connection between the Confederacy and modern technology. In the background, a steamship traverses the ocean, perhaps representing the profitable export of southern staples or the hope for direct trade with Europe. Agriculture also appears on the note, but not in the form of large plantations or cotton fields. Instead, a milkmaid and a dairy farm appear in the foreground, linking the railroad to agricultural diversification.

These images of a modern southern economy—appearing on the Confederacy's most visible and widely circulated emblems of national authority—symbolized how secessionists made economic development a rationale for southern independence. Confederate currency also provides a clue as to how Confederates sought to modernize their economy. A popular trope appearing on various Confederate notes was a larger-than-life picture of a statehouse or other government building (Illustration 5, bottom). The large size of the statehouse dwarfs the persons milling about—a perfect symbol of how government authority and the need for collective action dwarfed the needs of individuals. The symbolic rendering of state over individuals is hardly surprising given the program of state activism that secessionists had pursued throughout the antebellum decades. To reform and diversify southern agriculture, secessionists had supported state backing of experimental farms, agricultural societies, and university professorships. To build railroads to the West, secessionists had enthusiastically supported state investment to complement (and sometimes supplant) private capital. To encourage direct trade with Europe and spur southern manufacturing, secessionists had strongly endorsed tariffs on northern goods. Secessionists, in short, had envisioned that the "visible hand" of an activist state would guide economic development.

This chapter shows how that visible hand made Confederates more likely to resort to far stronger state action when war endangered the survival of slavery. Whether it was government investment in railroads, government ownership of key industries, or government regulation of commerce, Confederates adopted centralized control of the economy with surprisingly little opposition. States' rights objections to a strong central government, so prominent in the South under the old Union, did little to slow down the growth of the Confederate state. In antebellum debates, secessionists never imagined creating a Confederate Leviathan, but their general economic philosophy certainly helped make one possible.

The creation of a strong Confederate state revealed the powerful sense of nationalism that knit together the supporters of the Confederacy's slave society. In many ways, the nationalistic spirit grew stronger as the war progressed. Nationalism, though, had significant costs as well as benefits. Blinded by their fundamental assumption that "interests" dic-

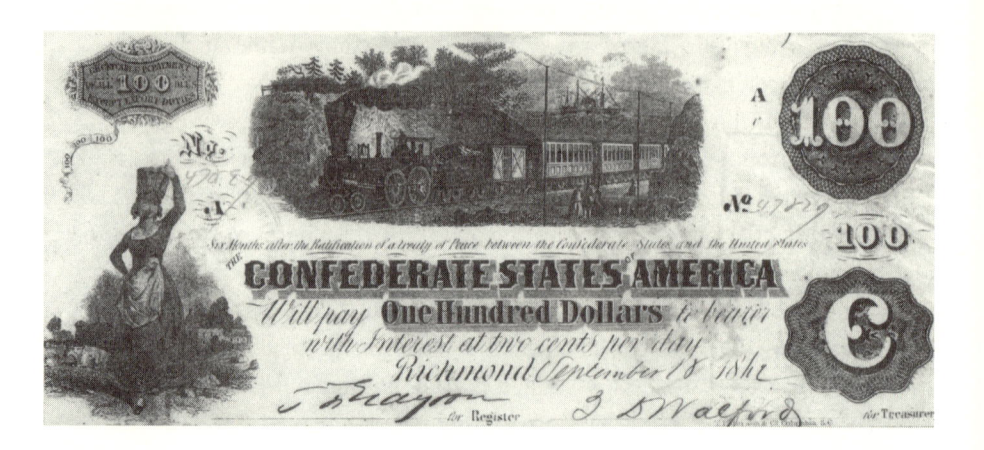

ILLUSTRATION 5   *The portraits on these notes symbolize a modern Confederate economy and a strong Confederate state. The small size of the persons relative to the state capitol suggests the primacy of government over that of the individual. (Currency from the collection of the author)*

tated human behavior, secessionists believed that the South's substantial population of Upcountry farmers and slaves would quietly acquiesce to the formation of a modern slaveholding republic. Supposing that they could manipulate and control others, secessionists resembled the "man of system" that Adam Smith described in *The Theory of Moral Sentiments*. Smith observed that the man of system "seems to imagine that he can arrange the different members of a great society with as much ease as the hand arranges the different pieces upon a chess-board." The man of system, Smith cautioned, invariably forgot that "in the great chess-board of human society, every single piece has a principle of motion of its own, altogether different from that which the legislature might chuse [*sic*] to impress upon it."[1] Confederates learned the hardest way imaginable how the pieces of the board could move on their own accord. During the Civil War, the Confederacy's "man of system" failed to master the force of human agency.

IDEOLOGICAL ORIGINS OF THE CONFEDERATE STATE

The transition from antebellum state activism to war socialism involved a complex series of ideological and policy shifts. In the antebellum era, government activism took place on the state level. When secessionists imagined national economic policies such as the Confederate tariff, they conceived of government intervention as a guiding hand that would gently nudge private economic interests to create a more modern economy. Precisely how, then, did the secessionists' vision of state activism lead the Confederacy to build a powerful wartime government that controlled most of the nation's economy? Military necessity certainly exerted great weight. A vast expansion in government power, after all, has accompanied most major conflicts, especially during the two world wars that dominated the first half of the twentieth century. The scale and size of the Civil War made the emergence of a strong central state seem almost natural. Yet if taken too far, the "wartime necessity" thesis obscures an important ideological precondition frequently articulated during the antebellum period: the preservation of slavery rested on notions of collective action and strong government, not on antistatism and individualism.

Scholars have tended to downplay the secessionist embrace of these principles because antebellum southerners sometimes articulated an alternative discourse focusing on states' rights and limited government.

Such discourses certainly served important purposes for southern extremists. In the antebellum period, antigovernment rhetoric gave extremists a powerful language from which to oppose federal initiatives that might endanger slavery. During the secession crisis and the Civil War, the language of states' rights and limited government connected the southern cause to the American Revolution, which may have helped gain foreign support (especially from Europeans hostile to slavery) and preserve internal unity (especially among nonslaveholding whites). Most secessionists, however, used states' rights doctrines in selective fashion. When secessionists perceived that states' rights doctrines would not serve their purposes, they readily abandoned them. States' rights and limited government thus reflected a rhetorical tradition—to be used or ignored depending on the context and situation—rather than a consistent political philosophy. Once the creation of the Confederacy made the protection of slavery a national issue, former advocates of states' rights shifted rather quickly to the support of a strong national government.

The career of Louis Wigfall demonstrates the instrumental nature of states' rights thinking among secessionists. Born into a prominent South Carolina family, Wigfall was one of the many Carolina planters who sought a fresh start in Texas. He enjoyed considerable political success in his new home, but his brand of southern extremism (which included calls for reopening the African slave trade) made him too radical for many Texans. In the emotional aftermath of John Brown's raid, Wigfall's extremist politics gained popularity, and in 1860 the Texas state legislature elected him to the U.S. Senate. The extremist Wigfall often embraced republican ideals celebrating limited government and states' rights; he proudly labeled himself as "one of the straitest of the sect of State-rights men."[2] In May 1861 Wigfall took his rhetoric one step further. The Texas senator famously told correspondent William Howard Russell of the *Times* (London) why southerners constituted a "peculiar people" who rejected much of the modern world: "We are an agricultural people; we are a primitive but a civilized people. We have no cities—we don't want them. We have no literature—we don't need any yet. We have no press—we are glad of it. . . . We want no manufactures: we desire no trading, no mechanical or manufacturing classes. As long as we have our rice, our sugar, our tobacco, and our cotton, we can command wealth to purchase all we want from those nations with which we are in amity, and lay up money besides."[3]

Several historians have cited Wigfall's vivid language as emblematic of Confederate opposition to economic modernization.[4] Given his interest in persuading Britons to support the Confederacy, should historians take Wigfall's position at face value? In talking to Russell, Wigfall was making a pitch for British recognition, highlighting the natural affinity of interests between the Confederacy (an exporter of staple crops and an importer of manufactured goods) and Britain (an importer of staple crops and an exporter of manufacturing goods). Wigfall's romantic agrarianism, with its echoes of contented yeoman farmers, avoided any mention of the Confederacy's 3 million slaves, a potentially sensitive issue for the antislavery readers of the *Times*.[5] Russell, for one, took Wigfall's "wonderful lucidity and odd affection of logic" far less seriously than have historians. The fawning Wigfall hovered so closely to the influential correspondent that Russell mockingly called him "my faithful Wigfall."[6]

Rather than reveal an antimodern streak within Confederate thought, Wigfall's rhetoric illustrates the ways in which southerners routinely contradicted their own republican critiques of activist government and economic modernity. Wigfall's comment—"We have no press—and are glad of it"—was particularly misleading. Before migrating to Texas, Wigfall controlled a South Carolina newspaper to advance his own political career. Like many other secessionists, Wigfall had long supported the southern press as part of a broader array of southern educational and cultural institutions that would combat the pernicious influence of abolitionist doctrines. While in the Texas legislature, Wigfall called for the creation of a free public university that would educate both men and women.[7] Wigfall's state activism went further; he also supported federal subsidies to encourage railroads. In 1860 the "straitest of the sect of State-Rights men" proposed a bill that would give two national railroads (one taking a northern route, the other taking a southern route through Texas) extensive land grants and sweetheart loans totaling $70 million. Wigfall believed that the federal government could invest in internal improvements as long as it enhanced national defense and facilitated mail delivery. One startled northern senator declared that Wigfall's position "exceeds in the latitudinarian construction of the Constitution anything that the Federalists ever dreamed of."[8] If secessionists could justify national railroad subsidies on the grounds of national defense and mail delivery, then they could also justify protective tariffs, conscription, or the government ownership of "essential" industries.

Confederate railroad policy, in fact, provides a microcosm for understanding how secessionists crossed the thin line separating antebellum state activism and a powerful, dynamic Confederate state. On the face of it, most Confederate leaders seemingly opposed national railroads. During the Confederate constitutional convention, South Carolina's Robert Barnwell Rhett and other secessionists sought to prohibit the central government from funding internal improvements. The Confederacy, they argued, should never allow internal improvements (at least on the national level) to generate the evils of logrolling, budget deficits, and higher taxes. Rhett won an important victory when the Confederate constitution specifically prohibited Congress from appropriating "money for any internal improvement intended to facilitate commerce." The constitution allowed the Confederate Congress to appropriate money to aid coastal navigation, improve harbors, or clear rivers, but only if it taxed the commerce that benefited from such improvements. "Internal improvements, by appropriations from the treasury of the Confederate States," Rhett's *Charleston Mercury* cheered, "is therefore rooted out of the system of Government the Constitution establishes."[9]

States' rights ideology, though, eventually lost to a more expansive vision of the Confederate central state. As Table 6 shows, the Confederate government chartered and subsidized four important lines to improve the movement of troops and supplies. Loans and appropriations for these lines amounted to almost $3.5 million, a significant sum given that a severe shortage of iron and other supplies necessarily limited southern railroad building. Jefferson Davis, who strongly backed these national projects, argued that military necessity rather than commercial ambition motivated national investment in these lines. The constitutional prohibition of funding internal improvements "for commercial purposes" was thus irrelevant. That Davis took this position during the Civil War followed naturally from his position on national railroads in the antebellum era. Like Wigfall, he believed that military necessity justified national railroad investment. As a U.S. senator, Davis told his colleagues in 1859 that a Pacific railroad "is to be absolutely necessary in time of war, and hence within the Constitutional power of the General Government."[10] Davis was more right than he realized. When the Republican-controlled Congress heavily subsidized the nation's first transcontinental railroad in 1862, military considerations constituted a key justification. Even after the Civil War, the military considered the transcontinental railroad as an

TABLE 6  Confederate National Investment in Railroads

| Railroad | Investment | Authorized | Completed |
|---|---|---|---|
| Danville, Va., to Greensborough, N.C. | $1 million loan | February 1862 | May 20, 1864 |
| Meridian, Miss., to Selma, Ala. | $150,000 advance | February 1862 | December 1862 |
| New Iberia, La., to Orange, Tex. | $1.5 million loan | April 1862 | NA |
| Rome, Ga., to Blue Mountain, Ala. | $1.12 million appropriation | October 1862 | NA |

Source: Derived from Charles W. Ramsdell, "The Confederate Government and the Railroads," *American Historical Review* 22 (July 1917): 794–810.

essential tool for subjugating the Sioux and other Native Americans resisting western settlement.[11]

When the Confederate Congress endorsed Davis's position on railroads, outraged supporters of states' rights strongly objected. Their petition against national railroads—inserted into the official record of the Confederate Congress—argued that the railroads in question might well have military value, "but the same may be said of any other road within our limits, great or small."[12] The constitutional prohibition against national internal improvements, the petition recognized, was essentially worthless if the "military value" argument carried the day. Essentially giving the Confederate government a means of avoiding almost any constitutional restrictions, the "military value" doctrine threatened to become the Confederacy's version of the "general welfare" clause that had done so much to justify the growth of government in the old Union. The elastic nature of "military value," however, hardly bothered the vast majority of representatives in the Confederate Congress. The bills for the railroad lines passed overwhelmingly in 1862 and 1863. As political scientist Richard Franklin Bensel has argued, the constitutional limitations on the Confederate central government "turned out to be little more than cosmetic adornments."[13]

Like Louis Wigfall's rambling interview with William Howard Russell, the "cosmetic adornments" in the Confederate constitution allowed secessionists to articulate republican principles without actually having to follow them. If Confederate delegates in Montgomery really wanted to stop all national improvements, they could have simply prohibited the Confederate Congress from appropriating "money for any internal improvements" rather than insert the qualifying phrase "intended to facilitate commerce." It is hard to believe that the inclusion of the "commerce" qualification was accidental. Having spent much of their careers debating the old federal Constitution, the delegates at Montgomery carefully considered the implications of every phrase they wrote.[14] The delegates surely knew that men such as Wigfall and Davis had used the national defense argument to justify federal spending on internal improvements. As it was, the delegates ritualistically invoked states' rights without having to worry about the consequences. Historian Don E. Fehrenbacher has argued that the Confederate constitution was written "by men committed to the principle of states' rights but addicted, in many instances, to the exercise of national power."[15] Perhaps it would be more accurate to say that Confederates were committed to the *language* of states' rights in a way that rarely prevented the growth of national power.[16]

The decision to subsidize railroads, while ideologically important, was only a small part of the overall growth of the Confederate state. Other elements of Confederate state building, in fact, proved less controversial. When a shortage of pig iron threatened ordnance production, Davis told Congress in early 1862 that the "exigency is believed to be such as to require the aid of the Government."[17] In April 1862 the Confederate Congress passed legislation that offered no-interest loans to iron masters who expanded their forges. The loans would only pay half the cost of the additional investment, but the Confederate government also offered to make advances up to one-third the value of contracts. To help forges secure additional raw materials, the Confederate Congress set up the Niter Bureau in 1862, which quickly became involved in exploration for new sources of iron. The Confederacy sometimes used private firms to produce ordnance—the famous Tredegar Iron Works is a good example—but the Confederacy's Ordnance Bureau also built and operated its own arsenals, mills, and factories throughout the South. The arsenal at Selma, Alabama, for example, employed 3,000 civilians, while the Ordnance Bureau's powder factory in Augusta, Georgia, was the second largest in the world. Whereas the North tended to rely on government contracts with private firms to meet the needs of wartime production, the Confederacy, with surprisingly little opposition, produced much of the military supplies consumed by its armies.[18]

The story of the Quartermaster Department is similar to the Ordnance Bureau. Historian Harold S. Wilson describes Confederate efforts to outfit soldiers with uniforms, shoes, blankets, and tents as the "brink of military socialism."[19] The Quartermaster Department of the Confederacy operated its own factories and workshops, employing some 50,000 workers (many of them seamstresses). To obtain cloth for these factories and workshops, the Quartermaster Department exerted immense control over privately owned textile mills. Mills that refused to submit to Confederate controls on prices and profits faced the prospect of having their workers conscripted into the Confederate army. When wool supplies ran short—largely because Union forces captured most of the major wool-producing areas early in the war—the Confederate Congress authorized quartermasters to impress whatever supplies they could find.[20] The Confederate Congress also allowed the Quartermaster Department (under the auspices of the Bureau of Foreign Supplies) to regulate and control most blockade runners. In early 1864 the Confederate government prohibited private shipments of cotton, tobacco, and other staple crops; required that private blockade runners devote half of all cargo space to the war department; and prohibited luxuries from entering the South. The Confederacy had essentially nationalized much of its foreign commerce.[21]

These interventions were significant, but no single policy was as important as conscription. Short of manpower against the North's larger population, the Confederate government resorted to conscription in April 1862. Any southern man age eighteen to thirty-five (even if he was already in the military) was liable to serve three years in the Confederate army. The conscription legislation provided exemptions (such as for militia officers and apothecaries) and allowed men to pay for substitutes. Subsequent legislation, though, prohibited substitutes and eliminated many of the exemptions. In February 1864 the draft had been expanded to cover men between the ages of seventeen and fifty.[22] Despite corruption, inefficiency, and sometimes violent opposition, Confederate conscription policies worked remarkably well. In Mississippi, for example, some 73 percent of whites between the ages of eighteen and twenty-four enlisted in the Confederate army; the comparable figure for northern localities was 40 percent.[23] The draft also served to give the Confederate government additional leverage over private industry. Railroads, mills, and factories that failed to serve the needs of the Confederate government might find their entire workforce forced into the army.

Historians have stressed that the Confederate draft faced substantial opposition. Those opposing the draft ranged from important political figures such as Georgia governor Joseph E. Brown to many ordinary farmers and artisans. The source of that opposition is not hard to understand: many considered conscription as inimical to republican ideals of personal freedom and limited government.[24] Yet, as in the case of government subsidies to railroads and other elements of the Confederate state, opposition did little to derail actual legislation. More than two-thirds of Confederate senators and congressmen voted for the initial draft legislation in April 1862. Some of the secessionists who had supported modernization policies in the antebellum era enthusiastically embraced conscription. The ever-present Wigfall, in fact, introduced the conscription bill to Congress, declaring that he "could not admit that the Southern States were joined in a 'loose league.'"[25] In April 1862 the *Charleston Mercury*, supposedly committed to a strong states' rights philosophy, criticized Jefferson Davis for not supporting conscription earlier in the war.[26] As casualties mounted, the *Mercury* ardently supported tightening exemption loopholes. Calling conscription "that law to which we owe our salvation," the *Mercury* argued in January 1864 that "exemptions must be diminished.... Young men must not be permitted to evade their duty by slipping into safe places."[27] Edmund Ruffin, true to the state activism he articulated during the antebellum decades, also supported conscription. Upon reading that the governor of Georgia opposed conscription, Ruffin wrote in his diary: "This is an unfortunate occurrence. What trouble it may bring I cannot understand, or conceive the end of. Many other persons, public & private, have held the like opinion. But all others waived their difficulties on account of the great military necessities of the Confederacy."[28]

Confederate officials, much like Ruffin, used military necessity to justify measures such as conscription. It is important to recognize, though, that Confederate war socialism had important antecedents in the antebellum era. The Niter Bureau's search for essential minerals and the Ordnance Bureau's experimental laboratory resembled the geological surveys and experimental farms that the agricultural reform movement had long advocated. Government ownership of essential industries had roots in the antebellum era, when state investment in railroads was the norm. And if government could own railroads, why could it not also own blockade runners and other forms of transportation? In the antebellum period, southerners framed activist government as part of a long-term defense of slavery. The creation of the Confederacy linked interventionist policies to the defense of slavery in a far more direct way. States' rights ideology quickly wavered; it seemed either overly philosophical in rejecting needed measures or unpatriotically narrow-minded in putting local interests above national concerns. The willingness of southerners to frame the defense of slavery as a collective endeavor—during both the antebellum period and the war itself—helps explain the emergence of a strong Confederate state. When debating conscription, the ever-quotable Wigfall put the nationalistic principles of the Confederacy into their baldest form: "No man has any individual rights, which come into conflict with the welfare of the country."[29]

## THE PARADOXES OF CONFEDERATE NATIONALISM

Few Confederate politicians would endorse Wigfall's wholesale rejection of individual rights in favor of a strong national government. On the other hand, the tremendous growth of the Confederate state suggests that powerful nationalistic beliefs influenced Confederate leaders and their supporters. Northerners expected Confederate nationalism to quickly collapse, but it grew stronger as the war progressed.[30] The economic attitudes in the antebellum era contributed to the development of nationalism. At its most basic level, secessionist political economy assumed that southern whites had a fundamental interest in slavery. A modern, slaveholding republic, secessionists predicted, would provide benefits for *all* southern whites. In a widely circulated 1860 essay titled "The Interest in Slavery of the Southern Non-Slaveholder," journalist J. D. B. De Bow concluded that all southern whites had a stake in a modern slaveholding republic. The Confederacy would allow southerners to "build up our towns and cities, to extend our railroads, and increase our shipping. . . . [O]pulence would be diffused throughout all classes, and we should become the freest, the happiest and most prosperous and powerful nation on earth."[31]

Slavery remained the foundation of Confederate nationalism, but Confederate nationalism blossomed well beyond in the emphasis on interests. Historians have noted, for example, how Confederates embraced the image of the genteel cavaliers to distinguish themselves from crass, money-mad Yankees. The cavalier image appeared frequently in Confederate newspapers, pamphlets, and broadsides, giving hope that the South's superior values—its citizens greater sense of patriotism, courage, and valor—would eventually triumph over the North's superior numbers.[32] In similar fashion, Confederates often portrayed themselves as devout Christians morally superior to the spiritual decadence of amoral Yankees.[33] Because modernization and slavery coexisted so easily within the secessionist imagination, secessionists could still embrace honor and piety even as their political economy envisioned sprawling cities and new factories. Images of a gallant Jeb Stuart or a dignified Robert E. Lee could thus help sustain Confederate nationalism during wartime crisis without undermining the Confederacy's economic ambitions. Secessionists believed that southerners could be cavaliers and capitalists at the same time.

For modernizing secessionists who wanted to transcend the parochial political culture of the Old South, the creation of a vibrant Confederate nationalism was a great success. The strength of Confederate nationalism was certainly far stronger than the nationalism that animated the American Revolution. During the American Revolution, the Continental Congress struggled to create the most rudimentary national institutions. The national government that emerged from the revolution—based on the highly decentralized Articles of Confederation—lacked the power to levy its own taxes.[34] In sharp contrast, Confederate nationalism supported the creation of extensive bureaucracies, government-owned ordnance facilities, and draconian conscription policies. No wonder that historians have been more inclined to compare Confederate state building to authoritarian states such as Prussia and the Soviet Union rather than to America's own revolutionary heritage.[35] The tremendous growth of the Confederate state undermines arguments that Confederates lost the Civil War because they lacked a coherent national identity. The Confederacy endured four years of brutal combat and a staggering casualty rate in its quest for independence; one-quarter of its white men of military age and nearly 4 percent of the total population perished. No nation in World War I lost a higher percentage of its population.[36] It seems hard to believe that Confederates would have sacrificed so much unless they had developed a strong sense of nationalism.

Perhaps the Confederates lost the war not because their sense of nationalism was too weak, but because it was too strong. Even as nationalistic sentiment helped sustain the Confederate effort, the same nationalism simultaneously helped destroy the Confederacy from within. The strength of Confederate nationalism, so successful in uniting the planting class and its allies, made Confederate ideals far less effective in uniting other elements of southern society. Confederate nationalism assumed that various groups within the South—such as Upcountry farmers or even the slaves themselves—had an "interest" in the success of the Confederacy. Yet did Upcountry farmers really have an interest in making tremendous sacrifices on behalf of a slaveholders' republic? Did slaves really have an interest in perpetuating their own bondage? Secessionists, reflecting an overbearing chauvinism, answered both questions in the affirmative. Just as they assumed that cotton would force Europe to support the Confederate cause or the northern economy would collapse without southern trade, secessionists confidently believed that both Upcountry farmers and slaves could be manipulated, cajoled, or forced to serve the ends of the Confederacy. The result was a serious miscalculation; many Upcountry yeomen and slaves fought against the Confederacy, not for it. Here, then, was the central paradox of Confederate nationalism: it certainly motivated some southerners to make staggering sacrifices to sustain the Confederacy, but it also led many southerners to make staggering sacrifices to defeat it. The surprising durability of Confederate nationalism among slaveholders and their allies came at the cost of forging a broader southern nationalism.

The complex wartime decisions of ordinary farm families demonstrated how Confederate nationalism became a double-edged sword for the secessionist cause. Secessionists expected the South's substantial population of yeoman farmers to support Confederate independence. Secessionists frequently portrayed the Confederacy as an essentially homogenous population of white men and women. "Are we not a people of homogeneous interests," asked Virginian John Goode in reference to the South. "Are we not a people of like habits, of like institutions, and like religion? Are we not all deeply and vitally concerned with the preservation of the institution of African slavery?"[37] The poorest yeoman farmer, secessionists argued, had no desire to see the South's several million slaves set free. Secessionists asserted that emancipation would quickly devolve into an apocalyptic race war that would endanger the lives and property of all whites, whether great masters or humble yeomen. Under Republican rule, wrote secessionist Stephen Hale of Alabama in 1860, "the slave-holder and the non-slave-holder must ultimately share the same fate." Either the white southerners must accept full equality of blacks—which would invariably lead to "amalgamation" of the races—or "there will be an eternal war of races, desolating the land with blood, and utterly wasting and destroying all the resources of the country."[38]

Appeals to racism and economic mobility helped rally yeomen support. Numerous yeomen families, especially those living among slaveholders, willingly joined the Confederate cause, where they made tremendous sacrifices on behalf of their new nation. In places such as the South Carolina Lowcountry or the Virginia piedmont, white families owning a modest number of slaves or even no slaves at all often belonged to kinship networks that included wealthier slaveholders. These kinship networks, which could provide financial assistance in times of need, helped solidify political support for wealthier slaveholders.[39] The ambition to become a slaveholding patriarch—with its attendant social and political status—undoubtedly led some small farmers to identify with their wealthy neighbors.[40] Southerners, in fact, asserted that economic mobility in their region was open to all hardworking and industrious white men, regardless of their initial economic and social position.[41] These claims helped motivate a good many yeomen households to support the Confederacy.

In both Virginia and South Carolina, an overwhelming number of whites supported the Confederacy. What, though, of the substantial areas of the southern Upcountry (such as the Appalachian region), where slavery was far weaker? Confident assertions of an essentially "homogeneous" southern population failed to capture the reality that many Upcountry yeomen had no real interest in preserving slavery. Western Virginia, for example, had long been at loggerheads with eastern slaveholders over legislative representation, internal improvements, and tax policy.[42] The creation of a strong Confederate state—with its draconian draft policy, high taxes, and inflationary fiscal polices—hardly added to the appeal of the Confederacy in western Virginia and other portions of southern Appalachia. The oft-quoted phrase "rich man's war, poor man's fight" demonstrated the divergence of interests between slaveholders and Upcountry yeomen. While many yeoman farmers in plantation districts fought and died for the Confederacy, others from areas that had little connection with slavery tended to remain neutral or support the Union.[43]

The case of western Virginia was particularly instructive. In July 1862 southern sympathizer G. W. Berlin informed Virginia governor John Letcher that thousands of "good and loyal citizens" in the western counties might support the Confederacy. A dismayed Berlin, however, soon found that these potential Confederate sympathizers ended up supporting the North because the "Mountains which separated them from the South & East, the want of Railroad or water communications with their friends [in the Confederacy], the fine R.R. & water communications from the Ohio River into the very heart of their country, & that in addition to all this the South was weak and the North strong." To make matters worse, bands of southern partisans had begun indiscriminately preying on local farmers, whether Unionist or not. If Confederate partisans continued to attack ordinary citizens, western Virginia might lose half its population. Such a scenario would not only "bankrupt the *state*, but would effect us individually in the same way, for as lands are valuable in proportion of the density of population, what would our lands be worth in N.W. Va. if half the people were driven away?"[44] Berlin's analysis remained steadfastly centered on economics in a way that recalled the secessionist focus on interests. This time, though, the tables were turned: economic interests did not unite white southerners but drove them apart. Perceiving that the region's citizens had no interests in a slaveholding regime, political leaders in western Virginia soon formed West Virginia the state. More than 25,000 West Virginians fought for the Union, as opposed to only 15,000 for the Confederacy. Strategically, West Virginia partially shielded the Ohio River and key Union railroads from direct Confederate attack. Although such factors were hardly decisive, the Confederacy nevertheless could ill afford to lose men and territory that Virginia secessionists assumed would fight on behalf of the South.[45]

THE INTERESTS OF SLAVES

Slaves—even more than Upcountry yeoman farmers—demonstrated the propensity of Confederate nationalism to produce enemies as well as supporters of the Confederacy. Secessionists believed that whereas free societies had to contend with the never-ending war between labor and capital, a southern confederacy had little reason to fear social unrest. In the transition to a more industrial economy, secessionists imagined their supposedly obedient and docile slaves as the perfect workforce for a modern economy. Charleston newspaper editor L. W. Spratt, for example, speculated that slavery would flourish in the South's new industrial economy because "improvements in machinery have superseded the necessity of more than mere manipulation upon the part of operatives." Indeed, when slavery expands into industry, "the institution will evolve an energy of light and life that will enable it to advance over existing forms of society with a desolating and restless power."[46] Spratt's rhetoric, however hyperbolic, captured the optimism of the many proslavery thinkers who believed that slavery and industry could coexist.[47] On one level, secessionists had a point. Antebellum slavery was a surprisingly flexible economic institution. If money could be made by moving slaves into industry and commerce, planters usually found a way to do so. The process, in fact, had already begun in Virginia, where slaves worked for iron forges, tobacco factories, and railroads.

What secessionist rhetoric failed to acknowledge was that slaves themselves could take advantage of the growth of industry and cities. Slavery, as historian Ira Berlin and others have forcefully argued, always involved some form of negotiation. Even in the most oppressive plantation environments, slaves could withhold their labor—through feigning illness, refusing to work, or damaging crops and equipment—so that they could negotiate a small and fragile sphere of autonomy.[48] Slaves in cities and industries frequently had far more power to bargain for autonomy than their plantation counterparts. Skilled slaves routinely worked for wages, which they used to purchase goods that they could call their own. Some masters even allowed skilled slaves to become something akin to independent contractors, making their own business arrangements as long as they paid their master a share of the profits. Such work occasionally provided slaves with the money to buy their own freedom. Most urban slaves had little chance of achieving freedom, but they nevertheless experienced greater autonomy in a more fluid and open urban environment. Owners often "hired out" slaves to urban employers, who had little inclination and opportunity to enforce the stifling discipline that prevailed on many plantations.[49]

Urban slavery's potential challenge to white authority resulted in a set of contradictory impulses within the secessionist movement. Even as secessionists predicted a glorious future for southern manufacturers, the growth of industrial and urban slavery created considerable anxiety. The fears surrounding urban slavery in Virginia and South Carolina, in fact, helped fuel the secession movement. The case of Jordan Hatcher—one of the many hired slaves working in Richmond's tobacco factories—symbolized growing anxieties over urban slavery. In February 1852 Hatcher struck and killed his overseer after having been beaten for shoddy work. A jury convicted Hatcher and sentenced him to be executed, but Governor Joseph Johnson commuted the sentence to sale and transportation outside of the state. While it remains unclear why Johnson commuted Hatcher's sentence, he soon came to regret his decision: a Richmond mob besieged the governor's mansion, labeling him an abolitionist and demanding his resignation. The Hatcher case became a statewide issue, and the legislature considered censuring Johnson. What made the Hatcher case important, historian William Link has explained, was the "context of deteriorating white authority in Richmond tobacco factories and across the entire commonwealth. Slaveholders were obviously anxious about urban slaves and their considerable freedom."[50] The situation in Charleston was similarly tense, as many in the "Queen City of the South" feared slave arson and slave rebellions.[51] These accumulated fears created an important contradiction that proslavery ideology had to answer. If slaves benefited from slavery, why did their masters worry so much about rebellions and uprisings?

Secessionist thinking about interests, buttressed by the racial assumptions of proslavery ideology, helps explain how secessionists counterpoised their constant fears of slave rebellion with the abiding faith in slave loyalty. Secessionists believed that slavery was literally in the interest of blacks. According to proslavery ideology, slavery uplifted blacks, taking them out of barbarous Africa and introducing them to Christianity and the comforts of Western society. Secessionists argued that slavery provided blacks with far more in food, shelter, and other material goods than most factory workers in the North and Britain could earn. Slaves instinctively realized that their true interests resided with their masters—unless seduced to rebel or run away by abolitionist propaganda or abolitionists agents. Simply preventing abolitionist propaganda from coming into the South would ensure the safety of slavery. "The Southern States have no danger to apprehend," wrote one South Carolina secessionist in 1850, "but the evils arising out of the too close connection we bear to the Northern States."[52] The repentant runaway slave—eagerly returning to servitude after having been misled by abolitionist agents—was a stock character in proslavery propaganda.[53]

By controlling the flow of information, southerners believed, they could control the interests of their slaves. Secessionists argued that southern independence would ensure that abolitionist propaganda would never reach their supposedly content (if somewhat gullible) slaves. Confederate independence would allow slaveholders to control the mail, the press, the military, and other national institutions, thus safely eradicating abolitionist propaganda. Just as the Confederate government could stop the flow of northern goods, it could also stop the flow of northern ideas. Henry Benning told the Virginia secession convention that the Confederate government would station customs agents along the Confederacy's border: "It could be easily made part of the duty of these officers to keep strict watch ... and intercept every slave, and keep surveillance on all who may come within the line of particular localities."[54] Within the Union, Ruffin pointed out, "mischievous agents of organized associations for stealing slaves, and exciting insurrection and massacre," could freely enter the South. With the power to question and investigate "those newly arrived and unknown," a Confederate government could ensure that abolitionists were "watched, detected, and by more stringent laws, speedily hung as soon as found guilty."[55] Sheltered from abolitionist propaganda by a vigilant central government, slaves would continue to see slavery as an institution that protected their interests.

Such logic led secessionists to believe that slaves, safe from pernicious abolitionist doctrines, would help the Confederacy defeat the North. Loyal to their masters, slaves would allow white men to serve in the armed forces with little in the way of lost production. Spratt, for example, believed that slaves would remain blissfully ignorant of the conflict and continue to diligently work on behalf of their masters: "The slaves, without knowledge of the war, or its aim, or purposes, will be as obedient to orders as in times of peace."[56] Ruffin took this argument a step further. In *Anticipations of the Future*, the Virginia planter imagined that slaves would man southern forts to repel the northern invaders. Were not southern slaves, after all, much better treated than the common sailors who allowed Britain's navy to rule the seas? Ruffin reasoned that slaves, well cared for by their southern masters, would become "zealous partisans, and as hostile in feeling to the northern enemy, as any citizen—and might well be relied upon as soldiers, unless incapacitated by their natural and constitutional cowardice." Their lack of courage might limit their use on battlefields, Ruffin conceded, but he nevertheless believed that the "implicit obedience and perfect subordination of Negroes to the authority of white men" would enable slaves to stand firm in the relative safety of fixed fortifications.[57]

Of all the miscalculations of the secessionists, underestimating the desire for freedom among their slaves was perhaps the most grievous to their cause. Slaves, to say the least, did not see slavery as in their best interests. Instead of working contentedly on their plantation or acting as the gullible "victims" of abolitionist propaganda, slaves took matters into their own hands. They used their own informal intelligence network to monitor the war's progress. When circumstances allowed, many made the hazardous journey to Union lines, where they often faced considerable suspicion, hostility, and racism. Many freed slaves volunteered for Union forces, where they worked as military laborers, acted as spies and scouts, or served as soldiers in the Union army.[58] Even those slaves who chose to stay behind often displayed far greater defiance and resistance to their masters. In helping to destroy slavery, slaves needed little prodding from abolitionist propaganda. Slaves, in fact, exerted great influence on northern public opinion and policy makers. The agency of slaves—their desire for freedom when offered even the faintest hint of liberty—helped transform northern war aims to include the end of slavery as well as the preservation of the Union.[59]

ECONOMIC MODERNIZATION AND THE NEW SOUTH

After their vision of a modern slaveholding economy failed so disastrously, how did the most devoted adherents of the Confederacy respond to national reunification? Some left for Mexico, Brazil, and other foreign lands, while Edmund Ruffin, ever the extremist, decided to end his life rather than submit to the "perfidious, malignant and vile Yankee race."[60] Other ex-Confederates, however, made a surprisingly swift transition back to the Union. Racism and the return to "home rule" after Reconstruction certainly made it far easier for ex-Confederates to return to the nation they had once denounced. Slavery may have been abolished, but the North's failure to protect the political and economic rights of African Americans allowed ex-Confederates to reestablish racial hierarchies through segregation and political disenfranchisement. By the late nineteenth century, racism provided an all-too-common bond that united white northerners and white southerners.

The modernizing impulse, so prominent in secessionist thought, also helped bridge the divide between the Old South and the New South. The same economic desires that captured the imagination of secessionists in the antebellum era—railroads, improved agriculture, and economic diversification—animated ex-Confederates during Reconstruction and the Gilded Age. Seeking to improve agricultural practices, late nineteenth-century southerners supported a network of experimental stations and agricultural colleges. They also expanded and solidified the region's railroad network. Big cities and small towns alike clamored for better railroad connections, often with great success. By 1890 nine out of every ten southerners lived in a railroad county.[61] City boosters, reiterating the promise of economic diversification, vigorously competed to capture trade and attract capital. "Agriculture, manufacturers, mining, and commerce must unite to make a state prosperous," proclaimed one southern newspaper in 1883.[62]

In their headlong pursuit of economic success, Gilded Age boosters believed that they were creating a "New South" that broke decisively with the nostalgic antebellum world of stately plantations, romantic cavaliers, and content slaves. Even younger Virginians who had supported economic modernization in the 1850s, historian Peter Carmichael has found, increasingly turned to nostalgic interpretations of the Old South.[63] The mythology of a valiant Confederacy—defending noble, if ultimately doomed, aristocratic ideals—allowed white southerners to reconcile their past and their present. They cherished memories of valor, sacrifice, and honor, while at the same time recognizing that the rise of big business and rapid economic change made the destruction of slavery inevitable. New South boosters, in fact, portrayed slavery and the values it spawned as antithetical to the modern world of industry and commerce. According to historian Paul M. Gaston, New South boosters believed that "slavery and a spirit of anti-industrialism had been responsible for the South's great failure; the New South must root out all remnants of that heritage."[64] Slavery thus belonged to a nostalgic world forever lost except in bittersweet memories.

In portraying plantation slavery and economic modernity as polar opposites, New South boosters presented themselves as revolutionaries seeking to modernize an agrarian, preindustrial economy. This bit of mythmaking gave New South boosters a ray of hope for their own economic future. Antebellum southerners had not built railroads and cities, the New South boosters reasoned, because they had not really tried to do so. In reality, the imagination of Confederate secessionists, filled with dreams of cities, factories, and commerce, had foreshadowed the ambitions of the New South. Though lost in a haze of nostalgia and romance, secessionist rhetoric and economic policies had established one of the most enduring continuities of southern history: the quest for a dynamic, diversified, and modern economy.

*statistical appendix*

# THE ORIGINS AND IMPACT
# OF SHIFTING CULTIVATION

Why did antebellum southerners cultivate significantly less land within their farms and plantations than northern farmers? A number of different factors may have been at work. Environmental conditions—such as poor soils, unfavorable climatic conditions, and difficult topography—might have played a significant role. The same might be said, though, for slavery (which may have encouraged ruthless mining of the soil), crop choice (cotton may have depleted the soil faster than grains), levels of economic development (proximity to railroads and markets might well have encouraged more intensive cultivation), and cultural factors (such as the greater love of leisure among southern yeomen). While historians are often leery of using statistics, such methods can test these differing explanations.

One of the most effective statistical tools for determining the role of certain variables is the multivariate regression. A regression might be thought of as a statistical equation with independent and dependent variables, here presented in tabular form. Independent variables can be thought of as the factors that may or may not influence the dependent variable, which is the percentage of improved land within southern farms. The independent variables—appearing on the left side of Table A.1—include geography and climate, railroads and urbanization, and crop choice. What makes regression analysis so useful is that it is relatively easy to determine whether or not an independent variable is influencing the dependent variable. Another important feature of regression analysis is that it holds constant all other specified independent variables when analyzing any one independent variable. Scholars can thus isolate the impact of particular variables in ways that other statistical methods (such as correlations) do not allow.

In the regressions in Table A.1, the data presented comes from the 1860 census, which reported the number of improved and unimproved acres in farms. The census data is most usefully analyzed on the county level; we can analyze variations in the percentage of improved land over nearly 700 counties in eight southern states. The independent variables classify each of these 700 counties according to soil type, topography, and level of economic development.[1] For soil type, I used data from the State Soil Geographic Database (STATSGO) to determine if alfisols were the primary soils of a county or at least important secondary soils. Out of the 698 southern counties, 110 counties contained mostly alfisols, while another 232 contained smaller stretches of alfisols. Ultisols (the acidic, infertile soils noted in chapter 1) dominated the rest of the counties. To capture the impact of topography, southern counties were grouped into seven major areas. Topography is important because one would naturally expect mountainous land in Appalachia or marshy land near the coast to have lower levels of improved land than easily drained plains. Another independent variable accounts for counties that most likely suffered from southern cattle fever.[2]

Most of the independent variables are dummy variables that are basically "yes" or "no" responses to a particular question. For the railroad variable, for example, a county with a railroad receives a value of 1 (a statistical "yes"), while a county without a railroad receives a value of 0 (a statistical "no"). The coefficient is the impact of a "yes" response. To use the railroad variable as an example, the coefficient reported in Table A.1 is 5.3, which means that a railroad added 5.3 percentage points to a county's percentage of improved land. Farmers and planters in a county without a railroad that cultivated 40 percent of its improved land, the regression predicts, would have cultivated 45.3 of its land if a railroad had been built. Notice that the coefficient is significant at the 99 percent level, which is an excellent indication that the result is not some sort of statistical illusion. As noted earlier, a regression holds the impact of all the specified variables constant. In this case, the coefficient of the railroad variable measures the impact of railroad access after taking into account soil type, topography, urbanization, and crop choice.

The regression results show the powerful impact of environmental factors on levels of improved land. Counties primarily composed of alfisols, in fact, added ten to twelve percentage points of improved land. The effect for counties that contained only partial strips of alfisols, as one would expect, was somewhat less, but both variables were statistically significant. As for topography, the limestone basins (which included the Kentucky Bluegrass region and the Nashville basin) had a higher percentage of improved land than the other areas. The large negative coefficient for the coastal flatwoods—an area well known for its pine barrens and poorly drained marshlands—is particularly striking because many of the South's largest port cities were located in that region. The negative coefficient for the cattle fever variable is also statistically significant, suggesting that livestock disease made continuous cultivation far more difficult in the Cotton South. Because the ticks that carried southern cattle fever thrived in heat and humidity, this variable could also be picking up the negative impact of the Deep South's climate on fodder crops and improved pastures.

Notice that the two indicators of general economic development—the presence of railroads and cities (defined as urban areas over 5,000 residents)—had relatively small impacts on levels of improved land. The railroad variable is positive and statistically significant, but the magnitude of the coefficient indicates that railroads had less impact than the environmental variables. As for cities, the regressions show no statistically significant relationship between urbanization and the percentage of improved land after controlling for other factors. Most southern cities were ports located in the marshy and sandy coastal plain that was poorly suited for intensive cultivation. Taken as a whole, the regression results indicate that shifting cultivation was the result of southern climate and geography and not a lack of markets.

Crop choice is another potentially important issue. Could southern

TABLE A.1 Determining the Percentage of Improved Land: County-Level Regression Results for Nine Southern States, 1860

| | (T-statistics below Coefficients) | | |
|---|---|---|---|
| Independent Variable or Diagnostic Statistic | Geography and Climate | Addition of Railroads and Cities | Addition of Crop Choice |
| Intercept (Piedmont counties) | 39.7** | 37.7** | 34.02** |
| | (31.57) | (29.2) | (23.48) |
| Coastal flatwood | −19.3** | −18.7** | −15.0** |
| | (−8.96) | (−8.78) | (−7.16) |
| Coastal plain | −6.9** | −6.39** | −6.1** |
| | (−4.76) | (−4.48) | (−4.42) |
| Mountains and ridges | −16.4** | −15.3** | −13.5** |
| | (−11.51) | (−10.70) | (−9.41) |
| Hills and valleys | −11.8** | −10.6** | −7.53** |
| | (−6.50) | (−5.91) | (−4.21) |
| Miss. alluvial and black prairies | −9.0* | −8.71** | −9.27** |
| | (−4.23) | (−4.20) | (−4.49) |
| Limestone basins | 15.8** | 16.3** | 18.23** |
| | (7.49) | (7.84) | (9.01) |
| Primary alfisol | 12.3** | 10.9** | 10.02** |
| | (7.72) | (6.84) | (6.55) |

**Significant at 1 percent level
*Significant at 5 percent level

|  | (T-statistics below Coefficients) | | |
| --- | --- | --- | --- |
| Independent Variable or Diagnostic Statistic | Geography and Climate | Addition of Railroads and Cities | Addition of Crop Choice |
| Secondary alfisol | 4.2** (2.75) | 3.74** (3.49) | 3.2** (3.11) |
| Southern cattle fever | −4.2** (−3.88) | −4.0** (−3.08) | −5.4** (−4.21) |
| Railroad county | — | 5.31** (5.05) | 3.8** (3.80) |
| Urban county | — | 0.01 (0.30) | 1.8 (.073) |
| Wheat | — | — | 8.10** (6.74) |
| Cotton | — | — | 8.99** (6.30) |
| Tobacco | — | — | −1.3 (−.07) |
| Adjusted R-squared | .476 | .500 | .556 |
| F-statistic | 71.29 | 63.13 | 61.19 |
| Degrees of freedom | 688 | 686 | 683 |

Sources: Census statistics at Geostat Center, University of Virginia Library, <http://fisher.lib.virginia.edu/collections/stats/histcensus/>; soil orders classified according using Soil Survey Staff, Natural Resources Conservation Service, USDA, "U.S. General Soil Map (STATSGO)," <http://soildatamart.nrcs.usda.gov>. Please see the appendix text for topographical classifications. Most counties in Mississippi, Alabama, Georgia, and South Carolina are classified as southern cattle fever counties.

staples such as cotton, tobacco, and corn deplete the land more rapidly than wheat and other crops more likely to grow in the North? To test this proposition, the regressions in Table A.1 contain dummy variables representing counties in the top quartile of wheat, cotton, and tobacco production. The wheat variable has a statistically significant and relatively large coefficient, which suggests that grain farmers in Virginia and other areas of the Upper South were more likely to integrate livestock and crops into a mixed-farming regime. The argument that special characteristics of cotton and tobacco accounted for shifting cultivation, however, receives little support. Cotton, in fact, was associated with more, not less, improved land. The large coefficient for the cotton variable suggests that planters brought more marginal land into cultivation in response to the high prices of the 1850s. Notice that, even with the inclusion of the crop-choice variables, almost all of the coefficients of the geographic and climatic variables remain statistically significant.

What about the relationship between slavery and shifting cultivation? As a first step to understanding the impact of slavery, Graph A.1 charts the percentage of improved land and the percentage of the population enslaved for each county. On the bottom left-hand corner there is a large clustering of counties with both a low percentage of improved land and a low percentage of slaves. Almost all of these counties, not surprisingly, were located in the mountainous southern Upcountry. In the middle of the graph are counties with intermediate to high percentages of slaves and intermediate or high levels of improved land, including counties in the Alabama and Mississippi Black Belt, the southern piedmont, and the limestone areas. ("Intermediate" and "high," of course, are only in relation to the South; planters in many of these counties improved less land than most northern farmers). On the bottom right-hand corner is a smaller group of counties with high concentrations of slaves but low levels of improved land. Most of these counties were located along the coast of the Carolinas and Georgia, where rice planters intensively cultivated a small number of acres and left most of their poorly drained "provisioning" lands unimproved. Overall, Figure A.1 indicates that antebellum slavery was a flexible institution suitable for both shifting cultivation and continuous cultivation.

Ideally, one would like to econometrically test the relationship between slavery and levels of improved land in a regression that holds soil quality, topography, and climate constant. When slavery is inserted into

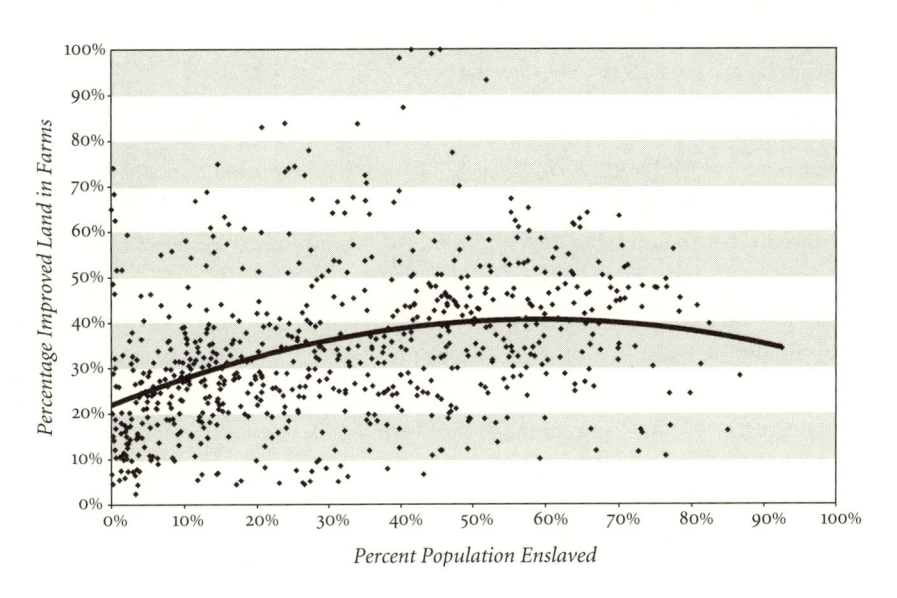

GRAPH A.1   THE RELATIONSHIP BETWEEN SLAVERY AND THE PERCENTAGE OF IMPROVED LAND IN FARMS

the equations in Table A.1, the coefficient shows a strongly positive (and statistically significant) relationship with higher levels of improved land. Counties with more slaves, simply put, had more improved land when all the other environmental and economic variables are taken into account. Adding slavery to the regressions, though, is bedeviled with what econometricians call an "endogeniety bias": it is impossible to tell with county-level data whether slavery caused more land to be improved or whether slaveholders simply preferred to locate in areas with the best soils and best access to transportation. Statistical tests can correct for the endogeniety bias, but they do not work well given the limitations of the census data.[3] The nonlinear relationship between slavery and levels of improved land increases skepticism about the econometric evidence. It makes little sense to suppose that the lack of slave labor was a major reason for low levels of improved land in the southern uplands; it also makes little sense to suppose that Carolina rice planters improved a small percentage of their land because they somehow possessed too many slaves.[4] The evidence suggests that the slavery coefficient reflected underlying environmental conditions rather than acting as an important variable in its own right. Slavery (or its absence) did not "cause" shifting cultivation, strengthening the point that environmental factors played the most important role.

*Statistical Appendix*

## MANUFACTURING AND SHIFTING CULTIVATION

From the standpoint of an individual planter or farmer, shifting cultivation could work reasonably well as long as there was enough reserve land. Having large tracts of unimproved land in reserve, though, was a major impediment to southern development. Adding unimproved acres led to larger farms and larger plantations without increasing the size of the workforce, thus reducing population densities. Regional comparisons highlight the inability of the rural South to replicate the dense settlement patterns that predominated in the North. Throughout the nineteenth century, the various subregions of the North had far denser rural populations than the subregions of the South (Table A.2). By 1860 even the recently settled Midwest had a nearly two-to-one advantage over the long-settled South Atlantic region in rural population density. When put in terms of *free* rural residents—the group much more likely to buy consumer goods, subscribe to newspapers, and support schools and voluntary societies—the northern advantage in 1860 was as high as five to one. Slavery and shifting cultivation worked together to stunt the development of southern markets.

One might worry that Table A.2 overstates the impact of shifting cultivation because it uses the census definition of "rural" as any town with less than 2,500 persons. Some of the North's higher rural population density might have resulted from small-town artisans, merchants, and manufacturers rather than from thick networks of family farmers. The census did not distinguish between farm and nonfarm rural population until the twentieth century, but scholars have derived estimates from 1860 occupational data that indicates that 40 percent of the northern rural population lived in nonfarm households, while approximately 20 percent of the southern rural population lived in nonfarm households.[5] Subtracting each region's rural nonfarm households narrows the North's lead in farm population but hardly erases it. Northern states in 1860 still had a substantial advantage in farm population per square mile (23.3 to 15.9) and an overwhelming advantage in free farm population per square mile (23.3 to 10.3). The large nonfarm population of the rural North, of course, was not completely exogenous, as one would expect denser farm populations to create more demand for services and locally manufactured goods.

Facing low population densities and a large slave population, southern manufacturers would have served far smaller markets. To test the

TABLE A.2    Rural Population Densities, 1790–1890

| Region | 1790 | 1800 | 1810 | 1820 | 1830 | 1840 | 1850 | 1860 | 1870 | 1880 | 1890 |
|---|---|---|---|---|---|---|---|---|---|---|---|
| New England (w/o Maine) | 22.0 | 27.9 | 33.7 | 38.5 | 44.1 | 47.8 | 51.0 | 51.5 | 49.6 | 48.5 | 45.0 |
| Mid-Atlantic | 11.2 | 14.7 | 19.7 | 25.3 | 31.6 | 42.8 | 43.8 | 48.3 | 49.4 | 52.9 | 53.8 |
| Old Northwest | — | — | — | 5.8 | 10.6 | 19.4 | 26.2 | 35.0 | 40.5 | 44.5 | 44.3 |
| South Atlantic | 7.2 | 9.1 | 10.7 | 12.4 | 14.7 | 15.7 | 18.2 | 20.3 | 20.9 | 26.2 | 30.8 |
| (free pop.) | (4.6) | (5.7) | (6.4) | (7.2) | (8.5) | (9.2) | (10.6) | (11.7) | | | |
| South Central | 1.4 | 4.0 | 8.2 | 12.1 | 16.7 | 19.4 | 23.3 | 25.9 | 28.3 | 34.9 | 37.4 |
| (free pop.) | (1.2) | (3.4) | (6.7) | (9.5) | (12.9) | (14.9) | (17.8) | (19.7) | | | |
| Old Southwest | — | — | — | 2.3 | 4.3 | 8.5 | 12.1 | 15.6 | 16.0 | 21.2 | 24.2 |
| (free pop.) | | | | (1.3) | (2.2) | (4.1) | (5.8) | (7.1) | | | |

Notes and Sources: New England: Maine, New Hampshire, Vermont, Massachusetts, Rhode Island, and Connecticut; Mid-Atlantic: New York, New Jersey, Pennsylvania, Delaware, and Maryland; Old Northwest: Ohio, Indiana, and Illinois; South Atlantic: Virginia, West Virginia, North Carolina, South Carolina, and Georgia; South Central: Kentucky and Tennessee; Old Southwest: Alabama, Mississippi, and Louisiana. Calculated from *U.S. Census of Population: 1970*, vol. 1, pt. 1 (Washington, D.C., 1970), I-62–I-71.

proposition that these small markets retarded the development of local manufacturing, Table A.3 presents regressions that use the per capita value added of "demand-driven" manufacturing in 1860 as a dependent variable. Demand-driven manufacturing includes agricultural implements and wagons, building and construction, textiles, iron products, machinery, and a host of miscellaneous consumer goods.[6] Processing industries such as milling, lumber, and turpentine production, the location of which depended on proximity to key natural resources and not on consumer demand, were excluded from the calculations. Processing, of course, was an important element of early industrialization. America's vast timber reserves, for example, profoundly influenced the furniture industry and building trades. Yet timber became important for early industrialization only when it was converted to furniture, homes, buildings, tools, and implements, which is precisely what the "demand-driven"

*Statistical Appendix*

TABLE A.3  Shifting Cultivation, Slavery, and Per Capita Value Added for "Demand-Driven" Manufacturing, 1860

| | (T-statistics below Coefficients) | | | | | | |
|---|---|---|---|---|---|---|---|
| | Total Demand-Driven Manufacturing | Farm Implements and Wagons | Textiles | Building and Construction | Machinery | Iron Products | Consumer Goods and Miscellaneous |
| Intercept | .46 | −.108** | .16 | −.064 | .248 | .418* | −.106 |
| | (.96) | (−2.73) | (.35) | (−.69) | (1.85) | (2.27) | (−.42) |
| Percent improved land | .0823** | .0064** | .0044* | .016** | −.0033 | .36 | .0496** |
| | (6.59) | (5.92) | (2.39) | (6.3) | (−.94) | (.73) | (7.2) |
| Percent population enslaved | −.0466** | −.0065 | −.0021 | −.0074** | −.0054 | −1.52** | −.016** |
| | (−4.18) | (−.67) | (−.54) | (−3.26) | (−1.67) | (−3.4) | (−2.61) |
| Railroad | 1.85** | .028 | .49** | .16 | .14 | .409** | .616** |
| | (4.51) | (.79) | (3.33) | (1.88) | (1.16) | (2.49) | (2.72) |
| City greater than 5,000 | 15.54** | .51** | 1.41** | 1.48** | 2.7** | 1.98** | 7.48** |
| | (15.62) | (5.98) | (4.01) | (7.3) | (9.36) | (4.98) | (13.64) |
| Wheat | −.37 | .011 | −.18 | −.13 | .007 | .18 | −.26 |
| | (−.79) | (.48) | (−1.06) | (.096) | (.052) | (.96) | (−1.0) |

**Significant at the 1 percent level
*Significant at the 5 percent level

|  | Total Demand-Driven Manu-facturing | Farm Implements and Wagons | Textiles | Building and Construction | Machinery | Iron Products | Consumer Goods and Miscellaneous |
|---|---|---|---|---|---|---|---|
| Cotton | .94 | .06 | −.001 | .119 | .44** | .055 | .313 |
|  | (1.66) | (1.23) | (−.006) | (1.72) | (2.69) | (.24) | (.634) |
| Tobacco | −.22 | .096* | −.21 | −.02 | −.013 | .198 | −.262 |
|  | (−.49) | (2.47) | (−1.3) | (−.23) | (−.099) | (1.09) | (−1.05) |
| Mean of dependent variable | 3.14 | .17 | .48 | .38 | .21 | .38 | 1.53 |
| Adjusted R-square | .380 | .139 | .07 | .156 | .136 | .073 | .33 |
| F-statistic | 55.98 | 15.44 | 7.02 | 17.5 | 15.14 | 8.11 | 43.78 |
| Degrees of freedom | 621 | 621 | 621 | 621 | 621 | 621 | 621 |

(T-statistics below Coefficients)

Notes and Sources: "Demand-driven manufacturing" excludes processing industries (flour and meal, leather, distilled liquor, lumber, provisions, rice cleaning, sugar refining, timber cutting, manufactured tobacco, and tar and turpentine) and mining (coal, copper, gold, iron, and salt). I thank Viken Tchakerian for graciously providing the manufacturing data, which was derived from *Manufacturers of the United States in 1860* (Washington, D.C.: Government Printing Office, 1865).

variable measures.⁷ Acting alone and without links to other markets, processing industries were not likely to lead to widespread industrialization.

To test the impact of shifting cultivation and other variables on demand-driven manufacturing, Table A.3 shows a series of regressions. Because it contains such a large amount of information, Table A.3 is somewhat tricky to read. Each column is a separate regression with a different dependent variable. The dependent variable for the first regression is the per capita value added of demand-driven manufacturing on the county level; the independent variables include percentage of improved land, percentage of population enslaved, the presence of a city, the presence of railroads, and various crop-choice variables. The other six columns essentially break down demand-driven manufacturing into six separate categories: farm implements and wagons, textiles, building and construction, machinery, iron, and consumer goods (ranging from shoes to books and clocks). Each of these variables acts as a dependent variable as one reads down the column to see the impact of the various independent variables.

The results show a strong relationship between access to markets and demand-driven manufacturing. Urbanization and railroads, two proxies for market access, clearly spurred more demand-driven industry. The performance of the urbanization variable is especially impressive. With all other factors held constant, southern counties with a city larger than 5,000 residents had more than four times per capita value added than the southern average. Most southern cities specialized in the collection of staples, but they nevertheless created an agglomeration of consumers that led to far more demand-driven manufacturing than other counties. Some historians have argued that cotton, tobacco, and other southern staple crops provided far fewer linkages to local manufacturing that wheat and other grains. The regression results provide little support for such arguments. The coefficient for the wheat variable (a dummy representing the top quarter of wheat-producing counties) is statistically insignificant and has the wrong expected sign.

The regression results indicate that both slavery and shifting cultivation limited demand-driven manufacturing in the South. Results show that, while holding the other variables constant, a county with half of its population enslaved would have about 50 percent less demand-driven manufacturing (in per capita value-added terms) than a county with no slaves. These results strongly support a long literature that has argued that slaves purchased painfully few consumer goods, while wealthy planters often bypassed local manufacturers in favor of imported goods from the North or abroad.[8] Shifting cultivation had an even bigger impact than slavery; the regression implies that if southerners had improved the same percentage of the land as the nation as a whole in 1860, they would have increased per capita value added in demand-driven industries by 58.4 percent.

To ensure that the results are not the product of the industrial classifications, I estimated regressions for more specific industries. Improving more land had little impact on the production of machinery and iron products, which presumably required larger, more capital-intensive plants better suited to urban locations than rural ones. On the other extreme, a higher percentage of improved land was associated with a large increase in the building and construction trades, as more people created more demand for these highly localized industries. Higher levels of improved land were also positively associated with increased production of textiles, agricultural implements, and a host of consumer goods. Although these goods were often traded regionally or even nationally, it seems reasonable to surmise that dense rural populations still supported considerable local production. The recent literature on early industrialization has demonstrated how fairly modest workshops subdivided routine tasks and made incremental technological advances to increase productivity.[9] In such an economic environment, local producers could find important niches even in the face of national competition. The key requirement for such local manufacturing was a large market, something that both slavery and shifting cultivation clearly discouraged.

SHIFTING CULTIVATION IN THE POSTBELLUM ERA

In the postbellum era, the continued development of the railroad network—combined with greater investment in agricultural research—gradually raised the percentage of improved land in southern farms. After the Civil War, the region's railroad network expanded dramatically, so that by 1890 90 percent of the southern population lived in a county that had a least one railroad station. The quality of rail service also improved, as large trunk lines integrated individual lines into coherent networks with standardized gauges. The expansion of the region's railroad network contributed to a dramatic increase in urbanization, particularly in upland

TABLE A.4  The Continuing Importance of Environmental Factors in the Postbellum Era: County-Level Regression Results for Nine Southern States, 1890

|  | (T-statistics below Coefficients) | | |
| --- | --- | --- | --- |
| Independent Variable or Diagnostic Statistic | Geography and Climate | Addition of Railroads and Cities | Addition of Crop Choice |
| Intercept (Piedmont counties) | 50.6** | 45.0** | 43.2** |
|  | (32.0) | (25.2) | (22.8) |
| Coastal flatwood | −19.6** | −19.5** | −15.2** |
|  | (−9.4) | (−9.6) | (−7.3) |
| Coastal plain | −7.4** | −6.6** | −4.7** |
|  | (−5.1) | (−4.6) | (−3.2) |
| Mountains and ridges | −12.5** | −11.5** | −9.5** |
|  | (−7.9) | (−7.44) | (−6.0) |
| Hills and valleys | −5.5** | −4.6** | −3.9* |
|  | (−2.8) | (−2.6) | (−2.2) |
| Miss. alluvial and black prairies | −2.0** | −1.9** | −4.2** |
|  | (−.9) | (−.9) | (−2.15) |
| Limestone plains | 16.6** | 15.3** | 16.5** |
|  | (7.9) | (6.7) | (7.5) |
| Primary alfisol | 13.3** | 11.6** | 11.4** |
|  | (8.4) | (7.4) | (7.5) |

**Significant at 1 percent level
*Significant at 5 percent level

|  | (T-statistics below Coefficients) | | |
| --- | --- | --- | --- |
| Independent Variable or Diagnostic Statistic | Geography and Climate | Addition of Railroads and Cities | Addition of Crop Choice |
| Secondary alfisol | 3.2** | 2.6** | 2.5* |
|  | (3.0) | (2.5) | (2.4) |
| Southern cattle fever | −7.9** | −8.9** | −12.0** |
|  | (−6.5) | (−7.3) | (−9.5) |
| Railroad county | — | 6.9** | 6.68** |
|  |  | (5.6) | (5.6) |
| Urban county | — | 6.6** | 7.7** |
|  |  | (4.1) | (4.8) |
| Wheat | — | — | 1.4 |
|  |  |  | (1.2) |
| Cotton | — | — | 9.8** |
|  |  |  | (7.5) |
| Tobacco | — | — | .8 |
|  |  |  | (.71) |
| Adjusted R-squared | .48 | .52 | .55 |
| F-statistic | 81.2 | 75.8 | 67.9 |
| Degrees of freedom | 766 | 764 | 761 |

Sources: Census statistics at Geostat Center, University of Virginia Library, <http://fisher.lib.virginia.edu/collections/stats/histcensus/>. Soil orders classified according using Soil Survey Staff, Natural Resources Conservation Service, USDA, "U.S. General Soil Map STATSGO)," <http://soildatamart.nrcs.usda.gov>. Please see the appendix text for topographical classifications. Counties with southern cattle fever classified according to "Map Showing Boundary Line of District Infected with Splenetic or Southern Cattle Fever, as Defined in Order of Hon. J. M. Rusk, Secretary of Agriculture" (Washington, D.C., 1891).

areas that had been relatively isolated before the Civil War.[10] Within agriculture itself, phosphate emerged as a relatively inexpensive fertilizer for southern planters and farmers. Federal and state experimental stations provided advice and technical support about fertilizers and other cultivation practices for those wishing to adopt more intensive agriculture. In light of these changes, it is not surprising that shifting cultivation gradually declined and the percentage of improved land within southern farms gradually increased between 1880 and 1920. By the turn of the century, southerners improved a higher percentage of their land than did farmers in New England, where a sharp drop in wool prices led farmers to abandon many of their improved pastures.[11]

These important technological developments and institutional changes, however, did not suddenly sweep aside the South's severe environmental constraints. The regional differences in land-use patterns remained, as farmers in the cotton states still lagged far behind their middle Atlantic and midwestern counterparts. In 1920 farmers in North Carolina, South Carolina, Georgia, Alabama, Mississippi, and Louisiana—despite the spread of railroads, the growth of cities, and the introduction of new fertilizers—still cultivated a lower percentage of their land than Ohio farmers had in 1850. Advocates of continuous cultivation within the South, according to historian Gilbert Fite, often expressed keen disappointment at the slow rate of progress. Fite attributes the southern failure to fully adopt continuous cultivation to ingrained traditionalism and the South's reliance on cotton, but he also notes that environmental factors hindered progress: "The natural grasses and forage in much of the South were less nutritious than those found in the Midwest. To get satisfactory pastures and hay in the Deep South the soil had to be plowed, planted, and fertilized at considerable expense.... In addition, southern livestock was subject to diseases that caused heavy losses. Swine and fowl cholera were common, and Texas fever became so widespread that in the early 1880s it was being referred to by a veterinarian in the USDA as 'Southern Cattle fever.'"[12]

Regression analysis for 1890, using many of the same variables as the 1860 specifications, confirms Fite's observations (Table A.4). Initial soil quality, despite the introduction of cheaper fertilizers, still had a significant impact. Counties composed mostly of alfisols continued to improve at least 10 percent more land than counties possessing ultisols or other soils. The coefficients for the 1890 topographical variables generally remain statistically significant and have the same signs as those in the 1860 regressions. Farmers on limestone plains continued to cultivate a far higher percentage of their land than farmers living in other topographical regions, while the marshy, coastal flatwoods lagged especially far behind. Southern cattle fever, which had spread to several areas in the Upper South during the Civil War, grew even worse in 1890. Farmers in counties with southern cattle fever cultivated 8 to 12 percent less land after taking into account the other variables. In Virginia, for example, the percentage of improved land in twenty-three newly infected counties declined from 44 percent to less than 40 percent between 1860 and 1890, whereas the percentage of improved land within the state as a whole increased from 37 percent to 48 percent.[13]

In contrast to the 1860 results, the regressions show that cities and railroads in the 1890s significantly influenced land-use patterns. In 1860 railroads and cities had only a small impact on the percentage of improved land, but by 1890 farmers in a county with a railroad connection and a city improved nearly 14 percent more land than their nonrailroad, nonurban counterparts. What accounts for this change? Southern railroads and urbanization before the Civil War had been focused on linking plantation districts to port cities. The postbellum extension of the rail network to the southern uplands, working in conjunction with increased urbanization, seems to have "unlocked" high-quality alfisol soils in Appalachia. Indeed, the percentage of improved land between 1860 and 1890 increased faster in the southern uplands than in any other region. Notice, too, that the dummy variable representing a county in the top quartile in cotton production is statistically significant. The continued expansion of the South's cotton culture might well have incorporated previously marginal acreage that had gone unimproved. The completion of levees on the Mississippi River, in particular, created rich new land for cotton in Black Belt areas.[14] Within the state of Mississippi, for example, farmers and planters in the eleven counties bordering the Mississippi River increased the percentage of improved land from 36 percent in 1860 to 52.5 percent in 1890, a figure far higher than the statewide average of 40 percent. The struggle to achieve even modest increases in improved acreage via expensive levee shows how southerners were still struggling to conquer nature in 1890.

# NOTES

INTRODUCTION

1 "A Century Hence," undated manuscript, John C. Rutherfoord Papers, Virginia Historical Society, MSS 1R9337632–50. For information on Rutherfoord, see William A Link, *Roots of Secession: Slavery and Politics in Antebellum Virginia* (Chapel Hill: University of North Carolina Press, 2003), 142–44. Peter S. Carmichael analyzes young Virginia secessionists—most of whom stressed bringing about a more modern economy—in *The Last Generation: Young Virginians in Peace, War, and Revolution* (Chapel Hill: University of North Carolina Press, 2005), 35–58.
2 L.C.B. [pseud.], "The Country in 1950; or, The Conservatism of Slavery," *Southern Literary Messenger* 22 (June 1856): 426.
3 Ibid., 438–39.
4 Benedict Anderson, *Imagined Communities: Reflections on the Origin and Spread of Nationalism* (New York: Verso Press, 1983). For an application of Anderson's framework to the Confederacy, see Drew Faust, *The Creation of*

*Confederate Nationalism: Ideology and Identity in the Civil War South* (Baton Rouge: Louisiana State University Press, 1988), 1–21.

5 George W. Randolph in *Proceedings of the Virginia State Convention of 1861*, vol. 1, ed. George H. Reese (Richmond: Virginia State Library, 1965), 740.

6 John Townsend, *The Southern States, Their Present Peril and Their Certain Remedy* (Charleston: E. C. Councell, 1850), 21. It should be noted that at this point in his career, Townsend was a cooperationist who opposed independent state secession in favor of united action by a number of southern states. By 1860 he had become a supporter of independent state secession.

7 For an excellent discussion of why extremism flourished in South Carolina, see William W. Freehling, *The Road to Disunion*, vol. 1, *Secessionists at Bay, 1776–1854* (New York: Oxford University Press, 1990), 213–52.

8 The phrase is borrowed from Edward L. Ayers, Gary W. Gallagher, and Andrew J. Torget, *The Crucible of the Civil War: Virginia from Secession to Commemoration* (Charlottesville: University of Virginia Press, 2006).

9 Using a neo-Marxist theoretical framework, Eugene Genovese interpreted southern planters as "an essentially prebourgeois ruling class." See, for example, the Wesleyan edition of *The World the Slaveholders Made: Two Essays in Interpretation* (Middletown, Conn.: Wesleyan University Press, 1988), xxvi, 3–20, 95–102. Genovese added more nuance to his argument in *The Slaveholders' Dilemma: Freedom and Progress in Southern Conservative Thought, 1820–1860* (Columbia: University of South Carolina Press, 1992).

10 James M. McPherson, *Drawn with the Sword* (New York: Oxford University Press, 1996), 22. For a similar take on the antebellum South and the Confederacy, see Marc Egnal, *Divergent Paths: How Culture and Institutions Have Shaped North American Growth* (New York: Oxford University Press, 1996), 52–68, 87–101. Roger L. Ransom's sophisticated counterfactual analysis argues that Confederates would have rejected measures to modernize their economy; see *The Confederate States of America: What Might Have Been* (New York: W. W. Norton, 2005), 188–97.

11 John Lauritz Larson, *Internal Improvement: National Public Works and the Promise of Popular Government in the Early United States* (Chapel Hill: University of North Carolina Press, 2001), 115. For a critical analysis of the broader Jacksonian opposition to federal improvements, see Richard R. John, *Spreading the News: The American Postal System from Franklin to Morse* (Cambridge: Harvard University Press, 1995), 206–56. Robin L. Einhorn connects slavery to antigovernment sentiments in *American Taxation, American Slavery* (Chicago: University of Chicago Press, 2006).

12 James McCardell, *The Idea of a Southern Nation: Southern Nationalists and Southern Nationalism, 1830–1860* (New York: W. W. Norton, 1979), 91–240.

William Barney offers a somewhat similar analysis in *The Road to Secession: A New Perspective on the Old South* (New York: Praeger Publishers, 1972), 3–48.

13  Lacy K. Ford Jr., *The Origins of Southern Radicalism: The South Carolina Upcountry, 1800–1860* (New York: Oxford University Press, 1988), 215–77.

14  Ford, *Origins of Southern Radicalism*, 337. Link, *Roots of Secession*, adds another layer to Ford's argument. Economic development, Link argues, led to practices such as slave hiring in Virginia's cities. With few controls over slaves in the cities, many white Virginians became increasingly sensitive to internal divisions and the infiltration of abolitionist doctrines, thus feeding the secessionist impulse.

15  Margaret Mitchell, *Gone with the Wind* (New York: Macmillan Company, 1936), 6, 108.

16  Tony Horwitz, *Confederates in the Attic: Dispatches from the Unfinished Civil War* (New York: Vintage Books, 1998), 77.

17  The historical literature that stresses the essentially modern character of the southern economy and southern planters is quite large. Robert William Fogel and Stanley L. Engerman stress the modern, capitalistic elements of southern slavery in *Time on the Cross: The Economics of American Negro Slavery* (Boston: Little, Brown and Company, 1974). For an updated version of the Fogel and Engerman arguments, see Robert William Fogel, *Without Consent or Contract: The Rise and Fall of American Slavery* (New York: W. W. Norton, 1989), 60–153. A number of economists have criticized Fogel and Engerman's specific conclusions, but even these critics largely portray southern planters as capitalistic. See, for example, Gavin Wright, *Slavery and American Economic Development* (Baton Rouge: Louisiana State University Press, 2006). Among historians, the current tendency is to stress modern elements within the southern political economy. Examples of this type of analysis include James Oakes, *The Ruling Race: A History of American Slaveholders* (New York: Alfred A. Knopf, 1982), 69–95; James L. Huston, *Calculating the Value of the Union: Slavery, Property Rights, and the Economic Origins of the Civil War* (Chapel Hill: University of North Carolina Press, 2003), 24–41; Brian Schoen, "The Fragile Fabric of Union: The Cotton South, Federal Politics, and the Atlantic World, 1783–1861" (Ph.D. diss., University of Virginia, 2004); William Dusinberre, *Them Dark Days: Slavery in the American Rice Swamps* (New York: Oxford University Press, 1996), 285–301; and Mark M. Smith, *Mastered by the Clock: Time, Slavery, and Freedom in the American South* (Chapel Hill: University of North Carolina Press, 1997), 69–92. In 1924 Robert Royal Russel described progovernment impulses within secessionist thought in *Economic Aspects of Southern Sectionalism, 1840–1861* (Urbana: University

of Illinois Press, 1924). Russel later expressed disappointment that his "findings have not been incorporated to a great extent in general accounts" of southern secession (*Critical Studies in Antebellum Sectionalism: Essays in American Political and Economic History* [Westport, Conn.: Greenwood Publishing Company, 1972], xiv).

18  John Majewski, *A House Dividing: Economic Development in Pennsylvania and Virginia before the Civil War* (New York: Cambridge University Press, 2000), 12–36; David R. Goldfield, *Urban Growth in the Age of Sectionalism: Virginia, 1847–1861* (Baton Rouge: Louisiana University Press, 1977).

19  Rutledge [pseud.], *Separate State Secession Practically Discussed* (Charleston, 1851), 18.

20  On "war socialism" and the growth of the Confederate state, see Raimondo Luraghi, *The Rise and Fall of the Plantation South* (New York: New Viewpoints, 1978), 112–32; and Jeffrey Rogers Hummel, *Emancipating Slaves, Enslaving Free Men: A History of the American Civil War* (Chicago: Open Court, 1996), 227–30, 235–38.

21  Paul P. Van Riper and Harry N. Scheiber, "The Confederate Civil Service," *Journal of Southern History* 25 (November 1959): 450.

22  Mark E. Neely Jr., *Southern Rights: Political Prisoners and the Myth of Confederate Constitutionalism* (Charlottesville: University of Virginia Press, 1999), 1–6.

23  Richard Franklin Bensel, *Yankee Leviathan: The Origins of Central State Authority in America, 1859–1877* (New York: Cambridge University Press, 1990), 14.

24  Emory M. Thomas, *The Confederacy as a Revolutionary Experience* (Englewood Cliffs, N.J.: Prentice Hall, 1971), 58–59. In *The Confederate Nation, 1861–1865* (New York: Harper & Row, 1979), Thomas expounded on this theme: "Though the change was often subtle and unintended, the Confederates' revolution, in the name of survival, altered many, if not most, of those traditional Southern characteristics it was designed to preserve" (147).

25  Quoted in Huston, *Calculating the Value of the Union*, 45.

26  Henry Mayer, *All on Fire: William Lloyd Garrison and the Abolition of Slavery* (New York: St. Martin's Press, 1998), 300–329. On the need for government support (such as slave patrols) to make slavery profitable to individual slaveholders, see Hummel, *Emancipating Slaves, Enslaving Free Men*, 37–60. On the political organization of slave patrols, see Sally E. Hadden, *Slave Patrols: Law and Violence in Virginia and the Carolinas* (Cambridge: Harvard University Press, 2001), 41–104.

27  G.F. [George Fitzhugh], "Political Economy," *Charleston Mercury*, November 11, 1856.

28 William Howard Russell, *My Diary North and South*, ed. Eugene H. Berwanger (New York: McGraw Hill, 1988), 131–32.

29 Barrington Moore Jr., *Social Origins of Dictatorship and Democracy: Lord and Peasant in the Making of the Modern World* (Boston: Beacon Press, 1966). The emphasis on the manipulation of private interests in my conception of state activism is different from Chad Morgan's "inverted Prussian Road," which focuses more on direct control (*Planters' Progress: Modernizing Confederate Georgia* [Gainesville: University Press of Florida, 2005], 67–69).

30 For an overview of Hamilton's political economy, see John R. Nelson Jr., *Liberty and Property: Political Economy and Policymaking in the New Nation, 1789–1812* (Baltimore: Johns Hopkins University Press, 1987), 22–65. As Nelson perceptively notes, Hamilton needed trade with Great Britain to fund his fiscal programs. Confederates, on the other hand, incessantly worked to establish commercial independence from the North. Given Hamilton's desire for close relations with Great Britain, one could argue that the Confederates supported a far stronger form of economic nationalism.

31 James McPherson and Manisha Sinha have stressed the "counterrevolutionary" element of secessionist thought. See McPherson, *Battle Cry of Freedom: The Civil War Era* (New York: Oxford University Press, 1988), 234–75; and Sinha, *The Counter-Revolution of Slavery: Politics and Ideology in Antebellum South Carolina* (Chapel Hill: University of North Carolina Press, 2000).

32 L. W. Spratt, *A Series of Articles on the Value of the Union to the South* (Charleston: James, Williams & Gitsinger, 1855), 4.

33 William J. Cooper, *Liberty and Slavery: Southern Politics to 1860* (New York: Alfred A. Knopf, 1983), 285.

34 Russell, *Critical Studies in Antebellum Sectionalism*, 122–23.

35 Quoted in Philip M. Hamer, *The Secession Movement in South Carolina, 1847–1852* (New York: Da Capo Press, 1971), 22–23.

36 On the importance of interests in the formulation of early U.S. nationalism, see Cathy D. Matson and Peter S. Onuf, *A Union of Interests: Political and Economic Thought in Revolutionary America* (Lawrence: University Press of Kansas, 1990), 90–100, 147–62. For an application to the South in the early nineteenth century, see Brian Schoen, "Calculating the Price of Union: Republican Economic Nationalism and the Origins of Southern Sectionalism, 1790–1828," *Journal of the Early Republic* 23 (Summer 2003): 173–206.

37 For an excellent account of the debate over separate state secession, see Sinha, *The Counter-Revolution of Slavery*, 94–123.

38 James Henry Hammond, "Speech Delivered at Barnwell Court House, October 29, 1858," in *Selections from the Letters and Speeches of the Hon. James H. Hammond of South Carolina* (Spartanburg, S.C.: Reprint Co., 1978), 323–57.

39 On the importance of Wise during the Virginia secession convention, see Nelson D. Lankford, *Cry Havoc! The Crooked Road to the Civil War, 1861* (New York: Viking, 2007), 50–51.

40 Freehling uses the term "extremists" throughout *Secessionists at Bay, 1776–1854*.

41 Hammond, "Speech Delivered at Barnwell Court House," 351.

42 Most South Carolinians identified with the Democratic Party. Virginia had a strong Whig Party, but most Whigs opposed secession. Secessionists who promoted southern economic modernization—such as Garnett, Wise, Floyd, and Ruffin—tended to be Democrats.

43 "A Citizen of Virginia" [Muscoe Russell Hunter Garnett], *The Union, Past and Future: How It Works and How to Save It* (Washington, D.C.: Jno. T. Towers, 1850).

44 Stephanie McCurry, *Masters of Small Worlds: Yeoman Households, Gender Relations, and the Political Culture of the Antebellum South Carolina Low Country* (New York: Oxford University Press, 1995), 280–82; Sinha, *Counter-Revolution of Slavery*, 232–33; and William W. Freehling, *The Road to Disunion*, vol. 2, *Secessionists Triumphant, 1854–1861* (New York: Oxford University Press, 2007), 390–94.

45 James Henley Thornwell, *The State of the Country: An Article Republished from the Southern Presbyterian Review*, 3rd ed. (Columbia, S.C.: Southern Guardian Steam-Power Press, 1861), 7.

46 One exception to this general point was the economic writings of William Manning, an ordinary Massachusetts farmer who penned a vision of the U.S. economy in his 1799 essay "The Key of Liberty." The essay was never published during Manning's lifetime, but its exceptional nature helps account for why it is published today. See William Manning, *The Key of Liberty: The Life and Democratic Writings of William Manning, a Laborer, 1747–1814*, ed. Michael Merrill and Sean Wilentz (Cambridge: Harvard University Press, 1993).

47 See, for example, Tom Downey, *Planting the Capitalist South: Masters, Merchants, and Manufacturers in the Southern Interior, 1790–1860* (Baton Rouge: Louisiana State University Press, 2006), 92–117; Ford, *Origins of Southern Radicalism*, 219–43; and Majewski, *House Dividing*, 59–110. These works make clear that a strong consensus about the general desirability of railroads did not preclude conflict over issues such as location and eminent domain.

48 This evidence is analyzed in chapter 4.

49 Henry L. Benning in *Proceedings of the Va. Convention*, vol. 1, 71.

50 Drew Gilpin Faust, *James Henry Hammond and the Old South: A Design for Mastery* (Baton Rouge: Louisiana State University Press, 1982).

CHAPTER ONE

1 William J. Cooper, *Liberty and Slavery: Southern Politics to 1860* (New York: Alfred A. Knopf, 1983), 6–8, 248.
2 William E. Sparkman Plantation Journal, 681z, Southern Historical Collection, University of North Carolina at Chapel Hill.
3 Farm Journal of Julian Ruffin, Ruffin Papers, MSS 1:R838a 818, Virginia Historical Society, Richmond.
4 On Ruffin's continued use of shifting cultivation, see Jack Temple Kirby, *Poquosin: A Study in Rural Landscape and Society* (Chapel Hill: University of North Carolina Press, 1995), 111.
5 For an analysis of environmental constraints in the tropics, see, for example, Andrew D. Mellinger, Jeffrey D. Sachs, and Anthony J. Venables, "Climate, Coastal Proximity, and Development," in *The Oxford Handbook of Economic Geography*, ed. Gordon L. Clark, Maryann P. Feldman, and Meric S. Gertler (New York: Oxford University Press, 2000), 169–94. In many respects, my focus on environmental conditions follows the example of Julius Rubin, "The Limits of Agricultural Progress in the Nineteenth-Century South," *Agricultural History* 49 (April 1975): 362–73.
6 J. S. Otto and N. E. Anderson, "Slash-and-Burn Cultivation in the Highlands South: A Problem in Comparative Agricultural History," *Comparative Studies in Society and History* 24 (January 1982): 136–49; William Cronon, *Changes in the Land: Indians, Colonists, and the Ecology of New England* (New York: Hill and Wang, 1983), 43–53.
7 Lewis Cecil Gray, *History of Agriculture in the Southern United States to 1860*, vol. 1 (Gloucester, Mass.: Peter Smith, 1958), 438–42.
8 Lois Green Carr, Russell R. Menard, and Lorena S. Walsh, *Robert Cole's World: Agriculture and Society in Early Maryland* (Chapel Hill: University of North Carolina Press, 1991), 39.
9 Allan Kulikoff, *Tobacco and Slaves: The Development of Southern Cultures in the Chesapeake, 1680–1800* (Chapel Hill: University of North Carolina Press for the Institute of Early American History and Culture, 1986), 48; Virginia DeJohn Anderson, *Creatures of Empire: How Domestic Animals Transformed Early America* (New York: Oxford University Press, 2004) 107–40; Stanley Wayne Trimble, *Man-Induced Soil Erosion on the Southern Piedmont, 1700–1970* (Ankeny, Iowa: Soil Conservation Society of America, 1974), 43–51; Lois Green Carr and Russell R. Menard, "Land, Labor, and Economies of Scale in Early Maryland: Some Limits to Growth in the Chesapeake System of Husbandry," *Journal of Economic History* 49 (June 1982): 407–18.
10 Quoted in Trimble, *Man-Induced Soil Erosion*, 45.

11  Carr and Menard, "Land, Labor, and Economies of Scale in Early Maryland," 413–18. Note that Carr and Menard focus on Maryland, which generally had better soils than Virginia.
12  Kirby, *Poquosin*, 95–125.
13  Daniel W. Crofts, *Cobb's Ordeal: The Diaries of a Virginia Farmer, 1842–1872* (Athens: University of Georgia Press, 1997), 71. According to Crofts, "Cobb replicated patterns of slash-and-burn agriculture that had been practiced in Virginia long before the arrival of Europeans" (64).
14  Frederick Law Olmsted, *A Journey in the Seaboard Slave States, with Remarks on Their Economy* (New York: Mason Brothers, 1859), 65.
15  Olmsted, *Journey in the Seaboard Slaves States*, 413.
16  Solon Robinson, "Mr. Robinson's Tour—No. 20," *American Agriculturalist* 9 (August 1850): 225.
17  "Plantation Journal of John D. Ashmore," Ashmore Papers, #2343, Southern Historical Collection, Manuscripts Department, Wilson Library, University of North Carolina at Chapel Hill.
18  John Hebron Moore, *The Emergence of the Cotton Kingdom in the Old Southwest: Mississippi, 1770–1860* (Baton Rouge: Louisiana State University Press, 1988), 86.
19  Otto and Anderson, "Slash-and-Burn Cultivation in the Highlands South," 141–42.
20  For a general summary of the dual economy thesis that stresses the different orientation of commercial planters and isolated yeomen families, see Harry L. Watson, "Slavery and Development in a Dual Economy: The South and the Market Revolution," in *The Market Revolution in America: Social, Political, and Religious Expressions, 1800–1880*, ed. Melvyn Stokes and Stephen Conway (Charlottesville: University of Virginia Press, 1996), 43–73.
21  Jeremy Atack and Fred Bateman, *To Their Own Soil: Agriculture in the Antebellum North* (Ames: Iowa State University Press, 1987), 118–19. According to special instructions to the 1860 census, marshals were to exclude "irreclaimable marshes" and large bodies of water from total acreage.
22  Trimble, *Man-Induced Soil Erosion*, 153.
23  Calculated from *Manufactures in the United States in 1860* (Washington, D.C.: Government Printing Office, 1865), 682, 695, 708, 716.
24  Edward L. Ayers, *The Promise of the New South: Life after Reconstruction* (New York: Oxford University Press, 1992), 124–25.
25  Steven Stoll, *Larding the Lean Earth: Soil and Society in Nineteenth-Century America* (New York: Hill and Wang, 2002), 82–83; Moore, *Cotton Kingdom*, 26–27.
26  For southern attitudes and practices concerning hogs, see Kirby, *Poquosin*,

98–103, and Frank. L. Owsley, *Plain Folk of the Old South* (Baton Rouge: Louisiana State University Press, 1949, 1982), 23–50.
27 S.D.M. [pseud.], "Lands," *Southern Planter* 5 (February 1846): 30–31.
28 A.G.W. [pseud.], "Agriculture," *Southern Planter* 8 (June 1848): 172–73.
29 Robert Mills, *Statistics of South Carolina* (Charleston: Hurlbut and Lloyd, 1826), 637.
30 "Agricultural Survey of the Parish of St. Matthews," *Southern Cabinet of Agriculture, Horticulture, Rural, and Domestic Economy* 1 (April 1840): 199.
31 For a recent statement of this view, see Roger G. Kennedy, *Mr. Jefferson's Lost Cause: Land, Farmers, Slavery, and the Louisiana Purchase* (New York: Oxford, 2003), 11–25.
32 Gray, *History of Agriculture in the Southern United States*, vol. 1, 448. See also John Solomon Otto, *Southern Agriculture during the Civil War Era, 1860–1880* (Westport, Conn.: Greenwood Press, 1994), 4–6.
33 Grady McWhiney, *Cracker Culture: Celtic Ways in the Old South* (Tuscaloosa: University of Alabama Press, 1988), 51–79.
34 Historians have noted that some ethnic groups—settlers of German descent, for example—practiced continuous cultivation more readily than other groups. This is certainly true, but it is important to keep in mind that German settlers sought out soils that allowed them to practice their preferred mode of agriculture. See, for example, Douglas Helms, "Soil and Southern History," *Agricultural History* 74 (Autumn 2000): 736–43. If we can imagine a world in which the Germans were forced to settle the poor soils of the coastal plain or the slopes of southern Appalachia, their agricultural practices would almost certainly have changed.
35 Olmsted, *A Journey in the Seaboard Slave States*, 382.
36 Helms, "Soil and Southern History"; S. W. Buol, F. D. Hole, R. J. McCracken, and R. J. Southard, *Soil Genesis and Classification*, 4th ed. (Ames: Iowa State University Press, 1997); and Henry D. Foth and John W. Schaffer, *Soil Geography and Land Use* (New York: John Wiley and Sons, 1980), 177–98.
37 On the fertilizing properties of ash, see Kirby, *Poquosin*, 111–14.
38 "Leached Ashes as a Manure," *Southern Agriculturalist* 1 (September 1841): 479–80.
39 National Research Council, *Sustainable Agriculture*, 53–57.
40 On the importance of livestock to intensive land use among northern farmers, see Donald H. Parkerson, *The Agricultural Transition in New York State: Markets and Migration in Mid-Nineteenth-Century America* (Ames: Iowa State University Press, 1995), 94–98.
41 Stoll, *Larding the Lean Earth*, 49–54.
42 Tamara Miner Haygood, "Cows, Ticks, and Disease: A Medical Interpreta-

tion of the Southern Cattle Industry," *Journal of Southern History* 52 (November 1986): 551–64.

43  Northern cattle that did not have the chance to develop immunity at a young age frequently died when exposed to southern cattle fever. See Haygood, "Cows, Ticks, and Disease," 553.

44  Anderson, *Creatures of Empire*, 111–12.

45  W. H. Wischmeier and D. D. Smith, *Predicting Rainfall Erosion Losses: A Guide to Conservation Planning* (Washington, D.C.: U.S. Department of Agriculture, 1978), 5–6; Trimble, *Man-Induced Soil Erosion*, 12–13; Stoll, *Larding the Lean Earth*, 134–43.

46  Trimble, *Man-Induced Soil Erosion*, 153–56.

47  Quoted in Boynton Merrill Jr., *Jefferson's Nephews: A Frontier Tragedy*, 2nd ed. (Lexington: University of Kentucky Press, 1987), 47.

48  For a good summary of this view, see Sara T. Phillips, "Antebellum Agricultural Reform: Republican Ideology, Sectional Tension," *Agricultural History* 74 (Autumn 2000): 799–822.

49  David R. Meyer, *The Roots of American Industrialization* (Baltimore: Johns Hopkins University Press, 2003), 162–88.

50  Olmsted, *Journey in the Seaboard Slave States*, 137.

51  Peter A. Coclanis and Lacy K. Ford, "The South Carolina Economy Reconstructed and Reconsidered: Structure, Output, and Performance, 1670–1985," in *Developing Dixie: Modernization in a Traditional Society*, ed. Winfred B. Moore Jr., Joseph F. Tripp, and Lyon G. Tyler Jr. (New York: Greenwood Press, 1988), 98–101; Daniel W. Crofts, "Late Antebellum Virginia Reconsidered," *Virginia Magazine of History and Biography* 107 (Summer 1999), 253–86.

52  Robert William Fogel, *Without Consent or Contract: The Rise and Fall of American Slavery* (New York: W. W. Norton, 1989), 84.

53  T. H. Breen, *Tobacco Culture: The Mentality of the Great Tidewater Planters on the Eve of Revolution* (Princeton: Princeton University Press, 1985), 40–83. On productivity improvements in tobacco growing, see John J. McCusker and Russell R. Menard, *The Economy of British America, 1607–1789* (Chapel Hill: University of North Carolina Press, 1985), 122–23.

54  Moore, *Cotton Kingdom*, 18–36; Fogel, *Without Consent or Contract*, 60–107.

55  Otto and Anderson, "Slash-and-Burn Cultivation in the Highlands South"; Kirby, *Poquosin*, 109–11.

56  Please see the statistical appendix (especially table A.2) for more analysis of population densities.

57  Breen, *Tobacco Culture*, 43.

58 Adam Smith, *An Inquiry into the Nature and Causes of the Wealth of Nations*, vol. 1, ed. R. H. Campbell, A. S. Skinner, and W. B. Todd (Oxford: Clarendon Press, 1979; repr., Indianapolis: LibertyClassics, 1981), 13–36.

59 Meyer, *Roots of American Industrialization*, 15–54, 162–88. See also John Majewski and Viken Tchakerian, "Markets and Manufacturing: Industry and Agriculture in the Antebellum South and Midwest," in *Global Perspectives on Industrial Transformation in the American South*, ed. Susanna Delfino and Michele Gillespie (St. Louis: University of Missouri Press, 2005), 131–50.

60 Allan R. Pred, *Urban Growth and City-Systems in the United States, 1840–1860* (Cambridge: Harvard University Press, 1980); Diane Lindstrom, *Economic Development in the Philadelphia Region, 1810–1850* (New York: Columbia University Press, 1978).

61 Kenneth Sokoloff, "Invention, Innovation, and Manufacturing Productivity Growth in the Antebellum Northeast," in *American Economic Growth and Standards of Living before the Civil War*, ed. Robert E. Gallman and John Joseph Wallis (Chicago: University of Chicago Press, 1992), 345–78; Jeremy Atack, "Returns to Scale in Antebellum United States Manufacturing," *Explorations in Economic History* 14 (June 1978): 337–59; Viken Tchakerian, "Productivity, Extent of Markets, and Manufacturing in the Late Antebellum South and Midwest," *Journal of Economic History* 54 (September 1994), 500; Sean Wilentz, *Chant's Democratic: New York City and the Rise of the American Working Class, 1788–1850* (New York: Oxford University Press, 1984), 107–42.

62 Ralph V. Anderson and Robert E. Gallman, "Slaves as Fixed Capital: Slave Labor and Southern Economic Development," *Journal of American History* 64 (June 1977): 24–46.

63 Eugene D. Genovese, *The Political Economy of Slavery: Studies in the Economy and Society of the Slave South*, 2nd ed. (Middletown, Conn.: Wesleyan University Press, 1989), 157–79; John Majewski, *A House Dividing: Economic Development in Pennsylvania and Virginia before the Civil War* (New York: Cambridge University Press, 2000), 158–61.

64 The modest size of most manufacturing establishments (whether northern or southern) indicated that antebellum industry enjoyed only modest economies of scale. See Atack, "Returns to Scale," 337–59. Genovese may have also underestimated the ability of some slaves—either through special bonuses and overtime payments or their own independent production—to own their own goods. See, for example, Dylan C. Penningroth, *The Claims of Kinfolk: African American Property and Community in the Nineteenth-Century South* (Chapel Hill: University of North Carolina Press, 2003), 45–78.

65 William E. Sparkman Plantation Journal, 681z, Southern Historical Collection, University of North Carolina, Chapel Hill.

66 Peter A. Coclanis, *The Shadow of a Dream: Economic Life and Death in the South Carolina Low Country, 1670–1920* (New York: Oxford University Press, 1989), 143–50; David L. Carlton, "Antebellum Southern Urbanization," in *The South, the Nation, and the World: Perspectives on Southern Economic Development*, by David L. Carlton and Peter A. Coclanis (Charlottesville: University of Virginia Press, 2003), 39–41; and William M. Mathew, *Edmund Ruffin and the Crisis of Slavery in the Old South: The Failure of Agricultural Reform* (Athens: University of Georgia Press, 1988), 162.

67 Coclanis, *Shadow of a Dream*, 116.

68 McCusker and Menard, *The Economy of British America*, 131. For the population of Baltimore and Norfolk in 1860, see Stewart Blumin, *The Urban Threshold: Growth and Change in a Nineteenth-Century American Community* (Chicago: University of Chicago Press, 1976), 223–26.

69 Blumin, *The Urban Threshold*, 223–24.

70 Majewski, *House Dividing*, 161–67.

71 Lee Soltow and Edward Stevens, *The Rise of Literacy and the Common Schools in the United States: A Socioeconomic Analysis to 1870* (Chicago: University of Chicago Press, 1981), 166–76.

72 Soltow and Stevens, *The Rise of Literacy and the Common Schools*, 155–66; and James M. McPherson, *Ordeal by Fire: The Civil War and Reconstruction*, 3rd ed. (New York: McGraw-Hill, 2001), 27–29.

73 On the lackluster state of the southern publishing industry, see Alice Fahs, *The Imagined Civil War: Popular Literature of the North and South, 1861–1865* (Chapel Hill: North Carolina University Press, 2001), 21–41; and Drew Gilpin Faust, *The Creation of Confederate Nationalism: Ideology and Identity in the Civil War South* (Baton Rouge: Louisiana State University Press, 1988), 16–18.

74 James David Miller, *South by Southwest: Planter Emigration and Identity in the Slave South* (Charlottesville: University of Virginia Press, 2002), 26–38; William W. Freehling, *Prelude to Civil War: The Nullification Controversy in South Carolina, 1816–1836* (New York: Oxford University Press, 1965), 25–48.

75 The economic desperation of some antebellum northern communities led them to invest heavily in plank roads as a means of reviving their fortunes. John Majewski, Christopher Baer, and Daniel B. Klein, "Responding to Relative Decline: The Plank Road Boom of Antebellum New York," *Journal of Economic History* 53 (March 1993): 106–22.

76 Parkerson, *Agricultural Transition in New York State*, 25–38.

77 Quoted in Heather Cox Richardson, *The Greatest Nation of the Earth: Re-*

*publican Economic Policies during the Civil War* (Cambridge: Harvard University Press, 1997), 157.

78  Richard L. Bushman, *The Refinement of America: Persons, Houses, and Cities* (New York: Vintage Books, 1992), 390–98.

79  Eric Foner, *Free Soil, Free Labor, Free Men: The Ideology of the Republican Party before the Civil War* (New York: Oxford University Press, 1970), 40–72; Eric Foner, "Free Labor and Nineteenth-Century Political Ideology," in *The Market Revolution in America: Social, Political, and Religious Expressions, 1800–1880*, ed. Melvyn Stokes and Stephen Conway (Charlottesville: University of Virginia Press, 1996), 99–127; John Ashworth, "Free Labor, Wage Labor, and the Slave Power: Republicanism and the Republican Party in the 1850s," in *The Market Revolution*, 128–46.

80  Quoted in Joshua Michael Zeitz, "The Missouri Compromise Reconsidered: Antislavery Rhetoric and the Emergence of the Free Labor Synthesis," *Journal of the Early Republic* 20 (Autumn 2000), 477.

81  Quoted in Zeitz, "Missouri Compromise," 476.

82  Alexis de Tocqueville, *Democracy in America*, trans. and ed. Harvey C. Mansfield and Delba Winthrop (Chicago: University of Chicago Press, 2000), 333.

83  Olmsted, *Journey in the Seaboard Slave States*, 65–74.

84  Ibid., 454.

85  Quoted in Jonathan H. Earle, *Jacksonian Antislavery and the Politics of Free Soil, 1824–1854* (Chapel Hill: University of North Carolina Press, 2004), 136.

86  *Congressional Globe*, 34th Cong., 1st sess., app., 637.

87  *Congressional Globe*, 33rd Cong., 1st sess., app., 664.

88  Quoted in John Ashworth, *Slavery, Capitalism, and Politics in the Antebellum Republic*, vol. 1, *Commerce and Compromise* (New York: Cambridge University Press, 1995), 80.

89  Abraham Lincoln, "Annual Address before the Wisconsin State Agricultural Society at Milwaukee, Wisconsin. September 30, 1859," in *Abraham Lincoln: His Speeches and Writings*, ed. Roy P. Basler (Cleveland: World Publishing Company, 1946), 495–99.

90  Ibid., 502.

91  Ibid., 503–4.

92  Gavin Wright, *Slavery and American Economic Development* (Baton Rouge: Louisiana State University Press, 2006), 49.

93  P. [pseud.], "Southern Productions," *Plough, the Loom, and the Anvil*, February 1856, 458–59. For an analysis of this article and similar southern critiques of North-South comparisons, see Phillips, "Antebellum Agricultural Reform," 811.

94  "To Southern Planters," *Southern Cultivator*, March 1, 1843, 6.

95 Jacob Cardozo, "Agriculture," *Charleston Courier*, November 6, 1848.
96 See, for example, Senator Washburn's quotation of southern sources in his speech in *Congressional Globe*, 34th Cong., 1st sess., app., 636–37.
97 Quoted in Peter S. Carmichael, *The Last Generation: Young Virginians in Peace, War, and Revolution* (Chapel Hill: University of North Carolina Press, 2005), 44.
98 *Congressional Globe*, 34th Cong., 1st sess., app., 636–37.

CHAPTER TWO

1 Avery O. Craven, *Edmund Ruffin, Southerner: A Study in Secession* (New York: D. Appleton and Co., 1932; repr. Baton Rouge: Louisiana State University Press, 1972), 56.
2 Quoted in ibid., 179.
3 See, for example, Charles G. Steffen, "In Search of the Good Overseer: The Failure of the Agricultural Reform Movement in Lowcountry South Carolina, 1821–1834," *Journal of Southern History* 63 (November 1997): 753–802; Drew Gilpin Faust, "The Rhetoric and Ritual of Agriculture in Antebellum South Carolina," *Journal of Southern History* 45 (November 1979): 541–68; Drew Gilpin Faust, *A Sacred Circle: The Dilemma of the Intellectual in the Old South, 1840–1860* (Baltimore: Johns Hopkins University Press, 1977), 7–14.
4 The story of Ruffin's discovery of marl has been told many times. See, for example, Craven, *Edmund Ruffin*, 54–56; William W. Mathew, *Edmund Ruffin and the Crisis of Slavery in the Old South: The Failure of Agricultural Reform* (Athens: University of Georgia Press, 1988), 21; Jack Temple Kirby, ed., *Nature's Management: Writings on Landscape and Reform, 1822–1859* (Athens: University of Georgia Press, 2000), xxii–xxiii.
5 Steffen, "In Search of the Good Overseer," 794.
6 Publishing information about southern agricultural periodicals are found in Albert Lowther Demaree, *The American Agricultural Press, 1819–1860* (New York: Columbia University Press, 1941), 356–75.
7 Examples of agricultural articles appearing in the *Mercury* in 1856 and 1857 include: "Chinese Sugar Cane," *Charleston Mercury*, April 1, 1857; "A Practical Test of the Chinese Sugar Cane," *Charleston Mercury*, August 24, 1857; "The Dhoora Corn, or Egyptian Millet," *Charleston Mercury*, January 24, 1856; "Prolific Corn," *Charleston Mercury*, September 10, 1856; "Carolina Planters," *Charleston Mercury*, May 6, 1857; and "Agriculture in Our Schools," *Charleston Mercury*, March 4, 1856.
8 Edmund Ruffin, *Essay on Calcareous Manures*, ed. J. Carlyle Sitterson (Cambridge: Harvard University Press, 1961), 190.

9 Mathew, *Edmund Ruffin and the Crisis of Slavery*, 3.
10 Edmund Ruffin, "The Old Dominion's Declension" (1836), in *Nature's Management: Writings on Landscape and Reform, 1822–1859*, ed. Jack Temple Kirby (Athens: University of Georgia Press, 2000), 26, 27.
11 Edmund Ruffin, "The Morals of Agriculture" (1822), in *Nature's Management: Writings on Landscape and Reform, 1822–1859*, ed. Jack Temple Kirby (Athens: University of Georgia Press, 2000).
12 Edmund Ruffin, "An Address on the Opposite Results of Exhausting and Fertilizing Systems of Agriculture" (1852), in *Nature's Management: Writings on Landscape and Reform, 1822–1859*, ed. Jack Temple Kirby (Athens: University of Georgia Press, 2000), 341.
13 Whitemarsh B. Seabrook, *An Address, Delivered at the First Anniversary Meeting of the United Agricultural Society of South Carolina* (Charleston: A. E. Miller, 1828), 38.
14 A South Carolinian [Whitemarsh B. Seabrook], *An Appeal to the People of the Northern and Eastern States on the Subject of Negro Slavery in South Carolina* (New York, 1834), 3.
15 Seabrook, *An Address*, 29.
16 Quoted in Mathew, *Edmund Ruffin and the Crisis of Slavery*, 11.
17 N. Herbemont, "Address to the President and Members of the United Agricultural Society of South Carolina," *Southern Agriculturalist* 2 (July 1829): 292, 296–97.
18 N. Herbemont, "On Manures," *Farmers' Register* 3 (February 1836): 605.
19 Ibid., 604.
20 "Constitution of the Albemarle Hole and Corner Club, No. 1," *Southern Planter* 2 (July 1842): 154.
21 "Address of Mr. Ruffin," *Journal of Transactions of the Virginia State Agricultural Society* (Richmond: P. D. Bernard, 1853), 16. See also Edmund Ruffin, "Address," *Southern Planter* 12 (February 1852): A8, for a full reprint of Ruffin's address.
22 Faust, "Rhetoric and Ritual," 558–60. For an analysis of the connection between agricultural reform, proslavery politics and secession in Virginia, see William Blair, *Virginia's Private War: Feeding Body and Soul in the Confederacy, 1861–65* (New York: Oxford University Press, 1998), 25–29.
23 Seabrook, *An Address*, 33.
24 Ruffin, "The Morals of Agriculture," 28.
25 "Legislative Aid to Agriculture—No. 1," *Farmers' Register* 6 (February 1838): 698.
26 N. Herbemont, "Remarks on Some Parts of Mr. Garnett's Address," *Farmers' Register* 6 (May 1838): 93.

27 Whitemarsh Seabrook, *An Essay on the Agricultural Capabilities of S. Carolina* (Columbia: John G. Bowman, 1848), 21.
28 "The Agricultural Convention," *Southern Agriculturalist and Register of Rural Affairs* 12 (December 1839): 636–37.
29 "Southern Agricultural Convention," *De Bow's Review* 16 (March 1854): 331.
30 Whitemarsh Seabrook, "Extract from an Address, Delivered before the United Agricultural Society of South Carolina," *Southern Agricultural and Register of Rural Affairs* 2 (March 1829): 114, 115.
31 Edmund Ruffin, *Incidents of My Life: Edmund Ruffin's Autobiographical Essays*, ed. David F. Allmendinger Jr. (Charlottesville: University of Virginia Press, 1990), 55.
32 Edmund Ruffin, "To the Friends and Supporters of the Farmers' Register," *Farmers' Register* 6 (April 1838): 64.
33 R.N. [pseud.], "On the Necessity and Means for Legislative Aid to Agriculture—No. 2," *Farmers' Register* 2 (June 1834): 62, 63.
34 James Barbour, "On the Improvement of Agriculture, and the Importance of Legislative Aid to that Object: Description of the South West Mountain Lands," *Farmers' Register* 2 (April 1835): 704.
35 "Legislative Aid to Agriculture—No. 1," 695.
36 Eric Hobsbawm and Terence Ranger, eds., *The Invention of Tradition* (New York: Cambridge University Press, 1983). The articles in this collection refer to traditions in the sense of rituals rather than intellectual constructions, but the analogy is still apt in the case of southern agricultural reformers.
37 D. F. Jamison, "Annual Address before the State Agricultural Society of South Carolina," in *Proceedings of the State Agricultural Society* (n.p., 1856), 345, 341.
38 Jamison, "Annual Address," 349.
39 A Well Wisher to Agriculture [pseud.], "To the President and Members of the Agricultural Society of Charleston, SC," *Carolina Journal of Medicine, Science, and Agriculture* 1 (July 1825): 365–66.
40 Whitemarsh Seabrook, "Reflections on the Theory and Practice of Agriculture," *Southern Agriculturist and Register of Rural Affairs* 5 (May 1832): 226.
41 "Late Works of Massachusetts in Aid of Agricultural Improvement," *Farmers' Register* 6 (May 1838): 117.
42 "State Aid to Agriculture—Letter from Hon. B. P. Johnson, Secretary of the New York State Agricultural Society," *Southern Cultivator* 17 (November 1859): 327.
43 Thomas Legare, "An Address Delivered from the Agricultural and Police Society of St. Andrew's, before the Agricultural Society of Edisto-Island," *Southern Agriculturalist and Register of Rural Affairs* 9 (August 1836): 396.

44 Clairborne W. Gooch, "Legislative Action Required to Aid Agriculture," *Farmers' Register* 4 (September 1836): 283.
45 Seabrook, *An Essay on the Agricultural Capabilities of S. Carolina*, 19.
46 William Gilmore Simms, "The Good Farmer," *Ladies' Companion*, August 1841, 156.
47 See, for example, "Emigration," *Southern Planter* 4 (June 1844): 124–25.
48 Simms, "The Good Farmer," 157.
49 Dr. Thomas Legare, "Original Communications—An Address . . .," *Southern Agriculturalist and Register of Rural Affairs* 9 (August 1836): 397.
50 A Virginian [pseud.], "Review of Bruce's Address," *Southern Planter* 7 (October 1847): 300.
51 "Legislative Aid to Agriculture—No. 1," 697.
52 Herbemont, "On Manures," 605.
53 Edmund Ruffin, "Report to the Board of Agriculture—Continued from vol. x, page 514," *Farmers' Register*, n.s., 1 (February 28, 1843): 90.
54 E. [pseud.], "Great Improvements Made in Charlotte County, by Substituting Canals for Ponds," *Farmers' Register* 5 (May 1, 1837): 2.
55 Edmund Ruffin, "Malaria—Against Mill Ponds," in *Nature's Management: Writings on Landscape and Reform, 1822–1859*, ed. Jack Temple Kirby (Athens: University of Georgia Press, 2000), 115.
56 Ruffin, "Malaria," 127.
57 Edmund Ruffin, "Report to the State Board of Agriculture of Virginia," *Farmers' Register* 10 (November 30, 1842): 515, 516.
58 Seabrook, *An Address*, 11.
59 Edmund Ruffin, "The Recent Enactments of the Legislature of North Carolina," *Farmers' Register* 4 (April 1837): 767.
60 "Report of Major Gwynn on the Draining of the Swamp Lands," *Farmers' Register* 9 (January 31, 1841): 7.
61 Morton J. Horwitz argues that a general shift to an instrumentalist view of property occurred during the Early Republic. See Morton J. Horwitz, *The Transformation of American Law, 1780–1860* (Cambridge: Harvard University Press, 1977). Evidence from eminent domain cases, however, indicates that many Americans did not fully embrace these legal innovations. See, for example, Tony Freyer, *Producers versus Capitalists: Constitutional Conflict in Antebellum America* (Charlottesville: University Press of Virginia, 1994), 137–95.
62 Ruffin, "Report to the State Board of Agriculture of Virginia," 515, 516.
63 "Malaria and Millponds," *Farmers' Register* 8 (March 31, 1840): 141.
64 An older historical literature credits Ruffin and the reform movement with instigating a revolution in Virginia's farming practices. Emblematic of this approach is Craven, *Edmund Ruffin*, 63–64.

65 Mathew, *Edmund Ruffin and the Crisis of Slavery*, 112, 115.
66 "An Essay on Calcareous Manures, by Ed. Ruffin," *Journal of Transactions of the Virginia Historical Society* (Richmond: P. D. Bernard, 1853), 82.
67 Quoted in Mathew, *Edmund Ruffin and the Crisis of Slavery*, 156.
68 Jimmy M. Skaggs, *The Great Guano Rush: Entrepreneurs and American Overseas Expansion* (New York: St. Martin's Press, 1994), 9–11.
69 These calculations assume that a planter would need 3,000 bushels of marl at 6 cents a bushel (a total of $1,800) and 12.5 tons of guano at $50 per ton (a total of $562) to effectively fertilize 100 acres. See Mathew, *Edmund Ruffin and the Crisis of Slavery*, 155. Stanley Lebergott performed similar calculations using somewhat different data. He found that it was far more profitable to cultivate new land in the West than to renovate older land in the Southeast. See Stanley Lebergott, "The Demand for Land: The United States, 1820–1860," *Journal of Economic History* 45 (June 1985): 190–92.
70 "Desultory Hints to Southern Planters," *Southern Cabinet of Agriculture, Horticulture, Rural, and Domestic Economy* 1 (November 1840): 659.
71 Hammond to Ruffin, November 9, 1849, Ruffin Papers, Virginia Historical Society, Richmond, Virginia.
72 Ibid., August 7, 1845.
73 Ibid., February 8, 1850.
74 "Report on the Geology of South-Carolina," *Southern Quarterly Review* 16 (October 1849): 162.
75 Quoted in ibid.
76 Sean Patrick Adams, *Old Dominion, Industrial Commonwealth: Coal, Politics, and Economy in Antebellum America* (Baltimore: Johns Hopkins University Press, 2004), 119–51.
77 Ruffin, *Incidents of My Life*, 63–64. The Monticello Agricultural Society of South Carolina similarly indicted that "little or nothing has been done to assist agriculture by State Legislation." See "Proceedings of the Monticello Planters' Society," *Southern Agriculturalist and Register of Rural Affairs* 12 (June 1839): 285.
78 Expenditures on geological surveys and the South Carolina State Agricultural Society were taken from the annual session laws published in Columbia (usually titled *Acts of the General Assembly of the State of South Carolina*). State budget data was taken from Lacy K. Ford, *Origins of Southern Radicalism: The South Carolina Upcountry, 1800–1860* (New York: Oxford University Press, 1988), 311.
79 "Gov. Floyd's Message," *Southern Planter* 9 (December 1849): 376.
80 James Barbour, "On the Improvement of Agriculture, and the Importance of Legislative Aid to That Object," *Farmers' Register* 2 (April 1835): 704.

81  Herbemont, "Remarks on Some Parts of Mr. Garnett's Address," 94.
82  "Committee on Agriculture, Report and Resolution on the Petition of Alexander Herbemont on Means to Advance the Agricultural Interests of South Carolina," ca. 1827, S165005, item 00316, South Carolina State Archives, Columbia, South Carolina.
83  Hammond to Ruffin, December 18, 1842. Hammond seems to have consistently opposed the ambitious legislative agendas of other reformers. During an 1839 agricultural convention, he spoke against a set of five legislative proposals for state-supported agricultural research and education. There is no record of Hammond's speech, but the minutes of the meeting record that "John A. Calhoun, Esq. also addressed the Convention in reply to Mr. Hammond—and condemned the ultra course he had taken." See "The Agricultural Convention," *Southern Agriculturalist and Register of Rural Affairs* 12 (December 1839): 630.
84  P. T. Spratley, "Legislation for Agriculture," *Farmers' Register* 7 (January 1839): 40.
85  Edmund Ruffin, "Communication to the Virginia State Agricultural Society," in *Journal of Transactions of the Virginia State Agricultural Society* (Richmond: P. D. Bernard, 1853), 23.
86  "State Aid to Agriculture," *De Bow's Review* 28, o.s. (April 1860): 470. See also Gould D. Coleman, "Government and Agriculture in New York State," *Agricultural History* 39 (January 1965): 41. Coleman concludes that New York farmers "had only a casual relationship" with the state government prior to 1880.
87  Ruffin, "A Common Objection to Agricultural Periodicals," *Farmers' Register* 9 (January 1841): 40.
88  "Agricultural Convention," *Farmers' Register* 3 (February 1836): 619–20.
89  According to public-choice economics, large but disorganized groups (such as "farmers" or "planters") often have less legislative influence than smaller but better organized groups. Twentieth-century American agriculture exemplifies this dynamic. As the number of farmers and their overall economic importance declined over the twentieth century, the ability of the farm lobby to extract research funds, price supports, and other government subsides steadily grew. For helpful explanations of why some groups succeed in lobbying government and others do not, see Mancur Olson, *The Logic of Collective Action: Public Goods and the Theory of Groups* (Cambridge: Harvard University Press, 1965), 53–65, 148–59.
90  Gooch, "Legislative Aid to Agriculture," 281–84.
91  "Editorial and Original—The Agricultural Convention," *Southern Agriculturalist and Register of Rural Affairs* 12 (December 1839): 637.

92 Willoughby Newton, *Address before the Virginia State Agricultural Society* (Richmond, 1852), 11.
93 "New Hampshire and Virginia," *Southern Planter* 17 (February 1857): 3.
94 Ruffin, *Incidents of My Life*, 127.
95 Quoted in Harry L. Watson, *Liberty and Power: The Politics of Jacksonian America* (New York: Noonday Press, 1990), 83.
96 Gilbert C. Fite, *Cotton Fields No More: Southern Agriculture, 1865–1980* (Lexington: University Press of Kentucky, 1984), 68–90.
97 Lex Renda, "The Advent of Agricultural Progressivism in Virginia," *Virginia Magazine of History and Biography* 96 (January 1988): 55–82; G. Terry Sharrer, *A Kind of Fate: Agricultural Change in Virginia, 1861–1920* (Ames: Iowa State University Press, 2000), 111–45.
98 Emory Thomas, *The Confederacy as a Revolutionary Experience* (New Jersey: Prentice Hall, 1971), 114.

CHAPTER THREE

1 Quoted in Manisha Sinha, *The Counterrevolution of Slavery: Politics and Ideology in Antebellum South Carolina* (Chapel Hill: University of North Carolina Press, 2000), 246.
2 Gavin Wright, *Old South, New South: Revolutions in the Southern Economy since the Civil War* (New York: Basic Books, 1986), 22. Wright's statistics cover Virginia, North Carolina, Georgia, South Carolina, Alabama, Mississippi, and Louisiana. Inclusion of Kentucky and Tennessee would have made the increase in mileage even more impressive. In the aftermath of the panic of 1857, southerners built far more railroad mileage between 1857 and 1860 than did northerners, despite a substantially smaller population. See James L. Huston, *The Panic of 1857 and the Coming of the Civil War* (Baton Rouge: Louisiana State University Press, 1987), 216–17.
3 Carter Goodrich, "The Revulsion against Internal Improvements," *Journal of Economic History* 10 (November 1950): 145–69.
4 James A. Ward, "A New Look at Antebellum Southern Railroad Development," *Journal of Southern History* 39 (August 1973): 413.
5 For an overview of southern state investment, see Robert C. Black III, *The Railroads of the Confederacy* (Chapel Hill: University of North Carolina Press, 1952), 40–48.
6 Two of the best studies of state railroad policy in the South cover Georgia, which actually ranked in the middle of the pack when it came to public investment per capita. See Peter Wallenstein, *From Slave South to New South: Public Policy in Nineteenth-Century Georgia* (Chapel Hill: University of

North Carolina Press, 1987), 23–39; and Milton Sydney Heath, *Constructive Liberalism: The Role of the State in Economic Development in Georgia to 1860* (Cambridge: Harvard University Press, 1954), 254–92. For an excellent analysis of railroad investment in South Carolina, see Lacy K. Ford Jr., *Origins of Southern Radicalism: The South Carolina Upcountry, 1800–1860* (New York: Oxford University Press, 1988), 215–43.

7 John Lauritz Larson, *Internal Improvement: National Public Works and the Promise of Popular Government in the Early United States* (Chapel Hill: University of North Carolina Press, 2001), 225–55.

8 Thomas R. Dew, *Review of the Debate in the Virginia Legislature of 1831 and 1832* (Richmond: T. W. White, 1832; repr. Negro Universities Press, 1970), 123.

9 Ulrich Bonnell Phillips, *A History of Transportation in the Eastern Cotton Belt to 1860* (Columbia University Press, 1908; repr. New York: Octagon Books, 1968), 173–82.

10 As historian Scott Reynolds Nelson notes, "With limited inbound traffic to carry, many Southern railroads would continually struggle to pay back investors" (*Iron Confederacies: Southern Railways, Klan Violence, and Reconstruction* [Chapel Hill: University of North Carolina Press, 1999], 13). On the lack of internal demand and the development of an inferior "linear" transportation system in South Carolina, see Peter A. Coclanis, *The Shadow of a Dream: Economic Life and Death in the South Carolina Low Country, 1670–1920* (New York: Oxford University Press, 1989), 147.

11 Anti-Debt [pseud.], *The Railroad Mania: And Review of the Bank of the State of South Carolina, A Series of Essays Published in the Charleston Mercury* (Charleston: Burges, James, and Paxton, 1848), 28, 29–30.

12 Fishlow notes that transportation projects built ahead of demand usually required some sort of government subsidy. See Albert Fishlow, *American Railroads and the Transformation of the Antebellum Economy* (Cambridge: Harvard University Press, 1965), 189–96.

13 See Goodrich, "Revulsion against Internal Improvements"; L. Ray Gunn, *The Decline of Authority: Public Economic Policy and Political Development in New York State, 1800–1860* (Ithaca: Cornell University Press, 1988), esp. chapters 5–8; Louis Hartz, *Economic Policy and Democratic Thought: Pennsylvania, 1776–1860* (Cambridge: Harvard University Press, 1948), 309–20.

14 Goodrich, for example, documents state investment policies in the 1830s and 1840s, but these tailed off considerably. Underdeveloped states such as Maine and Missouri continued state investment policies, and some northern cities offered municipal aid. Yet private investment was clearly the norm. Chicago —barely a generation removed from its initial settlement in the 1850s— provided no municipal investment to its burgeoning railroad network. Even

relatively young cities could dispense with public investment and use private capital instead. Carter Goodrich, *Government Promotion of American Canals and Railroads, 1800–1890* (New York: Columbia University Press, 1960), 121–65.

15  Hartz, *Economic Policy and Democratic Thought*, 161–80.

16  D. W. Menig, *The Shaping of America: A Geographical Perspective on 500 Years of History*, vol. 2, *Continental America, 1800–1867* (New Haven: Yale University Press, 1993), 388–89; Charles B. Dew, *Ironmaker to the Confederacy: Joseph R. Anderson and the Tredegar Iron Works* (New Haven: Yale University Press, 1966), 32–37.

17  William Gregg, *Speech of William Gregg of Edgefield on a Bill to Amend an Act Entitled "An Act to Authorize Aid to the Blue Ridge Railroad Company in South Carolina"* (Columbia: R. W. Gibbes, 1857), 14.

18  Quoted in Ford, *Origins of Southern Radicalism*, 220.

19  Petition from the Blue Ridge Railroad Company, S165015, item 03471, n.d. (ca. 1859), State Archives of South Carolina.

20  Phillips, *History of Transportation in the Eastern Cotton Belt*, 375–80; Ford, *Origins of Southern Radicalism*, 228–29.

21  For key examples of this dynamic at work, see Daniel B. Klein, "The Voluntary Provision of Public Goods? The Turnpike Companies of Early America," *Economic Inquiry* 28 (October 1990): 788–812; and Carter Goodrich, "Public Spirit and American Improvements," *Proceedings of the American Philosophical Society* 92 (October 1948): 305–9.

22  *First Annual Report of the Directors of the Pennsylvania Rail-Road Company* (Philadelphia, 1847), 9.

23  John C. Calhoun to Jacob P. Reed, June 1, 1848, in *The Papers of John C. Calhoun*, vol. 25, ed. Clyde N. Wilson and Shirley Bright Cook (Columbia: University of South Carolina Press, 1999), 450.

24  Historians sometimes argue that investment in slavery deflected investment in railroads and other internal improvements. In their most simplistic form, such arguments make little sense. Since southerners, almost by definition, owned all of the slaves, the purchase of a slave merely transferred capital from one southerner to another. Moreover, slaveholders could mortgage their slaves for additional capital if a particular lucrative investment opportunity presented itself. The most pressing problem for southern railroads was not a regional shortage of capital but an acute lack of profits.

25  Colleen A. Dunlavy, *Politics and Industrialization: Early Railroads in the United States and Prussia* (Princeton: Princeton University Press, 1994), 106.

26  Robert Y. Hayne, *Address in Behalf of the Knoxville Convention [on] . . . The*

*Proposed Louisville, Cincinnati, and Charleston Railroad* (Charleston: A. E. Miller, 1836), 24.

27 David Johnson, "Message Regarding the Desirability of Investing in Construction of Railroads, and the Improvement of Sundry Rivers" (1847), S165008, 6, South Carolina Department of Archives and Manuscripts.

28 *Letter from the Memphis and Charleston Rail Road Company to the Senate and House of Representatives of the State of Alabama* (n.p., n.d.), 6.

29 "Roads," *Southern Planter* 7 (September 1847): 273–74.

30 "Manufactures," *Southern Planter* 5 (July 1845): 156.

31 Dew, *Review of the Debate in the Virginia Legislature*, 122.

32 Ibid., 123.

33 Joseph Segar, *Speech of Mr. Segar, of Northampton, on the Subject of a General System of Internal Improvements* (Richmond: Bailie and Gallaher, 1838), 18, 4, 5.

34 Joseph Segar, *Speech of Mr. Segar, of Elizabeth City, on the Bill Authorizing a Loan of State Bonds to the South-Side Rail Road Company* (Richmond: H. K. Ellyson, 1853), 21.

35 *Letter from the Memphis and Charleston Rail Road Company*, 6.

36 Quoted in Ford, *Origins of Southern Radicalism*, 235.

37 John C. Calhoun to J. P. Reed, June 1, 1848, *The Papers of John C. Calhoun*, vol. 25, 450.

38 J. P. Reed to John C. Calhoun, September 8, 1848, *The Papers of John C. Calhoun*, vol. 26, 40.

39 *Fourth Report of the President of the Charleston & Savannah Railroad to the Stockholders, January 20, 1858* (Charleston: Walker, Evans, and Co., 1858), 11.

40 Joseph Segar, *Proceedings of the Internal Improvement Convention Held at White Sulphur Springs* (Richmond: The Dispatch), 17.

41 William M. Burwell, *An Address on the Commercial Future of Virginia* (Richmond: Ritchie and Dunnavant, 1851), 2–4.

42 "Speech of Gov. Henry A. Wise," doc. 1, *Journal of the House of Delegates, Session 1857–58* (Richmond: William F. Ritchie, 1857), cxxiv.

43 Craig M. Simpson, *A Good Southerner: The Life of Henry A. Wise of Virginia* (Chapel Hill: University of North Carolina Press, 1985), 135–56.

44 "Message [from the Governor]," doc. 1, *Senate Documents* (Richmond, 1849), 8–9.

45 Joseph Johnson, "Governor's Message," *Governor's Message and Annual Reports of the Public Offices of the Boards of Directors* (Richmond: William F. Ritchie, 1852), 11.

46 For a summary of these policies, see Brian Shoen, "Alternatives to Depen-

dence: The Lower South's Antebellum Pursuit of Sectional Development through Global Interdependence," in *Global Perspectives on Industrial Transformation in the American South*, ed. Susanna Delfino and Michel Gillespie (Columbia: University of Missouri Press, 2005), 50–75.

47  Maury to Calhoun, March 29, 1848, *The Papers of John C. Calhoun*, vol. 25, 278.
48  *Ibid*, 278.
49  "Report of the Committee of Roads and Internal Navigation," in *Supplemental Report of the President and Directors of the Board of Public Works* (Richmond, 1831), 242.
50  Ibid., 243.
51  Segar, *Speech of Mr. Segar . . . [on] a General System of Internal Improvements*, 14.
52  "Speech of R. G. Morriss," in *Proceedings of the Internal Improvement Convention Held at the White Sulphur Springs* (Richmond: The Dispatch, 1855), 9–10.
53  Ibid., 11.
54  Quoted in William A. Link, *Roots of Secession: Slavery and Politics in Antebellum Virginia* (Chapel Hill: University of North Carolina Press, 2003), 139.
55  *Southern Patriot*, October 21, 1835.
56  Quoted in Phillips, *History of Transportation in the Eastern Cotton Belt*,184.
57  *Proceedings of the Citizens of Charleston Embracing Report of the Committee . . . To the Proposed Railroad from Cincinnati to Charleston* (Charleston: A. E. Miller, 1835), 17.
58  For an analysis of Calhoun's Bonus Bill, see John Lauritz Larson, " 'Bind the Republic Together': The National Union and the Struggle for a System of Internal Improvements," *Journal of American History* 74 (1987): 377–81.
59  "Remarks on the Illinois Land Grant Bill," *The Papers of John C. Calhoun*, vol. 25, 380.
60  F. H. Elmore to John C. Calhoun, October 10, 1845, *The Papers of John C. Calhoun*, vol. 22, 218.
61  John C. Calhoun, "Address of Taking the Chair of the Southwestern Convention," *The Papers of John C. Calhoun*, vol. 22, 279.
62  "The Prospects and Policy of the South, as They Appear to a Planter," *Southern Quarterly Review* 9 (October 1854): 453.
63  Link, *Roots of Secession*, 146–48.
64  Carter Goodrich, "The Virginia System of Mixed Enterprise: A Study of State Planning and Internal Improvements," *Political Science Quarterly* 64 (September 1949): 369.

65 Raising taxes was never a popular position in Virginia—although Governor Henry Wise did so modestly in the late 1850s—so politicians had every incentive to resort to deficit spending. The conflict between eastern and western Virginians over how slaves should be taxed added to the political sensitivity of tax increases. On the issue of taxes in Virginia, see Robin L. Einhorn, *American Taxation, American Slavery* (Chicago: University of Chicago Press, 2006), 236–39, 251–55.

66 *The Diary of Edmund Ruffin*, vol. 1, *Toward Independence, October 1856–April 1861*, ed. William Kauffman Scarborough (Baton Rouge: Louisiana State University Press, 1972), 170.

67 Anti-Debt [pseud.], *The Railroad Mania*, 28.

68 Ibid., 26.

69 William Gregg, *Speech of William Gregg of Edgefield on a Bill to Amend an Act Entitled "An Act to Authorize Aid to the Blue Ridge Railroad Company in South Carolina"* (Columbia: R. W. Gibbes, 1857), 16–17, 19.

70 Louis Hartz, *Economic Policy and Democratic Thought: Pennsylvania, 1776–1860* (Cambridge: Harvard University Press, 1948), 309–20.

71 John L. Manning, "Governor's Message No. 1," *Journal of the House of Representatives of the State of South Carolina Being the Annual Session of 1853* (Charleston: R. W. Gibbs, 1853), 17.

72 Henry Wise, "Message I," *Governor's Message and Reports of the Public Officers of the State* (Richmond: William F. Ritchie, 1857), xxii–xxiii.

73 Anti-Debt [pseud.], *The Railroad Mania*, 24.

74 Gregg, *Speech of William Gregg*, 36.

75 John C. Rutherfoord, *Speech of John C. Rutherfoord* (Richmond, 1858), 7. Craig M. Simpson's otherwise superb biography of Wise misinterprets Rutherfoord's speech, arguing that it criticized state spending on internal improvements. Rutherfoord, like many Virginians, did indeed criticize spending public funds on local enterprises, but he clearly supported trunk lines such as the Ohio and Covington. See Simpson, *A Good Southerner*, 356 (n. 56).

76 John Majewski, *A House Dividing: Economic Development in Pennsylvania and Virginia before the Civil War* (New York: Cambridge University Press, 2000), 128–35.

77 Link, *Roots of Secession*, 32–33; David R. Goldfield, *Urban Growth in the Age of Sectionalism: Virginia, 1847–1861* (Baton Rouge: Louisiana University Press, 1977), 9–28; and William Shade, *Democratizing the Old Dominion: Virginia and the Second Party System, 1824–1861* (Charlottesville: University Press of Virginia, 1996), 35–49.

78 "A Citizen of Virginia" [Muscoe Russell Hunter Garnett], *The Union, Past and Future: How It Works and How To Save It* (Washington, D.C.: Jno. T. Towers, 1850), 16.
79 Vicki Vaughn Johnson, *The Men and the Vision of the Southern Commercial Conventions, 1845–1871* (Columbia: University of Missouri Press, 1992), 9; Ronald Takaki, *A Pro-Slavery Crusade: The Agitation to Reopen the African Slave Trade* (New York: Free Press, 1971), 148–56.
80 [Garnett], *The Union, Past and Future*, 20.
81 "Prospectus of the Charleston and Liverpool Steamship Company," *Charleston Mercury*, February 27, 1861.
82 "Governor's Letcher's Inaugural Message," doc. 39, *Governor's Message and Reports, 1859/1860* (Richmond, 1860), 6.
83 *Message of the Governor of Virginia and Accompanying Documents* (Richmond: William F. Ritchie, 1861), xxv, in *Confederate Imprints* (microfilm coll., New Haven, Conn.: Research Publications, 1974) #2356, reel 71.

CHAPTER FOUR

1 Quoted in Dumas Malone, *The Public Life of Thomas Cooper* (New Haven: Yale University Press, 1926; repr., New York: AMS, 1979), 292.
2 William W. Freehling, *Prelude to Civil War: The Nullification Controversy in South Carolina, 1816–1836* (New York: Oxford University Press, 1965), 193–96.
3 Jeremy Atack and Peter Passell, *A New Economic View of American History: From Colonial Times to 1940*, 2nd ed. (New York: W. W. Norton, 1994), 137–40.
4 "Special Committee Report and Resolutions Directing an Enquiry into the Nature and Origin of the Federal Government" (1827), S165005, item 00009, South Carolina Department of Archives and Manuscripts, 9, 36.
5 "Resolutions Requesting the Governor to Communicate with Other Southern States Regarding the Abolition, the Tariff, and Other Issues Threatening the South" (1844), S165018, item 00030, South Carolina Department of Archives and Manuscripts. For more on "Tariffs and the Indirect Defense of Slavery," see Freehling, *Prelude to Civil War*, 99–133.
6 Thomas R. Dew, *Lectures on the Restrictive System* (1829; New York: Augustus M. Kelley, 1969), 8.
7 "A Citizen of Virginia" [Muscoe Russell Hunter Garnett], *The Union, Past and Future: How It Works and How to Save It* (Washington, D.C.: Jno. T. Towers, 1850), 19.

8. Henry L. Benning in *Proceedings of the Virginia State Convention of 1861*, vol. 1, ed. George H. Reese (Richmond: Virginia State Library, 1965), 71.
9. The controversies in the West might be thought of as an extension and intensification of what Freehling calls "the direct defense of slavery" in the late 1830s. With abolitionism and the western extension of slavery openly debated, southerners no longer felt compelled to use the tariff as a proxy issue. See Freehling, *Prelude to Civil War*, 301–69.
10. According to Atack and Passell, "on the eve of the Civil War, American trade was as free as it was to be during the nineteenth century." See *A New Economic View*, 130.
11. John C. Calhoun to James H. Hammond, August 30, 1845, in *The Papers of John C. Calhoun*, vol. 32, ed. Clyde N. Wilson (Columbia: University of South Carolina Press, 1995), 101.
12. William A. Link, *Roots of Secession: Slavery and Politics in Antebellum Virginia* (Chapel Hill: University of North Carolina Press, 2003), 140. Robert Royal Russell similarly characterized Garnett as "an able and influential politician of the state rights school" (*Economic Aspects of Southern Sectionalism* [New York: Russell & Russell, University of Illinois, 1924], 80). For Garnett's influence in South Carolina, see Manisha Sinha, *The Counter-Revolution of Slavery: Politics and Ideology in Antebellum South Carolina* (Chapel Hill: University of North Carolina Press, 2000), 100–101.
13. [Garnett], *The Union, Past and Future*, 11.
14. Ibid., 16.
15. Rutledge [pseud.], *Separate State Secession Practically Discussed* (Charleston, 1851), 3.
16. L. W. Spratt, *A Series of Articles on the Value of the Union to the South, Lately Published in the Charleston Standard* (Charleston: James, Williams, and Gitsinger, 1855), 7.
17. *Congressional Globe*, 33rd Cong., 1st sess., app., 375.
18. *Congressional Globe*, 32nd Cong., 1st sess., app., 45–46.
19. "The Address to the South," *Charleston Mercury*, December 25, 1860.
20. "The Biter Bit," *Charleston Mercury*, March 29, 1861. Joseph J. Persky explores these arguments in *The Burden of Dependency: Colonial Themes in Southern Economic Thought* (Baltimore: Johns Hopkins University Press, 1992), 61–96.
21. [Garnett], *The Union, Past and Future*, 19.
22. Rutledge, *Separate State Secession*, 20, 21.
23. "Prospectus of the Charleston and Mercury Steamship Company," *Charleston Mercury*, February 27, 1861.

24 John Townsend, *The Southern States, Their Present Peril and Their Certain Remedy* (Charleston: E. C. Councell, 1850).
25 Ibid., 24–25.
26 John Townsend, *The South Alone, Should Govern the South* . . . (Charleston: Evans and Cogswell, 1860), 59.
27 Ibid., 59.
28 Edmund S. Morgan has explored the relationship between slavery and political stability in republican thought in *American Slavery, American Freedom: The Ordeal of Colonial Virginia* (New York: W. W. Norton, 1975), 363–87. James Henry Hammond most famously articulated the supposed social stability of slavery in his 1858 "mudsill" speech (*Congressional Globe*, 35th Cong., 1st sess., app., 71).
29 [Garnett], *The Union, Past and Future*, 22, 24.
30 Spratt, *Value of the Union to the South*, 4.
31 Edmund Ruffin, *Anticipations of the Future, to Serve as Lessons for the Present Times* (Richmond: J. W. Randolph, 1860), 332.
32 D. H. Hamilton, *An Oration upon the Policy of Separate Secession Delivered at Bluffton, South Carolina on the 4th July, 1851* (Charleston: Walker and James, 1851), 17.
33 Edward B. Bryan, *The Disunionist; or, Secession the Rightful Remedy* (Charleston, 1850), 67, 69.
34 *Congressional Globe*, 35th Cong., 1st sess., app., 70.
35 Townsend, *Southern States*, 18.
36 For more on "fanaticism" in proslavery thought, see Larry E. Tise, *Proslavery: A History of the Defense of Slavery in America, 1701–1840* (Athens: University of Georgia Press, 1987), 185–88, 252–54.
37 William Harper, "Slavery in the Light of Social Ethics" (originally published as "Memoir on Slavery," 1838), in *Cotton Is King, and Pro-Slavery Arguments*, by E. N. Elliott (Augusta, Ga.: Pritchard, Abbott, & Loomis, 1860), 625.
38 J. H. Hammond, "Slavery in the Light of Political Science" (originally published as "Gov. Hammond's Letters on Southern Slavery, Addressed to Thomas Clarkson, the English Abolitionist," 1845), in *Cotton Is King, and Pro-Slavery Arguments*, by E. N. Elliott (Augusta, Ga.: Pritchard, Abbott, & Loomis, 1860), 685, 687.
39 Wm. H. Trescot, *Position and Course of the South* (Charleston: Walker and James, 1850), 17–18.
40 Rutledge, *Separate State Secession*, 27.
41 Spratt, *Value of the Union*, 8.
42 David Christy, "Cotton Is King; or, Slavery in the Light of Political Econ-

omy," in *Cotton Is King, and Pro-Slavery Arguments*, by E. N. Elliott (Augusta, Ga.: Pritchard, Abbott, & Loomis, 1860), 94.
43 "Our Cincinnati Correspondent," *Charleston Mercury*, June 18, 1861.
44 Thomas Cooper, *Lectures on the Elements of Political Economy*, 2nd ed. (1830; New York: Augustus M. Kelley, 1971), 196.
45 Nicholas Onuf and Peter Onuf make a similar point, noting that "southern nationalists abandoned the liberal cosmopolitanism of an earlier generation of free traders." See *Nations, Markets, and War: Modern History and the American Civil War* (Charlottesville: University of Virginia Press, 2006), 324–33 (quote on 324).
46 Quoted in James McPherson, *Battle Cry of Freedom: The Civil War Era* (New York: Oxford University Press, 1988), 383.
47 William Howard Russell, *My Diary North and South*, ed. Eugene H. Berwanger (New York: McGraw Hill, 1988), 107. For more on the popularity of the "King Cotton" argument, see James L. Roark, *Masters without Slaves: Southern Planters in the Civil War and Reconstruction* (New York: W. W. Norton, 1977), 29–31.
48 *Proceedings of the Va. Convention*, vol. 1, 175.
49 Daniel W. Crofts, *Reluctant Confederates: Upper South Unionists in the Secession Crisis* (Chapel Hill: University of North Carolina Press, 1989), 107.
50 John P. Kennedy, *The Border States: Their Power and Duty in the Present Disordered Condition of the Country* (Philadelphia: J. B. Lippencott & Co., 1861), 17.
51 L. W. Spratt, *Speech on the Foreign Slave Trade before the Legislature of South Carolina* (Columbia: Steam Power Press Southern Guardian, 1858), 6. For a more general analysis of proposals to open the slave trade, see Ronald Takaki, *A Pro-Slavery Crusade: The Agitation to Reopen the African Slave Trade* (New York: Free Press, 1971), 23–80.
52 Many of the slaveholders who condemned the Atlantic slave trade saw no contradiction in engaging in the domestic slave trade. On the importance of slaveholders maintaining a paternalistic image—even when confronted with the outrages of the domestic slave trade—see Walter Johnson, *Soul by Soul: Life Inside the Antebellum Slave Market* (Cambridge: Harvard University Press, 1999), 19–44.
53 Takaki, *A Pro-Slavery Crusade*, 163–70.
54 "Message" [doc. 1], *Message of the Governor of Virginia and Accompanying Documents* (Richmond: William F. Ritchie, 1861), viii.
55 Even relative moderates such as University of Virginia political economist George Tucker, who had long endorsed a moderately protective tariff to

further southern industry, vaguely hinted at the utility of state tariffs. See Jay Carlander, "In Search of 'Industry': Slavery, Manufacturing, and the Language of Political Economy in the Antebellum South" (Ph.D. diss., University of California, Santa Barbara, 2003), 170.

56 Freehling, *Prelude to Civil War*, 147–48.
57 W. C. Rives, *Discourse on the Use and Importance of History, Illustrated by a Comparison of the American and French Revolutions* (Richmond: Shepard and Colin, 1847), 26–27. The copy with Preston's margin notes is at the Virginia Historical Society (Rare Books, D16 R62).
58 Minutes of the Central Southern Rights Association of Virginia, MSS4C3334a1, Virginia Historical Society, 17.
59 "Meeting in Chesterfield," *Richmond Whig*, January 3, 1860.
60 "Meeting in Fredericksburg," *Richmond Whig*, December 31, 1859.
61 "Meeting in Albemarle," *Richmond Whig*, January 11, 1860.
62 Quoted in Charles B. Dew, *Ironmaker to the Confederacy: Joseph R. Anderson and the Tredegar Iron Works* (New Haven: Yale University Press, 1966), 42–43.
63 W. A. Owens, *An Address to the People of Barnwell District on Separate State Secession* (Charleston: Walker and James, 1851), 25. Opponents of separate-state secession pointed out that South Carolinians would have to engage in widespread smuggling to avoid paying federal tariffs on exports to other states. Such smuggling would surely anger Charleston's southern rivals, thus fracturing the South. "How is such a scheme likely to be received by all those engaged in fair trade in the Southern States?" asked Christopher Memminger, who later would become the Confederacy's first secretary of the treasury. "Would it not rouse every honest trader throughout the South?" (*Southern Rights and Co-operation Documents, No. 7. Speech of Mr. Memminger at the Public Meeting of the Friends of Cooperation* [Charleston: Walker and James, 1851], 14).
64 Minutes of the Central Southern Rights Association of Virginia, MSS4C3334a1, Virginia Historical Society, 22.
65 Gregg D. Kimball, *American City, Southern Place: A Cultural History of Antebellum Richmond* (Athens: University of Georgia Press, 2000), 100–103.
66 Ibid., 103–8.
67 Drew Gilpin Faust, *Mothers of Invention: Women and the Slaveholding South in the American Civil War* (Chapel Hill: University of North Carolina Press, 1996), 46.
68 Quoted in J. D. B. De Bow, "Editorial Miscellany," *De Bow's Review* 25 (September 1858): 374.
69 Ruffin had, not coincidentally, strongly supported a licensing system that

Fitzhugh had favored. See "Slavery and Free Labor Defined and Compared," *Southern Planter* 19 (December 1859): 737–38.

70 Ruffin, *Anticipations of the Future*, 19–20.
71 *Proceedings of the Va. Convention*, vol. 1, 70.
72 Ibid., 200.
73 *Proceedings of the Va. Convention*, vol. 2, 267, 269.
74 Archer Jones, "Some Aspects of George W. Randolph's Service as Confederate Secretary of War," *Journal of Southern History* 26 (1960): 299–300.
75 *Proceedings of the Va. Convention*, vol. 1, 751.
76 *Proceedings of the Va. Convention*, vol. 2, 689.
77 Ibid., 263.
78 *Proceedings of the Va. Convention*, vol. 1., 747.
79 *Proceedings of the Va. Convention*, vol. 2, 267.
80 *Proceedings of the Va. Convention*, vol. 1, 750.
81 Ibid., 749.
82 See, for example, Douglas A. Irwin, *Free Trade under Fire*, 2nd ed. (Princeton: Princeton University Press, 2005), 25–60.
83 *Proceedings of the Va. Convention*, vol. 1, 70. Economic historians have debated the extent to which tariffs aided industrial development in the antebellum North. Douglas A. Irwin and Peter Temin, for example, argue that the U.S. textile industry "could easily have survived even if the tariff had been completely eliminated" ("The Antebellum Tariff on Cotton Textiles Revisited," *Journal of Economic History* 61 [September 2001]: 777–98).
84 Friedrich List, "Introduction to National System," in *Life of Friedrich List and Selections from His Writings*, ed. Margaret Ester Hirst (New York: A. M. Kelley, 1965), 307; *Proceedings of the Va. Convention*, vol. 2, 692.
85 Dew, *Ironmaker to the Confederacy*, 22–26. For a general discussion of slavery in antebellum southern industry see Robert S. Starobin, *Industrial Slavery in the Old South* (London and New York: Oxford University Press, 1970).
86 *Proceedings of the Va. Convention*, vol. 1, 753.
87 Ibid., 754.
88 *Proceedings of the Va. Convention*, vol. 2, 270.
89 "Shoes for the South," *Richmond Daily Dispatch*, March 7, 1861.
90 Richard Franklin Bensel, *Yankee Leviathan: The Origins of Central State Authority in America, 1859–1877* (New York: Cambridge University Press, 1990), 32.
91 "The Constitution of the Confederate States of America, March 11, 1861," in *Basic History of the Confederacy*, ed. Frank E. Vandiver (Princeton: Van Nostrand Company, 1962), 105.

92 *Journal of the Convention of the People of South Carolina, Held in 1860–61* (Charleston: Evans and Cogswell, 1861), 92.
93 W. W. Boyce, "The Tariff," *Congressional Globe*, 34th Cong., 3rd sess., app., 217.
94 "Our Montgomery Correspondence," *Charleston Mercury*, May 16, 1861.
95 *Congressional Globe*, 34th Cong., 3rd sess., app., 278.
96 "South Carolina White Lead, Zinc, and Color Works," *Charleston Mercury*, February 23, 1861.
97 *Tariff (of 1857) Made of Force by Act of Congress of the Confederates States of America, 9th February* (Charleston, 1861).
98 Richard Cecil Todd, *Confederate Finance* (Athens: University of Georgia Press, 1954), 121–24.
99 *Compilation of the Tariff Acts of the Confederate States of America* (New Orleans: Corson and Armstrong, 1861), 131–43.
100 Thomas F. Huertas, "Damnifying Growth in the Antebellum South," *Journal of Economic History* 39 (March 1979): 91.
101 For the 1860 figure, see Clayne L. Pope, *The Impact of the Ante-bellum Tariff on Income Distribution* (New York: Arno Press, 1975), 14.
102 U.S. revenues are from *Historical Statistics of the United States, Colonial Times to 1957* (Washington, D.C.: Government Printing Office, 1960), 539. One might argue that the $34 million figure is too high because it does not take into account factors such as decreased consumer demand and tax evasion. The Confederacy's first secretary of the treasury, Christopher Memminger, estimated in 1861 that the Confederacy would collect $25 million per year in tariff revenue. If Memminger had been correct, then southerners would have paid $4.46 worth of duties per free resident, which was still significantly higher than what southerners had paid under the old Union.
103 G. N. Reynolds to Wm. P. Miles, Feb. 23, 1861, #508, Miles Papers, Southern Historical Collection, Manuscripts Department, Wilson Library, University of North Carolina at Chapel Hill.
104 Russell, *My Diary North and South*, 131.
105 For an excellent discussion of Hamilton's trade policies, see John R. Nelson Jr., *Liberty and Property: Political Economy and Policymaking in the New Nation, 1789–1812* (Baltimore: Johns Hopkins University Press, 1987), 22–65.
106 Daniel Lord, *The Effect of Secession upon Commercial Relations between North and South, and upon Each Section* (New York: Office of New York Times, 1861), 15.
107 The embargo was never formally recognized by the Confederate government itself—it was enforced by state governments and more informal committees on public safety—but it nevertheless was clearly at odds with free-trade

principles. On enforcement of the embargo, see Jeffrey Rogers Hummel, *Emancipating Slaves, Enslaving Free Men: A History of the American Civil War* (Chicago: Open Court, 1996), 167; and Frank Lawrence Owsley, *King Cotton Diplomacy: Foreign Relations of the Confederate States of America*, 2nd ed. (Chicago: University of Chicago Press, 1959), 29–42

108 Quoted in McPherson, *The Battle Cry of Freedom*, 384–85.
109 L. Lynne Kiesling, "Collective Action and Assisting the Poor: The Political Economy of Income Assistance during the Lancashire Cotton Famine," *Journal of Economic History* 55 (June 1995): 380–83.
110 John Bright, "Speech on Slavery and Secession," in *Speeches of John Bright, M.P. on the American Question* (Boston: Little, Brown, and Company, 1865), 156–57.
111 Russell, *My Diary North and South*, 92.
112 C.R.C. [pseud.], "Existence and Prosperity of the Confederacy," *Southern Literary Messenger* 37 (September 1863): 529.
113 Paul D. Escott, *After Secession: Jefferson Davis and the Failure of Confederate Nationalism* (Baton Rouge: Louisiana State University Press, 1978), 60.

CHAPTER FIVE

1 Adam Smith, *The Theory of Moral Sentiments*, ed. D. D. Raphael and A. L. Macfie, vol. 1 of the *Glasgow Edition of the Works and Correspondence of Adam Smith* (Indianapolis: Liberty Fund, 1982), 247.
2 Quoted in Alvery L. King, *Louis T. Wigfall: Southern Fire-Eater* (Baton Rouge: Louisiana State University Press, 1970), 82.
3 William Howard Russell, *My Diary North and South*, ed. Eugene H. Berwanger (New York: McGraw Hill, 1988), 131.
4 See, for example, James M. McPherson, *Drawn with the Sword: Reflections on the American Civil War* (New York: Oxford University Press, 1996), 8, 14; and Gavin Wright, *Slavery and American Economic Development* (Baton Rouge: Louisiana State University Press, 2006), 82.
5 Deemphasizing slavery—and stressing the tyranny of the North—became a popular strategy for other Confederates seeking outside support. Jefferson Davis, for example, often avoided any direct reference to slavery when explaining the rationale for Confederate secession, preferring instead to stress the tyrannical nature of the Lincoln administration. These critiques, which emphasized links to the American Revolution, proved far more palatable to antislavery Europeans than an outright defense of slavery. Davis, for example, criticized Alexander Stephen's famous "Cornerstone" address, which forthrightly argued that slavery was the foundation of the Confederacy. Such

talk, Davis knew, would not serve the Confederacy well in its quest to gain foreign support. See Paul D. Escot, *After Secession: Jefferson Davis and the Failure of Confederate Nationalism* (Baton Rouge: Louisiana State University Press, 1978), 35–37.

6  Russell, *My Diary North and South*, 130.
7  King, *Wigfall*, 70.
8  *Congressional Globe*, 36th Cong., 1st sess., 1528.
9  "The Constitution of the Confederate States," *Charleston Mercury*, March 15, 1861.
10  Jefferson Davis, *Speech of the Hon. Jefferson Davis, of Mississippi, on the Pacific Railroad Bill* (Baltimore: J. Murphy & Co., 1859).
11  Robert C. Angevine, *The Railroad and the State: War, Politics, and Technology in Nineteenth-Century America* (Stanford: Stanford University Press, 2004), 165–92.
12  *Journal of the Provisional Congress*, February 10, 1862, 782.
13  Richard Franklin Bensel, *Yankee Leviathan: The Origins of Central State Authority in America, 1859–1877* (New York: Cambridge University Press, 1990), 100.
14  There was, in fact, a debate over the internal improvement clause during the Montgomery Convention. See Jeffrey A. Jenkins, "Why No Parties? Investigating the Disappearance of Democratic-Whig Divisions in the Confederacy," *Studies in American Political Development* 13 (October 1999): 257–61.
15  Don E. Fehrenbacker, *Constitutions and Constitutionalism in the Slaveholding South* (Athens: University of Georgia Press, 1989), 63–64.
16  On republicanism as a language, see Daniel T. Rodgers, "Republicanism: The Career of a Concept," *Journal of American History* 79 (June 1992): 11–38.
17  Quoted in Charles B. Dew, *Ironmaker of the Confederacy: Joseph R. Anderson and the Tredegar Iron Works* (New Haven and London: Yale University Press, 1966), 142.
18  On government ownership of armaments, see Raimondo Luraghi, *The Rise and Fall of the Plantation South* (New York: New Viewpoints, 1978), 126–30; Steven G. Collins, "System in the South: John W. Mallet, Josiah Gorgas, and Uniform Production at the Confederate Ordnance Department," *Technology and Culture* 40 (July 1999): 517–44; Jeffrey Rogers Hummel, *Emancipating Slaves, Enslaving Free Men: A History of the American Civil War* (Chicago: Open Court, 1996), 235–38.
19  Harold S. Wilson, *Confederate Industry: Manufacturers and Quartermasters in the Civil War* (Jackson: University Press of Mississippi, 2002), 42.
20  Ibid., 93–154. Charles W. Ramsdell emphasizes how army officials used control of raw materials and skilled labor (via conscription) as leverage over

mills and factories. See "The Control of Manufacturing by the Confederate Government," *Mississippi Valley Historical Review* 8 (December 1921): 231–49.

21  Mark Thornton and Robert B. Ekelund Jr., *Tariffs, Blockades, and Inflation: The Economics of the Civil War* (Wilmington, Del.: Scholarly Resources, 2004), 47–53; Hummel, *Emancipating Slaves, Enslaving Free Men*, 237–38.

22  For a summary of Confederate conscription policy, see James M. McPherson, *Ordeal by Fire: The Civil War and Reconstruction*, 3rd ed. (New York: McGraw-Hill, 2001), 202–4.

23  Larry M. Logue, "Who Joined the Confederate Army? Soldiers, Civilians, and Communities in Mississippi," *Journal of Social History* 26 (Spring 1993): 613.

24  George C. Rable, for example, stresses the conflict between a nationalistic and a libertarian political culture within the Confederacy. See *The Confederate Republic: A Revolution against Politics* (Chapel Hill: University of North Carolina, 1994), 174–294. Some Confederates certainly embraced a quasi-libertarian language to oppose Jefferson Davis, but they had little impact on the course of Confederate mobilization.

25  Quoted in King, *Wigfall*, 138.

26  "The President and Conscription—Better Late than Never," *Charleston Mercury*, April 3, 1862.

27  "The Crisis—Conscription," *Charleston Mercury*, January 21, 1863.

28  Edmund Ruffin, *The Diary of Edmund Ruffin*, vol. 1, *Toward Independence, October 1856–April 1861*, ed. William Kauffman Scarborough (Baton Rouge, Louisiana State University Press, 1972), 491.

29  Quoted in James M. McPherson, *Battle Cry of Freedom: The Civil War Era* (New York: Oxford University Press, 1988), 430.

30  Young army officers, for example, remained loyal to the Confederacy to the bitter end. Such loyalty undoubtedly stemmed from their status as slaveholders and from their desire to exact revenge upon Yankee invaders. See Gary W. Gallagher, *The Confederate War: How Popular Will, Nationalism, and Military Strategy Could Not Stave Off Defeat* (Cambridge: Harvard University Press, 1997), 63–111. For civilians, see William Blair, *Virginia's Private War: Feeding Body and Soul in the Confederacy, 1861–1865* (New York: Oxford University Press, 1998), 134–52.

31  James D. B. De Bow, "The Interest in Slavery of the Southern Non-Slaveholder," in *Southern Pamphlets on Secession, November 1860–April 1861*, ed. Jon L. Wakelyn (Chapel Hill: University of North Carolina Press, 1996), 87. Commercially minded yeomen were more likely to believe these claims. Even in yeomen strongholds in southern Appalachia, commercially minded

farmers and merchants (such as those who lived near railroads) typically provided the strongest support for secession, while farm families in more isolated areas remained loyal to the Union. See Noel Fisher, "Feelin' Mighty Southern: Recent Scholarship on Southern Appalachia in the Civil War," *Civil War History* 47 (December 2001): 339–42.

32  On the cavalier image in the Confederacy, see Mark E. Nealy Jr., Harold Holzer, and Gabor S. Boritt, *The Confederate Image: Prints of the Lost Cause* (Chapel Hill: University of North Carolina Press, 1987), 11–36.

33  Drew Gilpin Faust, *The Creation of Confederate Nationalism: Ideology and Identity in the Civil War South* (Baton Rouge: Louisiana State University Press, 1988), 22–40. See also Rable, *The Confederate Republic*, 75–77; and Anne Sarah Rubin, *A Shattered Nation: The Rise and Fall of the Confederacy, 1861–1868* (Chapel Hill: University of North Carolina Press, 2005), 34–42.

34  Edward Countryman, *The American Revolution* (New York: Hill and Wang, 1985), 179–85.

35  Historians, using Lenin's concept of the "Prussian Road," have compared southern planters and the Confederacy most often to Prussia's Junker aristocracy. See, for example, Steven Hahn, "Class and State in Postemancipation Societies: Southern Planters in Comparative Perspective," *American Historical Review* 95 (February 1990): 76–78; Jonathan M. Wiener, *Social Origins of the New South: Alabama, 1860–1885* (Baton Rouge: Louisiana State University Press, 1978), 137–61; and Chad Morgan, *Planters' Progress: Modernizing Confederate Georgia* (Gainesville: University Press of Florida, 2005), 67–69. For a critique of the Prussian Road framework as applied to southern industrialization, see Shearer Davis Bowman, *Masters and Lords: Mid-Nineteenth Century U.S. Planters and Prussian Junkers* (New York: Oxford University Press, 1993), 103–9. For comparisons to Soviet industrialization, see Luraghi, *The Rise and Fall of the Plantation South*, 112–18.

36  McPherson, *Drawn with the Sword*, 66.

37  George H. Reese, ed., *Proceedings of the Virginia State Convention of 1861* (Richmond: Virginia State Library, 1965), 198.

38  "Letter of Stephen F. Hale, Commissioner of Alabama, to Governor Beriah Magoffin of Kentucky, Dec. 27, 1860," in *Apostles of Disunion: Southern Secession Commissioners and the Causes of the Civil War*, by Charles B. Dew (Charlottesville: University of Virginia Press, 2001), 98–99.

39  On the development of kinship networks in the South, see Joan E. Cashin, *Family Venture: Men and Women on the Southern Frontier* (New York: Oxford University Press, 1991), 9–31; J. William Harris, *Plain Folk and Gentry in a Slave Society: White Liberty and Black Slavery in Augusta's Hinterlands* (Middletown, Conn.: Wesleyan University Press, 1985), 94–122; Robert C. Kenzer,

*Kinship and Neighborhood in a Southern Community: Orange County, North Carolina, 1849–1881* (Knoxville: University of Tennessee Press, 1987), 6–51; Alan Kulikoff, *Tobacco and Slaves: The Development of Southern Cultures in the Chesapeake, 1680–1800* (Chapel Hill: University of North Carolina Press, 1986), 205–60; and John Majewski, *A House Dividing: Economic Development in Pennsylvania and Virginia before the Civil War* (New York: Cambridge University Press, 2000), 14–17.

40 Stephanie McCurry, *Masters of Small Worlds: Yeoman Households, Gender Relations, and the Political Culture of the Antebellum South Carolina Low Country* (New York: Oxford University Press, 1995), 239–304.

41 James L. Huston, *Calculating the Value of the Union: Slavery, Property Rights, and the Economic Origins of the Civil War* (Chapel Hill: University of North Carolina Press, 2003), 36–45.

42 A lengthy literature documents this conflict. Two of the best books include Sean Patrick Adams, *Old Dominion, Industrial Commonwealth: Coal, Politics, and Economy in Antebellum America* (Baltimore: Johns Hopkins University Press, 2004); and Alison Goodyear Freehling, *Drift toward Disunion: The Virginia Slavery Debate of 1831–32* (Baton Rouge: Louisiana State University Press, 1982).

43 William C. Davis, *Look Away! A History of the Confederate States of America* (New York: Free Press, 2002), 259–79; David Williams, Teresa Crisp Williams, and David Carlson, *Plain Folk in a Rich Man's War: Class and Dissent in Confederate Georgia* (Gainesville: University Press of Florida, 2002), 131–94.

44 G. W. Berlin to Letcher, July 1862, John Letcher Papers, MSS lL5684a FA2, Virginia Historical Society.

45 McPherson, *Ordeal by Fire*, 173–76; William W. Freehling, *The South versus the South: How Anti-Confederate Southerners Shaped the Course of the Civil War* (New York: Oxford University Press, 2001), 17–82.

46 L. W. Spratt, *A Series of Articles on the Value of the Union to the South* (Charleston: James, Williams & Gitsinger, 1855), 22

47 Robert S. Starobin, *Industrial Slavery in the Old South* (New York: Oxford University Press, 1970), 230. Starobin writes: "By the time of secession in 1861, the use of slave labor to industrialize the South had become accepted in theory and practice."

48 Ira Berlin, *Many Thousands Gone: The First Two Centuries of Slavery in North America* (Cambridge: Harvard University Press, 1998), 1–14.

49 William A. Link, *Roots of Secession: Slavery and Politics in Antebellum Virginia* (Chapel Hill: University of North Carolina Press, 2003), 80–96; Richard C. Wade, *Slavery in the Cities: The South, 1820–1860* (New York: Oxford

University Press, 1964), 143–242; Midori Takagi, *Rearing Wolves to Our Own Destruction: Slavery in Richmond, Virginia, 1782–1865* (Charlottesville: University of Virginia Press, 1999).

50 Link, *Roots of Secession*, 94.

51 Steven A. Channing, *Crisis of Fear: Secession in South Carolina* (New York: Simon Schuster, 1970), 31–36, 43–44.

52 Edward B. Bryan, *The Rightful Remedy Addressed to the Slaveholders of the South* (Charleston, 1850), 47.

53 See, for example, J. W. Page, *Uncle Robin in His Cabin* (Richmond: J. W. Randolph, 1853).

54 Reese, *Proceedings of the Va. Convention*, 72.

55 Edmund Ruffin, "Consequences of Abolition Agitation," *De Bow's Review* 23 (November 1857): 549.

56 Spratt, *A Series of Articles on the Value of the Union to the South*, 11.

57 Edmund Ruffin, *Anticipations of the Future, To Serve as Lessons for the Present Times* (Richmond: J. W. Randolph, 1860), 130–31. Historian Alice Fahs shows that even during the midst of war, southerners continued to believe that slaves would loyally serve the Confederacy and refuse to join the Union army. See *The Imagined Civil War: Popular Literature of the North and South, 1861–1865* (Chapel Hill: University of North Carolina Press, 2001), 181–94.

58 Ira Berlin and others, eds., *Free at Last: A Documentary History of Slavery, Freedom, and the Civil War* (New York: New Press, 1992); Leon F. Litwack, *Been in the Storm So Long: The Aftermath of Slavery* (New York: Alfred A. Knopf, 1979), 3–103; Vincent Harding, *There Is a River: The Black Struggle for Freedom in America* (New York: Harcourt Brace Jovanovich, 1981), 219–41; Harris, *Plain Folk and Gentry in a Slave Society*, 167–91.

59 Freehling, *The South versus the South*, 85–114; Barbara J. Fields, "Who Freed the Slaves?," in *The Civil War: An Illustrated History*, by Geoffrey C. Ward with Ric Burns and Ken Burns (New York: Knopf, 1990), 179–81.

60 Quoted in Avery O. Craven, *Edmund Ruffin, Southerner: A Study in Secession* (1932; Baton Rouge: Louisiana State University Press, 1972), 259.

61 Edward L. Ayers, *The Promise of the New South: Life after Reconstruction* (New York: Oxford University Press, 1992), 9.

62 Quoted in ibid., 59.

63 Peter S. Carmichael, *The Last Generation: Young Virginians in Peace, War, and Reunion* (Chapel Hill: University of North Carolina Press, 2005), 234–36.

64 Paul M. Gaston, *The New South Creed: A Study in Southern Mythmaking* (New York: Alfred A. Knopf, 1970), 63.

STATISTICAL APPENDIX

1. The eight southern states are Virginia, Kentucky, Tennessee, North Carolina, South Carolina, Georgia, Alabama, and Mississippi. All states west of the Mississippi were excluded, as was Florida. The 1890 table includes West Virginia as well.
2. I classified all counties in Alabama, Mississippi, South Carolina, and Georgia as likely to have been infected. Portions of North Carolina and Virginia were infected in the late nineteenth century, but that was probably the result of a large influx of cattle from the Deep South during the Civil War. Before the Civil War, North Carolina banned cattle from the Lower South from entering the state between April 1 and November 1, which "largely kept cattle fever out of Virginia and states to the north before the Civil War" (G. Terry Sharrer, *A Kind of Fate: Agricultural Change in Virginia, 1861–1920* [Ames: Iowa State University Press, 2000], 18).
3. Various Hausman tests were tried to correct for endogeniety, but all conceivable instrumental variables—farm size, per capita personal wealth, per capita total wealth, or some measure of per capita agricultural output—are themselves associated (perhaps endogenously so) with high levels of improved land. This makes any result from such a test highly suspect.
4. A related problem is a possible missing variable bias. Any positive association between slavery and levels of improved land might be the result of variations in soil quality and commercial development not captured in our original specifications. Given the variations of soils and topography within our broad topographical categories, the possibility of a missing variable bias is quite strong.
5. For the northern figure, see Jeremy Atack and Fred Bateman, *To Their Own Soil: Agriculture in the Antebellum North* (Ames: Iowa State University Press, 1987), 225–26. I derive the percentage of nonfarm rural southern households from a sample of 4,016 households in four cotton counties reported in J. William Harris, *Plain Folk and Gentry in a Slave Society: White Liberty and Black Slavery in Augusta's Hinterlands* (Middletown, Conn.: Wesleyan University Press, 1985), 21. The weighted average of nonfarm rural population was 23.5 percent, but since some of the households listed in the "other, at home, none" category might have been farmers or farm laborers, 20 percent is perhaps a safe estimate.
6. I also included capital goods such as steam engines and railroad equipment, reasoning that the demand for such items ultimately depended upon local consumer demand.

7 Nathan Rosenberg, for example, notes the heavy use of lumber in the balloon-frame house that came about in the 1830s. Housing and building, of course, are classic "demand-driven" industries. See *Technology and American Economic Growth* (New York: Harper and Row, 1972), 27–30.

8 Eugene D. Genovese, *The Political Economy of Slavery: Studies in the Economy and Society of the Slave South* (1961; Middletown, Conn.: Wesleyan University Press, 1989), 157–79.

9 See, for example, Kenneth Sokoloff, "Invention, Innovation, and Manufacturing Productivity Growth in the Antebellum Northeast," in *American Economic Growth and Standards of Living before the Civil War*, ed. Robert E. Gallman and John Joseph Wallis (Chicago: University of Chicago Press, 1992), 345–78; and Jeremy Atack, "Returns to Scale in Antebellum United States Manufacturing," *Explorations in Economic History* 14 (November 1977): 337–59.

10 David F. Weiman, "The Economic Emancipation of the Non-Slaveholding Class: Upcountry Farmers in the Georgia Cotton Economy," *Journal of Economic History* 45 (March 1985): 83–88; Edward L. Ayers, *The Promise of the New South: Life after Reconstruction* (New York: Oxford University Press, 1992), 3–13; 55–62 ; Gavin Wright, *Old South, New South: Revolutions in the Southern Economy since the Civil War* (New York: Basic Books, 1986), 39–42.

11 Michael M. Bell, "Did New England Go Downhill?," *Geographical Review* 79 (October 1989): 460–61.

12 Gilbert C. Fite, *Cotton Fields No More: Southern Agriculture, 1865–1980* (Lexington: University of Kentucky Press, 1984), 85–86.

13 For infected counties, see U.S. Bureau of Animal Husbandry, *Map Showing Boundary Line of District Infected with Splenetic or Southern Cattle Fever* (Washington, D.C., 1891).

14 Albert E. Cowdrey, *This Land, This South: An Environmental History*, rev. ed. (Lexington: University of Kentucky Press, 1996), 122–23; Ayers, *Promise of the New South*, 194–95.

SECONDARY LITERATURE
AND PRIMARY SOURCES

The scholarship on the three interrelated topics of the antebellum South, slavery, and the Civil War is vast. So, too, are the breadth and depth of the primary sources—ranging from personal papers to census records and printed sources such as books, pamphlets, and newspaper articles. What follows is a brief summary, organized by topic, of the secondary and primary sources that I have found most important to this study. Given the intimidating size of the literature, the portion of the essay covering secondary works focuses on books and articles published in the last two decades. It would have been difficult—perhaps impossible—to write *Modernizing a Slave Economy* without such a strong secondary literature to draw upon.

CONFEDERATE NATIONALISM AND THE POLITICAL
ECONOMY OF SECESSION

The recent literature on secession is especially rich. William Freehling's two-volume study—*The Road to Disunion*, vol. 1, *Secessionists at Bay, 1776–1854* (New

York: Oxford University Press, 1990); and *The Road to Disunion*, vol. 2, *Secessionists Triumphant* (New York: Oxford University Press, 2007)—highlights how secessionist politics often reflect important regional divisions within the South. Freehling's work led me to take a comparative approach that resulted in Virginia and South Carolina becoming my two case studies. In selecting Virginia and South Carolina, I benefited from a number of state-level studies that draw complex linkages between economic development and the secessionist impulse. Lacy K. Ford's *The Origins of Southern Radicalism: The South Carolina Upcountry, 1800–1860* (New York: Oxford University Press, 1988) argues that even as Upcountry planters eagerly supported economic development, they feared losing control of their political destiny, making them more sensitive to the abolitionist threat. Manisha Sinha, *The Counter-Revolution of Slavery: Politics and Ideology in Antebellum South Carolina* (Chapel Hill: University of North Carolina Press, 2000), dispenses with Ford's republican framework and interprets South Carolina secessionists as antiliberal, antirepublican conservatives. Stephanie McCurry's *Masters of Small Worlds: Yeoman Households, Gender Relations, and the Political Culture of the Antebellum South Carolina Low Country* (New York: Oxford University Press, 1995) shows how gender ideology and evangelical religion served to unite yeomen and slaveholders, which ultimately helped generate a consensus favoring secession. William A. Link's *Roots of Secession: Slavery and Politics in Antebellum Virginia* (Chapel Hill: University of North Carolina Press, 2003) shows that the growing importance of railroads and cities made Virginians feel less secure about slavery, especially since the slaves themselves exerted more autonomy in urban areas such as Richmond. Daniel W. Crofts's *Reluctant Confederates: Upper South Unionists in the Secession Crisis* (Chapel Hill: University of North Carolina Press, 1989) provides a thorough analysis of the strong antisecession impulse in Virginia and other border states. In the same spirit, Nelson D. Lankford shows the importance of contingency and individual agency during the secession crisis in *Cry Havoc! The Crooked Road to Civil War, 1861* (New York: Viking, 2007).

The secession movement was intimately connected to the formation of Confederate nationalism. Like many historians focusing on Confederate nationalism, I have been influenced by Benedict Anderson's *Imagined Communities: Reflections on the Origin and Spread of Nationalism* (New York: Verso Press, 1983). It is not a big leap from "imagined communities" to "imagined economies." Anderson's focus on print culture also fits well with my study, as I found pamphlets, books, and newspaper editorials particularly important in reflecting secessionist thinking. Several other works on Confederate nationalism make use of Anderson, including Drew Gilpin Faust's *The Creation of Confederate Nationalism: Ideology and Identity in the Civil War South* (Baton Rouge: Louisiana State University Press, 1988) and Don H. Doyle's *Nations Divided: America, Italy, and the Southern*

*Question* (Athens: University of Georgia Press, 2002). Faust has also been at the forefront of analyzing the gendered meanings of Confederate nationalism. See *Mothers of Invention: Women of the Slaveholding South in the American Civil War* (Chapel Hill: University of North Carolina Press, 1996) for her penetrating analysis of how women of slaveholding families strongly supported—and sometimes strongly opposed—the Confederate cause. Anne Sarah Rubin's *A Shattered Nation: The Rise and Fall of the Confederacy, 1861–1868* (Chapel Hill: University of North Carolina Press, 2005) and George C. Rable's *The Confederate Republic: A Revolution against Politics* (Chapel Hill: University of North Carolina, 1994) emphasize religion and republicanism as essential components of Confederate nationalism, which is not inconsistent with the desire to create a more modern economy.

Confederate nationalism—or perhaps the lack of it—has been the subject of historical debate. Gary W. Gallagher, *The Confederate War: How Popular Will, Nationalism, and Military Strategy Could Not Stave Off Defeat* (Cambridge: Harvard University Press, 1997), makes a compelling case that Confederate nationalism was extraordinarily strong during the war. William W. Freehling, *The South vs. the South: How Anti-Confederate Southerners Shaped the Course of the Civil War* (New York: Oxford University Press, 2001), makes an equally compelling case that most slaves and a good many Upcountry yeomen opposed the Confederacy. As I suggest in the concluding chapter, Gallagher and Freehling are both right: Confederate nationalism attracted slaveholders and their allies even as it repelled many others. Alice Fahs's *The Imagined Civil War: Popular Literature of the North and South, 1861–1865* (Chapel Hill: University of North Carolina Press, 2001) shows how white Confederates convinced themselves that slaves would be loyal to the Confederacy. Like other recent interpreters of Confederate nationalism, I found several older studies invaluable, including Avery Craven's *The Growth of Southern Nationalism, 1848–1861* (Baton Rouge: Louisiana State University Press and the Littlefield Fund for Southern History of the University of Texas, 1953) and James McCardell's *The Idea of a Southern Nation: Southern Nationalists and Southern Nationalism, 1830–1860* (New York: W. W. Norton, 1979).

A closely related issue is the growth of the Confederate state. Emory M. Thomas, *The Confederacy as a Revolutionary Experience* (Englewood Cliffs, N.J.: Prentice Hall, 1971), sees a powerful Confederate state representing a decisive break with the past. Paul D. Escott's *After Secession: Jefferson Davis and the Failure of Confederate Nationalism* (Baton Rouge: Louisiana State University Press, 1978) argues that Jefferson Davis failed to unite the Confederacy around a strong central state. A number of other works—including Raimondo Luraghi's *The Rise and Fall of the Plantation South* (New York: New Viewpoints, 1978) and Jeffrey Rogers Hummel's *Emancipating Slaves, Enslaving Free Men: A History of the American*

*Civil War* (Chicago: Open Court, 1996) highlight the Confederacy's version of war socialism. Harold S. Wilson's *Confederate Industry: Manufacturers and Quartermasters in the Civil War* (Jackson: University Press of Mississippi, 2002) shows in great detail the vast power of the Confederacy's Quartermaster Department. Perhaps the most comprehensive analysis of Confederate state building is Richard Franklin Bensel's *Yankee Leviathan: The Origins of Central State Authority in America, 1859–1877* (New York: Cambridge Press, 1990). Bensel's argument that the Confederate state was more interventionist than its northern counterpart is consistent with my own claims.

As noted in the introduction, a number of influential scholars have portrayed the Confederacy as fundamentally antimodern in its economic orientation. James M. McPherson uses economic and social modernization as a central divide between North and South in his large corpus of works, including *Drawn with the Sword: Reflections on the American Civil War* (New York: Oxford University Press, 1996); his best-selling synthesis *Battle Cry of Freedom: The Civil War Era* (New York: Oxford University Press, 1988); and his well-known textbook *Ordeal by Fire: The Civil War and Reconstruction*, 3rd ed. (New York: McGraw-Hill, 2001). Eugene Genovese represents another strain in the literature that interprets the South as fundamentally antimodern. Genovese has modified his early neo-Marxist contributions—especially *The Political Economy of Slavery: Studies in the Economy and Society of the Slave South* (1961; Middletown, Conn.: Wesleyan University Press, 1989) and *The World the Slaveholders Made: Two Essays in Interpretation* (Middletown, Conn.: Wesleyan University Press, 1988)—to present a more subtle argument that sees southerners struggling to reconcile their conservative proslavery politics with their liberal belief in progress. I have found Genovese's *The Slaveholders' Dilemma: Freedom and Progress in Southern Conservative Thought, 1820–1860* (Columbia: University of South Carolina Press, 1992) particularly helpful. Elizabeth Fox-Genovese and Eugene Genovese, *The Mind of the Master Class: History and Faith in the Southern Slaveholders' Worldview* (Cambridge and New York: Cambridge University Press, 2005), is also extremely useful. While not necessarily accepting all of Genovese's arguments, many historians see southern economic backwardness as a product of traditional southern culture and values. Marc Egnal's comparative history *Divergent Paths: How Culture and Institutions Have Shaped North American Growth* (New York: Oxford University Press, 1996) exemplifies this approach.

Other scholars, focusing on the well-developed markets for southern staple crops, portray slaveholders as intensely capitalistic. Economists Robert William Fogel and Stanley L. Engerman's *Time on the Cross: The Economics of American Negro Slavery* (Boston: Little, Brown and Company, 1974) and Fogel's *Without Consent or Contract: The Rise and Fall of American Slavery* (New York: W. W.

Norton, 1989) argue that slavery was an efficient, capitalistic system that allowed planters to reap great profits. Although heavily criticized by economists and historians alike, Fogel and Engerman fundamentally changed the terms of the debate. While quite different in terms of method and evidence from Fogel and Engerman, most recent scholarship stresses that market-oriented, prodevelopment sentiments infused southern political economy. Two important state-level studies—Tom Downey's *Planting a Capitalist South: Masters, Merchants, and Manufacturers in the Southern Interior, 1790–1860* (Baton Rouge: Louisiana State University Press, 2006) and Peter S. Carmichael's *The Last Generation: Young Virginians in Peace, War, and Reunion* (Chapel Hill: University of North Carolina Press, 2005)—typify this trend. Historians working on the intersection of political economy and cultural history have shown that southerners fused a modern economic outlook with elements of a more traditional society. A superb example of this approach is Mark H. Smith's *Mastered by the Clock: Time, Slavery, and Freedom in the American South* (Chapel Hill: University of North Carolina Press, 1997). Many scholars, though, still remain skeptical of Fogel and Engerman's tendency to equate economic growth with economic development, which minimizes the regional differences in urbanization, manufacturing, and innovative activity. In *Slavery and American Economic Development* (Baton Rouge: Louisiana State University Press, 2006), Gavin Wright posits an economic "cold war" between North and South based on two differing models of economic growth: a slave-based system of extensive growth and geographic expansion and a free-labor system based on intensive growth and infrastructure improvements. Slavery, in Wright's view, produced profits without leading to development.

Given the profitability of slavery, it is not surprising that many scholars stress that secession was primarily a means of protecting the property rights to slave labor. Wright's *The Political Economy of the Cotton South: Households, Markets, and Wealth in the Nineteenth Century* (New York: Norton, 1978), Roger L. Ransom's *Conflict and Compromise: The Political Economy of Slavery, Emancipation, and the American Civil War* (Cambridge and New York: Cambridge University Press, 1989), and James L. Huston's *Calculating the Value of the Union: Slavery, Property Rights, and the Economic Origins of the Civil War* (Chapel Hill: University of North Carolina Press, 2003), make this basic argument, albeit in very different ways. Few scholars would disagree that the preservation of slavery was a key secessionist motivation, but framing the issue in such conservative terms leaves open the question of whether a more forward-looking vision existed within secessionist thought. A few historians note that the secessionists viewed the Confederacy as a way to encourage diversification and economic development. Mary A. DeCredico shows that Georgia's industrial entrepreneurs readily adapted to wartime conditions in *Patriotism for Profit: Georgia's Urban Entrepre-*

*neurs and the Confederate War Effort* (Chapel Hill: University of North Carolina Press, 1990). Robert Royal Russel's *Economic Aspects of Southern Sectionalism, 1840–1861* (Urbana: University of Illinois Press, 1924), while dated in certain respects, is too often overlooked. Chad Morgan usefully analyzes what he calls the "inverted Prussian Road" in *Planters' Progress: Modernizing Confederate Georgia* (Gainesville: University Press of Florida, 2005). For a critique of the Prussian-road model—which is most often applied to the postbellum era—see Shearer Davis Bowman, *Masters and Lords: Mid-19th-Century U.S. Planters and Prussian Junkers* (New York: Oxford University Press, 1993).

SHIFTING CULTIVATION AND AGRICULTURAL REFORM

When I first started investigating the high levels of unimproved land in the nineteenth-century South, I had barely heard of shifting cultivation. Steven Stoll's *Larding the Lean Earth: Soil and Society in Nineteenth-Century America* (New York: Hill and Wang, 2002) and Jack Temple Kirby's *Poquosin: A Study in Rural Landscape and Society* (Chapel Hill: University of North Carolina Press, 1995) alerted me to its importance in South Carolina and Virginia. While I ultimately disagree with some of the conclusions of Stoll and Kirby, it would have been difficult to write the shifting-cultivation chapter without their insightful accounts. Once I started looking for shifting cultivation, I found a number of helpful references within the agricultural history literature, especially in the following: Daniel W. Croft, *Cobb's Ordeal: The Diaries of a Virginia Farmer, 1842–1872* (Athens: University of Georgia Press, 1997); Stanley Wayne Trimble, *Man-Induced Soil Erosion on the Southern Piedmont, 1700–1970* (Ankeny, Iowa: Soil Conservation Society of America, 1974); and Lois Green Carr, Russell R. Menard, and Lorena S. Walsh, *Robert Cole's World: Agriculture and Society in Early Maryland* (Chapel Hill: University of North Carolina Press, 1991). As to the causes of shifting cultivation, perhaps the single best work is Douglas Helms, "Soil and Southern History," *Agricultural History* 74 (Autumn 2000): 736–43. Helms's detailed analysis highlights the important differences between ultisols and alfisols. G. Terry Sharrer's *A Kind of Fate: Agricultural Change in Virginia, 1861–1920* (Ames: Iowa State University Press, 2000) shows the continuing importance of environmental factors in the agriculture of postbellum Virginia. Helms and Sharrer hint at the wider economic implications of southern agricultural practices, but there has been little systematic study of the relationship between shifting cultivation and the development of the southern economy. Diane Lindstrom, *Economic Development in the Philadelphia Region, 1810–1850* (New York: Columbia University Press, 1978), and David R. Meyer, *The Roots of American Industrialization* (Baltimore: Johns Hopkins University Press, 2003), are among the works that make a compelling case that a densely populated countryside spurred northern development. Peter A. Coclanis usefully explores the concept of "market disarticulation" in *The Shadow of a Dream: Economic Life and Death in the South Carolina Low Country, 1670–1920* (New York: Oxford University Press, 1989). Nobody has done more research to show the importance of the "extent of markets" to early industrialization than Kenneth L. Sokoloff. See, for example, "Invention, Innovation, and Manufacturing Productivity Growth in the Antebellum Northeast," in *American Economic Growth and Standards of Living before the Civil War*, ed. Robert E. Gallman and John Joseph Wallis (Chicago: University of Chicago Press, 1992).

The large literature on southern agricultural reform has often centered on the effectiveness of the southern reformers. Older studies—exemplified by Avery O. Craven's *Edmund Ruffin, Southerner: A Study in Secession* (New York: D. Appleton and Co., 1932; repr. Baton Rouge: Louisiana State University Press, 1972)—argued that the reform movement largely succeeded in revolutionizing southern agriculture. More recent work—such as William W. Mathew's *Edmund Ruffin and the Crisis of Slavery in the Old South: The Failure of Agricultural Reform* (Athens: University of Georgia Press, 1988)—points out the shortcomings of the agricultural reform movement. Drew Gilpin Faust, "The Rhetoric and Ritual of Agriculture in Antebellum South Carolina," *Journal of Southern History* 45 (November 1979): 541–68, and Charles G. Steffen, "In Search of the Good Overseer: The Failure of the Agricultural Reform Movement in Lowcountry South Carolina, 1821–1834," *Journal of Southern History* 63 (November 1997): 753–802, investigate the relationship between agricultural reform and proslavery politics. Both Faust and Steffen attribute the movement's lack of success to a conservative bias among slaveholding planters. In many respects, my own work follows the footsteps of Julius Rubin's classic article, "The Limits of Agricultural Progress in the Nineteenth-Century South," *Agricultural History* 49 (April 1975): 362–73, which argues that the southern environment sharply limited the options available to southern planters and farmers.

I used a wide variety of primary sources to analyze shifting cultivation and agricultural reform. As noted in the statistical appendix, the census bureau began collecting information on improved-unimproved acreage beginning in 1850, providing an invaluable means of analyzing the extent of shifting cultivation. Historical census data is conveniently available online via the Historical Census Browser, which is sponsored by the University of Virginia's Geospatial and Statistical Data Center (<http://fisher.lib.virginia.edu/collections/stats/histcensus/index.html.>). Personal papers and journals—such as the Ruffin Papers (Virginia Historical Society), the Ashmore Papers (University of North Carolina at Chapel Hill), and the William E. Sparkman Journal (University of North Carolina at

Chapel Hill)—provided important firsthand accounts of southern agricultural practices. Frederick Law Olmsted's descriptions of the southern landscape, especially *A Journey in the Seaboard Slave States, with Remarks on Their Economy* (New York: Mason Brothers, 1859), revealed much about northern attitudes toward shifting cultivation. So did the many speeches made by northern congressmen during the 1850s. Published in the *Congressional Globe*, these speeches are readily available online at the Library of Congress website. *The Diary of Edmund Ruffin* (Baton Rouge: Louisiana State University Press, 1972), brilliantly edited by William Kauffman Scarborough, provides fascinating detail about Ruffin's role as an agricultural reformer and ardent secessionist. Jack Temple Kirby's *Nature's Management: Writings on Landscape and Reform, 1822–1859* (Athens: University of Georgia Press, 2000) reprints many of Ruffin's most important essays on agricultural reform and the southern environment. Ruffin, of course, published an important reform periodical, the *Farmer's Register*, which was part of a vibrant agricultural press that included journals such as the *Southern Planter* and the *Southern Cultivator*. Many of these periodicals are available online as part of "American Periodical Series Online, 1740–1900," an excellent collection that saved me from many blurry hours in front of a microfilm reader. The details of state agricultural policy were far harder to sort out than I first thought they would be. Legislative records and session laws available at the Virginia State Archives and the South Carolina State Archives proved helpful for understanding the small commitment to agricultural research in each state.

RAILROADS AND TRADE

An impressive literature traces the development of southern railroads. Although published more than a century ago, Ulrich Bonnell Phillips's *A History of Transportation in the Eastern Cotton Belt to 1860* (Columbia University Press, 1908; repr. New York: Octagon Books, 1968) is still useful. A large literature, beginning with the "Commonwealth School" of the 1950s, has investigated the relationship between public policy and railroad development. Louis Hartz, *Economic Policy and Democratic Thought: Pennsylvania, 1776–1860* (Cambridge: Harvard University Press, 1948), shows the transition from state-funded internal improvements to a more laissez-faire philosophy regarding railroads. While acknowledging a degree of public support, Albert Fishlow's *American Railroads and the Transformation of the Antebellum Economy* (Cambridge: Harvard University Press, 1965) finds that private investment had decisively superseded public investment, at least in the Northeast and Midwest. Carter Goodrich, *Government Promotion of American Canals and Railroads, 1800–1890* (New York: Columbia University Press, 1960), on the other hand, argues that while a more laissez-faire attitude prevailed by the

Civil War, government aid to railroads was still important. Colleen A. Dunlavy's *Politics and Industrialization: Early Railroads in the United States and Prussia* (Princeton: Princeton University Press, 1994) demonstrates that government aid was far more prominent in early railroad development than in Prussia. John Lauritz Larson's influential *Internal Improvement: National Public Works and the Promise of Popular Government in the Early United States* (Chapel Hill: University of North Carolina Press, 2001) shows how private and local interests ultimately derailed ambitious national plans.

A number of detailed state-level studies confirm how activist state governments continued to invest in railroads in the South. These studies include Peter Wallenstein, *From Slave South to New South: Public Policy in Nineteenth-Century Georgia* (Chapel Hill: University of North Carolina Press, 1987), and Milton Sydney Heath, *Constructive Liberalism: The Role of the State in Economic Development in Georgia to 1860* (Cambridge: Harvard University Press, 1954). Several studies have analyzed the growth of Virginia's railroad network, including David R. Goldfield, *Urban Growth in the Age of Sectionalism: Virginia, 1847–1861* (Baton Rouge: Louisiana University Press, 1977); William G. Shade, *Democratizing the Old Dominion: Virginia and the Second Party System, 1824–1861* (Charlottesville: University Press of Virginia, 1996); and William A. Link's aforementioned *Roots of Secession*. For South Carolina railroads, Ford's *The Origins of Southern Radicalism* and Downey's *Planting the Capitalist South* are two of the most important recent studies. In his influential *Old South, New South: Revolutions in the Southern Economy since the Civil War* (New York: Basic Books, 1986), Gavin Wright contends that the mobility of slave labor gave planters little incentive to invest in railroads and other improvements that might raise property values. The widespread boosterism that animated railroad construction in Virginia and South Carolina is somewhat at odds with Wright's argument. Sean Patrick Adams, in *Old Dominion, Industrial Commonwealth: Coal, Politics, and Economy in Antebellum America* (Baltimore: Johns Hopkins University Press, 2004), argues that Virginia's undemocratic, planter-dominated legislature short-circuited western internal improvements, a point that is consistent with my critique of the localism that so heavily influenced state railroad investment in both Virginia and South Carolina.

The literature on southerners and trade quite rightly stresses the South's opposition to protectionist measures in the antebellum period. I found William W. Freehling's important monograph on the nullification crisis, *Prelude to Civil War: The Nullification Controversy in South Carolina, 1816–1836* (New York: Oxford University Press, 1965), extremely helpful in linking slavery and antiprotectionist positions. Jeremy Atack and Peter Passell, *A New Economic View of American History: From Colonial Times to 1940*, 2nd ed. (New York: W. W. Norton, 1994), summarizes the econometric evidence that the tariff did indeed heavily penalize southerners. Joseph J. Persky's *The Burden of Dependency: Colonial Themes in Southern Economic Thought* (Baltimore: Johns Hopkins University Press, 1992) explores how perceived inequalities in trade sometimes led southerners to view themselves as colonial dependents. Beginning in the 1830s, southerners often met in commercial conventions to hatch plans to establish direct trade with Europe and escape their colonial dependency. For the most recent analysis of these meetings, see Vicki Vaughn Johnson, *The Men and the Vision of the Southern Commercial Conventions, 1845–1871* (Columbia: University of Missouri Press, 1992).

Despite their critique of trade with the North, southerners often saw trade (in the form of national and international markets) as a potent means of establishing national identity. In this regard, I have been very much influenced by Cathy D. Matson and Peter S. Onuf, *A Union of Interests: Political and Economic Thought in Revolutionary America* (Lawrence: University Press of Kansas, 1990), which shows how perceived "interests"—often generated from trade—formed much of the basis of nationalistic thinking in the early United States. Nicholas Onuf and Peter Onuf similarly note how the emergence of national and international markets generated differing conceptions of nationalism in *Nations, Markets, and War: Modern History and the American Civil War* (Charlottesville: University of Virginia Press, 2006). Brian Schoen argues that southerners (especially those in the Lower South) believed that King Cotton and free trade represented a decidedly modern economic order; see "Alternatives to Dependence: The Lower South's Antebellum Pursuit of Sectional Development through Global Interdependence," in *Global Perspectives on Industrial Transformation in the American South*, ed. Susanna Delfino and Michel Gillespie (Columbia: University of Missouri Press, 2005). Ronald Takaki, *A Pro-Slavery Crusade: The Agitation to Reopen the African Slave Trade* (New York: Free Press, 1971), documents the unsuccessful attempt of some southerners to take free trade to its ultimate extreme.

I used a number of different sources to understand how southern extremists viewed trade. Several prominent newspapers available on microfilm, including the *Charleston Mercury* and the *Richmond Enquirer*, proved invaluable. *De Bow's Review*, which combined southern extremism with calls for a modern economy, is available online via the American Periodical Series. Although published in New Orleans, *De Bow's Review* included a good many articles on Virginia and South Carolina. Other important periodicals available via the American Periodical Series include the *Southern Literary Messenger* and the *Southern Quarterly*. The *Richmond Daily Dispatch*, put online by the University of Richmond at <http://dlxs.richmond.edu/d/ddr/>, is an excellent source for Civil War historians. I also made extensive use of more traditional documentary collections. Clyde N. Wilson and various coeditors expertly collected *The Papers of John C. Calhoun* (Columbia: University of South Carolina Press, 1959–2003). The Calhoun papers provided a wealth of material about agriculture, railroads, and economic policy. I found the proceedings of the South Carolina Secession Convention, available on microfilm via the Confederate Imprint Series, useful for understanding debates between radical free traders and moderates advocating a revenue tariff. *The Proceedings of the Virginia State Convention of 1861*, ed. George Reese (Richmond: Virginia State Library, 1965), was even more valuable, as Virginia secessionists and Unionists debated the economic consequences of secession in scores of lengthy speeches. Virginia's *Annual Reports of the Board of Public Works* (Richmond, various years) contains a treasure trove of material related to internal improvements in the Old Dominion.

The many pamphlets published in antebellum Virginia and South Carolina provided another important source. Whether reprints of newspaper articles, public addresses, or original works, these pamphlets helped shape public opinion. The collections of the Virginia Historical Society, the Southern Historical Collection at UNC–Chapel Hill, and the South Caroliniana Library contain a large number of such pamphlets, and others are available via interlibrary loan. Some of the most useful include: Muscoe R. H. Garnett, *The Union, Past and Future: How It Works and How to Save It* (Washington, D.C.: Jno. T. Towers, 1850); L. W. Spratt, *A Series of Articles on the Value of the Union to the South, Lately Published in the Charleston Standard* (Charleston: James, Williams, and Gitsinger, 1855); E. N. Elliott, *Cotton Is King, and Pro-Slavery Arguments* (Augusta, Ga.: Pritchard, Abbott, & Loomis, 1860); John Townsend, *The Southern States, Their Present Peril and Their Certain Remedy* (Charleston: E. C. Councell, 1850); and John Townsend, *The South Alone, Should Govern the South . . .* (Charleston: Evans and Cogswell, 1860). Two books proved to be especially valuable primary sources: Edmund Ruffin's futuristic novel, *Anticipations of the Future, to Serve as Lessons for the Present Times* (Richmond: J. W. Randolph, 1860), and William Howard Russell's *My Diary North and South*, edited by Eugene H. Berwanger (New York: McGraw Hill, 1988). Ruffin unintentionally showed the miscalculations within secessionist thinking, while Russell's wry wit exposed the economic reductionism that lay at the heart of the South's "King Cotton" mentality.

INDEX

Abolitionism, 8; and southern fears of irrational fanaticism, 117–18; as threat to the South, 59–60, 98, 157–58. *See also* Brown, John
Adams, John Quincy, 80
Agricultural reform movement: and critiques of shifting cultivation and individualism, 31, 51–52, 56, 67–68, 79–80; and defense of slavery, 59–62; and failures to transform southern economy, 54–55, 72–74; political failures of, 55, 74–78; and support of southern state activism, 17–18, 54, 62–68, 69–70, 79–80; and use of state power to prevent malaria, 68–72; varied ideological strands of, 64–68. *See also* Shifting cultivation
Alabama, 28, 168
Albemarle County, Va., 123
Alexandria, Va., 88
Alfisols, fertility of, 36, 164–65, 179
American Revolution: and boycotts as model for the South, 121–22; compared to Confederacy, 140, 144, 152; influenced by republicanism, 10
American System, 109
Anderson, Joseph, 123
*Anticipations of the Future* (Ruffin), 116, 125, 158–59
Appalachia: agricultural practices of, 29–30, 179; difficult topography of,

164–65; and failure to support the Confederacy, 154–55
Ashmore, John D., 28–29
Augusta, Ga., 148

Bank of the United States, 9
Barbour, James, 64, 129
Barnwell Agricultural Society, 67
Benning, Henry, 125–26, 129, 158
Bensel, Richard Franklin, 7, 147
Berlin, G. W., 155
Berlin, Ira, 156
Blockade (Union), 138–39
Bluegrass Region, 32, 47, 165
Blue Ridge Railroad, 89
Board of Public Works, 97
Bonus Bill, 99
Boston, Mass., 25
*Boston Shoe and Leather Reporter*, 130
Botts, John Minor, 100–101
Boyce, W. W., 131
Boycotts, 121–25
Brazil, 94, 159
British Board of Agriculture, 65–66
Brown, John, 15–16, 53–54, 122–23, 124, 126, 144
Brown, Joseph E., 150
Breen, T. H., 39–40
Bright, John, 137–38
Brooks, Preston, 112–13
Bruce, James, 126, 130
Bryan, Edward B., 117
Buffalo, N.Y., 86
Burt, Armistead, 8
Burwell, William M., 94–95

Calhoun, John C., 11, 14, 111; strong support for railroads, 93, 99–100
Cardozo, Jacob, 51, 98

Carmichael, Peter, 160
Census of 1850, 29
Central Southern Rights Association, 122–23, 124
Charleston, S.C., 14, 17, 18, 25, 43, 88, 90, 157; and boosters' support for western railroads, 84–85, 89, 104; commercial promise within Confederacy, 102, 113–14, 131; small population and small markets of, 90, 137–38
Charleston and Savannah Railroad, 94
*Charleston Mercury*, 15, 106, 113, 114, 131, 146, 150
Chesapeake region, 27
Chesterfield County, Va., 123
China, 94, 95, 96–97
Christy, David, 118
Cities. *See* Urbanization
Clay, Henry, 109, 125
Climate, 16, 165
Clover, 27
Cobb, Daniel, 27
Cole, Robert, 27
Colonization Society, 59
Commercial conventions, 105–6
Confederate government, 132; and control of southern economy, 6–7, 148–50; draconian conscription policies of, 149–50; and elastic nature of constitution, 131, 146–48; images on currency of, 140–41; growth during Civil War, 141–43, 148–51; and origins of strong central state, 143–48; and political debate over subsides to railroads, 146–48. Confederate nationalism, 64; and economic imagination, 3–4, 16, 140–41; and importance of economic interests in creating, 11–

12, 97–100, 151, 153, 155–57; limitations of, 141–43; repelled Upcountry farmers and slaves, 153–55, 157–59; and strength among slaveholders, 151–52. *See also* Slavery

Confederate tariffs: broad consensus for revenue tariff, 131–33; and dreams of industrial economy, 19–20, 111–12, 125–30; probable economic impact of, 136–39; tied to national identity, 133–34. *See also* Free trade; Tariffs (U.S.)

Continuous cultivation, 32–36. *See also* Shifting cultivation

Cooper, Thomas, 108

Cotton, 21, 168–69, 179. *See also* King Cotton mentality

Craven, John H., 36

Dickinson College, 52

Davis, Jefferson, 7, 138–39, 146–47, 48

Davy, Humphry, 57

De Bow, J. D. B., 5, 151

*De Bow's Review*, 5

Democratic Party, 14, 95

Dew, Thomas R., 84, 92–93

Direct trade, 18–19, 94, 96, 105, 140

*Doom of Slavery, The* (Townsend), 15, 115

Dunlavy, Colleen, 90

Economic development. *See* Industrialization; Urbanization

Education, 44

Egypt, 137

*Elements of Agricultural Chemistry* (Davy), 57

Elmore, F. H., 99–100

Eminent domain, 70

Erosion, 36

*Farmers' Register*, 60, 63, 71–72, 77

Faust, Drew Gilpin, 21

Fehrenbacher, Don E., 148

Fite, Gilbert C., 80, 178

Fitzhugh, George, 8

Floyd, John B., 14, 18, 75, 95

Fodder, 35–36

Fredericksburg, Va., 123

Free-labor ideology, 46–47, 50, 52

Free trade: and imagined revival of the southern commerce, 111–16; modified by secessionists, 110–11, 128–29; radical supporters of, 130–31; and stronger ties to Europe and West, 118–19. *See also* Confederate tariffs; Tariffs (U.S.)

Fugitive Slave Act of 1850, 11, 122

Garnett, Muscoe H. R., 14, 105, 106, 110, 112–13, 116, 131

Garrison, William Lloyd, 8

Gaston, Paul M., 160

Genovese, Eugene, 41–42

Georgia, 168

*Gone with the Wind* (Mitchell), 6

Gooch, Clairborne W., 67, 78

Goode, John, Jr., 126, 153

Gray, Cecil Lewis, 26

Great Britain: Confederate attempts to appeal to, 45; rejection of King Cotton, 137–38; supposed dependence on cotton, 116–18

Great Dismal Swamp, 71

Gregg, William, 88, 102, 103

Hale, Stephen, 154

Hamburg, S.C., 88

Hamilton, Alexander, 9, 103, 133–34

Hamilton, D. H., 117

Hammond, James H., 13–14, 57, 73,

Index    235

111; and agricultural policies, 75–76; and King Cotton mentality, 117; opposition to railroad spending, 101–2, 103

Harper, William, 117

Hatcher, Jordan, 157

Hayne, Robert, 91, 98–99

Herbemont, Nicholas, 60, 69, 75–76

Homespun, 124–25

India, 95, 137

Individualism: rejected by secessionists, 56, 79–80, 109–10

Industrialization: dependence on extent of markets, 40–43, 172–75. *See also* Confederate tariffs; Railroads; Urbanization

Jamison, D. F., 64–66

Japan, 9, 94

Jefferson, Thomas, 3, 14, 126

Johnson, B. P., 66

Johnson, David, 88, 91

Johnson, Joseph, 95, 157

Kansas-Nebraska Act, 13

Kennedy, John, 120

Kentucky, 32, 47, 165

King Cotton mentality: predicted influence on Europe and the North, 116–19; ultimate failure of, 137–38

Kinzer, William, 52

Kirby, Jack Temple, 27

"L.C.B." (pseudonym), 2–3

Lancaster County, Pa., 42

Larson, John Lauritz, 5

Letcher, John, 106, 120–21

Lieber, Oscar M., 74

Lincoln, Abraham: critique of shifting cultivation, 49–50

Link, William, 157

List, Friedrich, 129

Livestock, 31. *See also* Fodder; Southern cattle fever

London, Daniel H., 14, 122–23, 124

Lord, Daniel, 136–37

Lost Cause mythology, 6

Louisville, Cincinnati, and Charleston Railroad, 84–85, 91. *See also* South Carolina Railroad

Lumber production, 30–31, 171–74

Mainline system, 86

Manning, John L., 102

Manufacturing. *See* Industrialization

Marl, 65. *See also* Ruffin, Edmund

Marlborough district, S.C., 31

Maryland, 27

Massachusetts, 77

Mathew, William, 59

Maury, Matthew F., 14, 38, 96–97

McCardell, John

McDuffie, George, 108–9

McPherson, James, 4–5

Memphis and Charleston Railroad, 91, 93, 99–100

Mexico, 159

Meyer, David R., 40

Midwest, 170, 178

Miles, William Porcher, 133

Millponds, 69–70

Mills, Robert, 31

Mississippi, 28, 130, 132, 149, 168, 179

Mississippi River, 21, 99, 179

Missouri Crisis, 46–47

Mitchell, Margaret, 6

Moore, Barrington, 9

Moore, John Hebron, 28

Moore, Samuel, 119
Morrill, Justin Smith, 45–46
Morriss, R. G., 98

Nashville basin, 165
Nationalism. *See* Confederate nationalism
Native Americans, 147
New South, 160–61
Newton, Willoughby, 14, 57, 72, 79, 125
New York City, 18, 86, 94, 116, 136
New York State Agricultural Society: supported by state government, 66–67, 77
Norfolk, Va., 17, 18, 88; in southern economic imagination, 38, 116; sparse hinterlands limiting development of, 25, 38, 43, 116
North Carolina, 71
Nullification, 45

Ohio and Covington Railroad, 94
Old Field. *See* Shifting cultivation
Olmsted, Frederick Law: description and critique of shifting cultivation, 27–28, 33, 38, 47–48
O'Neall, John B., 93
Owens, W. A., 123–24

Petersburg, Va., 88
Philadelphia, Pa., 25, 38, 90
Population densities, 39–40, 170–71
Preston, William Ballard, 121–22
Progressivism, 80
Prussia, 152

Railroads, 7, 15, 18–19, 77, 174–75; failure to revitalize the southern economy, 84, 104–6; impact on agriculture and land-use patterns, 37–38, 91–92, 164–65; impact on postbellum economy, 175–78; lack of steady profits, 82, 85–86, 88–90; large state and local investment in, 81–83, 100–104; relationship to slavery, 83–84, 90–91; as represented on Confederate currency, 140–42; and southern dreams of commercial expansion, 93–97; and southern support for transcontinental projects, 11, 145–47; and stronger national economic bonds, 97–100. *See also* Confederate government
Randolph, George W., 3, 14, 126–30
Reconstruction, 159–60
Reed, J. P., 93
Regression analysis, 163–64, 168–69
*Report on Manufacturers*, 133
Republicanism: compatible with modern economy, 102–3; definition of, 5–6; ignored in creation of Confederate state, 10–12. *See also* States' rights ideology
Reynolds, G. N., 133
Rhett, Robert Barnwell, 14, 106, 113, 146
Rice, 168
Richmond, 17, 25, 43, 88, 90, 124; manufacturing potential of, 126–27; as bastion of Whigs, 100–101, 127
*Richmond Daily Dispatch*, 15, 130
*Richmond Enquirer*, 15, 98
Richmond Howitzers, 126
*Richmond Whig*, 123
Rives, William C., 121–22
Robinson, Solon, 28
Rochdale, England, 138
Romans, 64–65, 69
Ruffin, Edmund, 13, 17, 18, 93, 101, 106, 116, 125, 150, 159; and battle against malaria, 68–72; as critic of democ-

racy, 79–80; and the defense of slavery, 59, 61, 158–59; and experiments with marl, 53, 56–58, 73–74; and legislative aid to agriculture, 62, 63–64, 74–78; as secessionist and southern extremist, 53–54
Ruffin, Julian, 23
Russell, Lord John, 137
Russell, William Howard, 8–9, 119; and Louis Wigfall, 144–45
Rutherfoord, John C., 1–2, 103
"Rutledge" (pseudonym), 112, 118

"S.D.M." (pseudonym), 31
St. Matthews Parish, S.C., 31
Scott, R. G., 122
Seabrook, Whitemarsh, 14, 57, 62, 65; and government drainage of wetlands, 70–71; support for activist government policies, 75–76
Secessionists: and critique of individualism, 56, 79–80; definition of, 12–16; and economic critique of the Union, 112–14; modern economic imagination of, 1–4, 80, 140–43; and movement to reopen the international slave trade, 119–20; prominence within agricultural reform movement, 53–54; and support of railroads, 107–8. *See also* Confederate government; Confederate nationalism; Confederate tariffs
Segar, Joseph, 93, 94, 97
Selma, Ala., 148
Seward, William, 48
Shenandoah Valley, 4, 32
Shifting cultivation, 16–17; definition of, 23–25; economic impact of, 25–26, 39–45, 171–75; environmental causes of, 25, 32–38, 163–70; extent of, 26–31; northern critique of, 26, 45–50; prevalence in postbellum era, 175–79
Simms, William Gilmore: calls for agricultural education by, 62–63; critique of shifting cultivation by, 67–68; as fearful of manufacturing in Confederacy, 130–31
Slavery: and agricultural practices, 31–32, 168–69; breakdown during Civil War, 158–59; economic impact of, 42–43, 129, 170–75; in industry and urban areas, 129–30, 155–57; and influence on Confederate identity and government, 7–9, 72, 116, 151–52; as justification for state activism, 7–9, 56–61, 72, 80, 90–94, 138–39. *See also* Agricultural reform; Confederate nationalism; Railroads
Slave trade, international, 106, 119–20
Smith, Adam: as critic of "man of system," 143; and extent of markets, 40; as supporter of state education, 64
Soil depletion. *See* Shifting cultivation
Soils. *See* Alfisols; Ultisols
*South Alone, Should Govern the South, The* (Townsend), 15, 115–16
South Carolina, 4, 5, 78, 130; agricultural practices in, 22–23, 28–29, 29–30; internal improvement policies of, 76, 82; government support of agriculture in, 74–75; land use in, 23, 72; population of, 17, 44–45; secession politics in, 12–13, 113; support for free trade in, 108–10, 130–31, 133.
South Carolina Agricultural Society, 57, 70

South Carolina Railroad, 28, 84–86, 88–90, 101
Southern cattle fever, 35–36, 165, 178–79
*Southern Cultivator*, 51, 66
*Southern Illustrated News*, 124–25
*Southern Literary Messenger*, 2, 138
*Southern Planter*, 31, 79, 92
*Southern Quarterly Review*, 73–74
*Southern States, Their Present Peril, The* (Townsend), 114
Southwest Railroad Bank, 85
Soviet Union, 152
Sparkman, William E., 22–23, 42–43
Spratley, P. T., 76
Spratt, L. W., 10, 14, 112, 116, 118, 120
State activism, 9–10
State Soil Geographic Database (STATSGO), 164
States' rights ideology, 5–7, 10–11; ignored during creation of strong Confederate state, 10–11, 143–48; as means of protecting slavery, 45; prominent in historiography, 5–7
Steffen, Charles G., 57

Tariffs (U.S.), 105, 128; blamed for southern decline, 111–13; and national identity, 109–10; and redistribution of resources, 108–9. *See also* Confederate tariffs
Taylor, John, 47
Texas, 144
*Theory of Moral Sentiments, The* (Smith), 143
Thomas, Emory M., 7, 80
Thornwell, James Henley, 15
*Times* (London), 144
Tocqueville, Alexis de, 47
Townsend, John, 14, 15, 114–15

Tredegar Iron Works, 4, 86–88, 129, 148
Tyler, John, 53

Ultisols, properties and impact of, 33–35, 164–65
*Union, Past and Future, The* (Garnett), 112–13
Unionism, 4, 13, 119–21
Upper South, 119–20, 130–31
Urbanization: impact on agricultural practices, 37–38, 179; impact on industry, 174–75; southerners as sometimes fearful of, 100–101; southern support for, 102–3. *See also* Charleston; Industrialization; Railroads; Richmond

Virginia, 4, 15–16, 27, 52; agricultural policies of, 74–75; divisions within, 77–78; internal improvement policies of, 76, 82, 101; land use in, 23, 29–30, 72, 179; and opposition to slave trade, 119–21; population of, 17, 44–45; secession politics in, 13–14, 119–21, 127. *See also* Boycotts; Virginia Secession Convention.
Virginia Agricultural Society, 59, 61, 79
Virginia Board of Agriculture, 69, 74–75
Virginia Secession Convention: and debate over trade policies, 125–30

Wade, Edward, 48
Washburn, Israel, 48, 52
Webster, Daniel, 53
West Virginia, 97, 130, 155
Wetlands, 70–71
Wheeling, Va., 130

*Index* 239

Whigs, 14, 94–95, 100–101, 121
Wigfall, Louis, 133; as exponent of strong Confederate state, 144–48, 150, 151
Wilmot, David, 48

Wilson, Harold S., 149
Wise, Henry A., 13–14, 18; support for railroads and urban growth, 95, 102–3
Wright, Gavin, 50